CONTENTS

Introduction
Principles of the School Learning Climate Program

Key Concepts and Considerations

- Common Factors Among High Achieving Schools
- School's Social System
- School's Learning Climate
- Organization, Ideology and Instructional Practices
- Climate and Background
- Research

Then and Now

In 1982, the first edition of *Creating Effective Schools* examined why some students succeed while others fail. Back then the problems of low academic achievement, low student self-conceptions of ability, high dropout rates, and overall school failure were critical elements contributing to student failure — and they still are important. This was especially true among schools serving predominately poor and minority children. Providing a quality education to these presumed "disadvantaged" children was seen as a positive blueprint for the future. It was feared that without needed changes in these schools, even more students would fail.

Today, to all our sadness, many of these schools have not changed. Many are still failing to meet the needs of students, and they are failing society as well. Coupled with their failure to foster academic skills is the problem many face with youth gangs and an increase in violence among students. It is easy to see, given the focus of the media on these failing schools, why there is a general perception that our schools are worse off today than in 1982.

It is true that many schools are failing. Yet it is also true that there are some shining lights — enough to show the way. There are schools in the poorest of neighborhoods with long histories of failure that are now succeeding. They are now doing well because they instituted fundamental changes in their ideologies, in their achievement expectations, and in their structures for fulfilling high expectations for students.

Equally important, the successes of these schools were brought about without significant increases in funding. The successes of these poorest schools suggest that every school has at its disposal the means for improvement. This is so because the most important factors influencing school effectiveness are qualitative in nature.

Successful schools have developed an expectation that all students are able to master the academic skills traditionally held for elite students. These are schools where the staff as a whole have an increased knowledge of how to employ effective interaction with their students; where they have increased the time students spend on academic tasks; and where they have provided safe and caring instructional environments. In these effective schools the staff worked to change those past practices that interfered with their being able to help students. What did these effective staffs do? The answer, of course, depends on each school.

Research on Effective Schools

"In effective schools administrators and teachers continually strive to improve instructional effectiveness."

Effective Schooling Practices: A Research Synthesis (1990),
Northwest Regional Educational Laboratory.

There are many ways that successful schools can structure effective educational environments. One common denominator is the emphasis on high achievement expectations for nearly every student. In successful schools, the staff holds high academic achievement expectations of their students, while providing safe and healthy environments in which to learn. The staff also reinforces high expectations among themselves and with new staff. They maintain high expectations while they respond to major changes in their communities. Whether it is a violent youth gang, a major drop in employment among parents, or some other social problem that impacts on their schools, they keep schools safe and secure, and they maintain high achievement expectations for their students. Simply stated, effective schools have clear norms and value systems of achievement, and staffs who are committed to them.

Research on Effective Schools

"Expect all students to perform at a level needed to be successful at the next level of learning."

Cotton, K. *Effective Schooling Practices: A Research Synthesis 1995 Update*, Northwest Regional Educational Laboratory.

Regardless of the type of problem they face, effective schools identified and corrected barriers that made it difficult to hold high expectations for the student body. A school in Arizona for example, faced an all too frequent dilemma. Should they promote students who do not pass all courses, or should they retain them? By passing students who were not performing at grade level, would they be promoting mediocrity? By retaining these students would they be negatively affecting student self-conceptions? Would this affect achievement levels and life chances? If they retained students, would they be communicating low expectations, thereby ensuring high drop-out rates?

Coupled with their belief that all students should be expected to learn, and that their past practice of retention was hurting two-in-three retained students, the school made a major change in their promotion policy. Their new policy was to promote students from the seventh to eighth grades in those subjects passed. Students repeated only the portions of courses they failed rather than the entire grade. In the repeated portions, students were provided with teacher mentors to help with homework, test preparation, study habits, and behavior. Mentors presumed each student who had failed could achieve at a much higher level with the mentor's help.

At the end of the first nine weeks of mentoring, 72 percent of students learned what was required and then passed to the eighth grade. It took longer for the few who did not quickly benefit from intensive remedial work, but they too eventually moved up in skill and knowledge. The point of the school's remedial effort was to help students catch up. It was not to lower the level of expectations. Achievement expectations were not lowered. Quite the opposite. Low- or under-achieving students were expected to learn and expected to pass. This effort was counter to the trend where students who fail to learn are simply taught less and seldom, if ever, catch up.

What Makes a School Ineffective?

If we educators seek to improve our schools, then we must learn from past mistakes and not repeat them. We must ask ourselves which variables are consistently linked to school failure, and then work to alter them. Past failure need not be a prologue to future failure. The following are several examples of modifiable conditions often associated with *ineffective* schools.

- Widely shared belief among school staff that the socioeconomic status of students alone will determine their achievement levels.

- The practice of identifying a significant proportion of the study body as slow learners.

- Widely shared belief among staff that the school can do little to impact on the academic performance of students who come from troubled homes.

- Frequent occurrence of violence or other disruptive acts among students.

- Failure to recognize and reward teachers and students who, despite considerable difficulties, still produce high levels of achievement.

- Failure to retrain, redirect, or otherwise alter the behavior of teachers who are widely recognized to be ineffective.

- The lack of a staff development program relevant to effective curriculum planning and instruction.

- The relative lack of time teachers spend in uninterrupted instruction which involves students in learning tasks directed to appropriate learning goals.

Consider another example of a high school in Texas. One out of every three of their students failed one or more classes in mathematics and English each year. The staff concluded that several factors accounted for most failure: incomplete homework, low student motivation, and lack of mastery of fundamental knowledge.

To combat these problems the staff developed a new master plan where each class period was reduced to 45 minutes from 50 minutes. The time gained was added to a special homeroom study period. This period was designated for students to work on homework assignments, do independent study, and receive reteaching/retesting over fundamental math and language skills that had not been learned in regular classroom sessions. In other words, time on task was increased for academic areas that were giving students trouble. Furthermore, mathematics and English teachers were given added time to work with students who scored less than 75 percent mastery in their classes.

By providing time for all students to master material, and by providing the instructional resources to help all students, the student success rate in one year increased dramatically. Prior to the program only 67 percent of students passed all classes. At the end of the first year the success rate had risen to 94 percent.

The message of such efforts is clear: virtually every student can succeed if schools, administrators, and teachers are willing to modify instructional practices accordingly.

A Matter of Quality and Commitment

Now, more than ever, quality education for all children must be the goal of every school. This is particularly true for schools serving low-income and minority students when there may be a history of school failure. Unfortunately, when failure is pervasive, many conclude that high levels of student performance are impossible, particularly in schools with student bodies drawn from lower socioeconomic status families. It is true that socioeconomic class status and minority composition are statistically associated with levels of student achievement. This does not mean, however, that class and race are causal factors. Schools in impoverished areas with high minority enrollment need not be doomed to a pattern of failure. The fact that there are many schools in the poorest and most educationally disadvantaged areas that are producing student bodies with high achievement levels, demonstrates that it is possible for other schools to succeed. Success is a matter of commitment to quality, coupled with the knowledge of how to create an effective school.

Research on Effective Schools

"Our findings show that student sense of current and future academic accomplishment and student sense of academic futility added the greatest non-SES variance to the prediction equation . . . [School climate] can dramatically affect student achievement, regardless of socioeconomic status."

"A Time to Summarize: The Louisiana School Effectiveness Study,"
S. Stringfield and C. Teddlie, *Educational Leadership*, October 1988.

For the past several decades, and even today, educators, researchers, and the public have usually sought to explain low student performance by emphasizing either characteristics of individual students, or family background. These explanations of student learning have largely ignored the influence of the principals, teachers, and other students, (i.e., the nature of the school) as critical to student achievement levels. Yet, the school makes a critical difference, regardless of individual or family characteristics. The discovery that some schools are effective in teaching disadvantaged students support this conclusion. In fact, there is a significant body of literature which suggests that essentially all children can learn what any child can learn.

Research on Effective Schools

The combined social interaction of teachers and students, parents and student, teachers and parents, and administrators, i.e., the school learning climate — is related to student learning.

School Learning Climate and Student Achievement:
A Social Systems Approach to Increased Student Learning (1980),
National Teachers Corps, Florida State University Foundation.

How do we as principals, teachers, district administrators, parents, and those concerned with providing a quality education to all students create an environment in which all children can learn? The answer, as demonstrated in research, is to be found in the school learning climate. This second edition of *Creating Effective Schools*, provides materials, references, ideas, and a framework for developing a positive learning environment — an effective school learning climate.

Climate and Background

The goal of *Creating Effective Schools* is to produce a learning climate in which students will master certain academic skills and knowledge, regardless of their socioeconomic or minority background. In our promotion of the mastery of certain basic skills and knowledge of mathematics, science, social studies and language, we do not imply in any way, that we are merely concerned with subject content and its recitation. We are concerned with the development of higher order thinking skills — skills which are critical in an emerging technological society. Thinking skills — from the point of many scholars — refer to those skills and subskills that govern a person's mental processes. These skills consist of knowledge, comprehension, and application at the metacognitive levels" (Cotton, 1992). When defined as critical thinking we are concerned that all students develop their facility to determine the authenticity, accuracy or value of something. We want them to increase their capability to seek reasons, to weigh evidence, to think about the consequences, in view of total situations.

As we move through the modules from raising expectations, mastering subject areas, engaging in cooperative planning inquiry and reporting, and reinforcement, we anticipate that no student can be expected to achieve higher order thinking without a mastery of certain fundamentals.

A student's social status, gender, race or ethnicity is neither a cause for student failure to develop a mastery of fundamentals, nor an acceptable reason for schools to "give up" on demanding such achievement. Students from all types of family backgrounds do learn at high levels. Whether students are from South Central Los Angeles or rural Pennsylvania, learn how to communicate with others, how to drive, and how to read. It is clear that all students can learn much more if provided with an appropriate learning climate. Any school in which a portion or all of the student body is failing to achieve at high levels will benefit from the *School Learning Climate Program* presented here. This program should, however, be particularly helpful in improving achievement in traditionally low achieving schools.

Research on Effective Schools

"Excellence in achievement and behavior is recognized and rewarded. Requirements for awards are clear; explicit procedures ensure consistency; evaluations are based on standards rather than on comparisons with peers."

Effective Schooling Practices: A Research Synthesis (1990),
Northwest Regional Educational Laboratory.

Research and Effective Schools

Great variation exists in the research on the characteristics of effective school learning climates. There is extensive research which demonstrates that the beliefs and evaluations concerning students' ability to learn, and the expectations that teachers hold for students, are highly related to the level of student achievement. Similarly, there is a body of research to support the conclusion that student achievement is related to the amount of engaged time devoted to learning. For these reasons, the model of the effective school learning climate presented here is not the product of a single study. Rather, our model derives from a series of studies and experiments which include efforts to raise achievement through: 1) modifying school organizations and leadership practices; 2) improving instructional practices supported by staff development; and 3) altering the ideologies of schools.

A word of caution — there is increasing evidence that some conditions function differently in different school social systems. For example, we emphasize instructional practice in accord with the *mastery learning* model. Some would apply mastery learning to group instruction, while others might apply it to individualized instruction. We have not advocated individualized instruction because we find little evidence to support this as a consistently effective teaching method. However, individualized instruction functions quite differently in different school contexts. If individualized instruction is used to assure that every student masters particular objectives, then this method would likely be quite effective. If, on the other hand, individualized instruction is used as a basis for differentiating among the students in a manner that identifies some students as not able to learn, or not ready to learn, then the resulting achievement outcome is likely to be reduced for a large proportion of students.

The modules of this book are based on research for how best to provide in-service training to a school staff that wishes to improve the learning climate of its school. Research indicates that it will not be effective for a school to concentrate on only one component or cluster of a school's learning climate. Thus the modules address school ideology, organization, and instructional practices as an interactive force for producing effective schools.

A Note on Documentation

The *School Learning Climate Program* is based on decades of solid research. We summarize several of the most basic research findings reported by the Northwest Regional Educational Laboratory and others in boxes throughout the text. This style allows one to skim over the citations while giving attention to the content of the reference. We are fortunate that the Northwest Regional Educational Laboratory in Portland, Oregon produces a synthesis every five years on factors associated with effective schools. We also value the *Effective Schools Research Abstracts* available from Effective Schools Products, Okemos, Michigan. We encourage you to make use of their valuable services.

Selected Bibliography

📖 Cotton, K. *Effective Schooling Practices: A Research Synthesis 1995 Update.* Portland, OR: Northwest Regional Educational Laboratory, 1995.

📖 Cotton, K. *School Improvement Research Series: Research You Can Use.* Portland, OR: Northwest Regional Educational Laboratory, 1994-95.

📖 *Effective Schooling Practices: A Research Synthesis.* Portland, OR: Northwest Regional Educational Laboratory, 1990.

📖 Lezotte, L. W. and B. C. Jacoby. *Effective Schools: Practices That Work.* Okemos, MI: Effective School Products, 1991.

📖 Mortimore, P. "School Effectiveness and the Management of Effective Learning and Teaching." *School Effectiveness and School Improvement* 4/4 (1993): 290-310.

📖 Sammons, P., Hillman, J. and P. Mortimore. *Key Characteristics of Effective Schools: A Review of School Effectiveness Research.* London: International School Effectiveness and Improvement Centre, University of London, 1994.

📖 *School Learning Climate and Student Achievement: A Social Systems Approach to Increased Student Learning.* Tallahassee, FL: National Teachers Corps, Florida State University Foundation, 1980.

📖 Stringfield, S. and C. Teddlie. "A Time to Summarize: The Louisiana School Effectiveness Study." *Educational Leadership*, October 1988.

Module 1
Preparation for In-service

Key Concepts and Considerations

- Keys for Implementation
- Involved Active Participation
- Building Leadership Team (BLT)
- Implementation Schedule
- Assistance Dyads

A Commitment to Excellence

The *School Learning Climate Program* presented here is based on the school as the unit of implementation. While this program may be implemented district wide, or in a classroom, the focus for change in this manual is at the school level.

Creating Effective Schools is a series of modules, each designed to contribute to one or more of the three components of a school learning climate: 1) school ideology, 2) school leadership and organization, and 3) instructional practices. While each of the modules contributes to the overall goal of creating an effective school learning climate, the whole is more than a sum of the modules. Failing to implement any module will reduce the overall effectiveness of the program and the chances of increased student achievement. When implementing the *School Learning Climate Program,* four rules are important:

- **Involve the Entire Staff**

  The School Learning Climate represents the COLLECTIVE norms, organization, and practices among school members. This means the combined efforts of the entire staff are necessary in order to be effective. There must be a unity of purpose to produce high levels of student achievement. This assumes collaboration in planning, a spirit of collegiality, and an atmosphere which rewards experimentation in instructional practices which enhance student achievement.

- **Use All Modules**

  Using only certain modules ignores the different aspects of the school learning climate that are interconnected and affect the other parts.

- **Do Not Expect A Quick Fix**

  Using the program does not guarantee quick success. The complete program must be implemented over time if maximum results are to be attained. Changing attitudes and expectations, coupled with changing organizational and instructional practices, will produce improvements in learning over time.

- **Expect Results for All Students**

  The *School Learning Climate Program* presented here is designed to assist principals and teachers to bring almost all students to high levels of achievement in the curriculum for their grade, particularly in the basic skill areas of reading and mathematics.

  With these considerations in mind, the first task of the principal is to form a *Building Leadership Team.* Each member should receive, prior to meeting collectively, a copy of this book so as to become familiar with the total program and the responsibilities of the team. They should then come together with the principal to discuss all facets of the program, carefully review the procedures in this manual, and address any concerns.

  Initial orientation to the *School Learning Climate Program* should, if at all possible, occur at a time when the staff is released from regular school responsibilities. Normally, it is best to provide this orientation prior to the beginning of the school year. At least two days are needed. In many cases, it is desirable to offer extended time if funds and schedules allow. We strongly suggest a Building Leadership Team be created to plan and conduct the initial orientation.

Research on Effective Schools

Principals and other school leaders:

- "The leader has a clear understanding of the school's mission and is able to state it in direct, concrete terms. Instructional focus is established that unifies the staff."

- "The principal and other leaders seek out [successful] innovative curricular programs, observe these, acquaint staff with them, and participate with staff in discussions about adopting or adapting them."

- "Leaders involve staff and others in planning implementation . . . enforce expectations for participation; commitments are made and followed through . . . "

- "There are high expectations for quality instruction. The principal and other school administrators hold high expectations of themselves, assuming responsibility for student outcomes, and being visible and accessible to staff, students, parents and community members."

Cotton, K. *School Improvement Research Series: Research You Can Use*, Northwest Regional Education Laboratory, 1994-95.

Building Leadership Team (BLT)

Purposes

- Develop an implementation team.
- Provide direction to the implementation of the *School Learning Climate Program*.
- Provide an organizational structure to assist in total staff involvement.
- Provide a vehicle for assessment.

Key Considerations

One of the most critical elements of the *School Learning Climate Program* is the BLT because it is this group which is responsible for providing the necessary leadership. The BLT should consist of the principal, and three or four teachers. Teachers selected for the BLT should be opinion leaders among the staff. They should also represent important organizational structures, such as department heads, grade level chairpersons, and other sub-groups within the school. Often these are the more enthusiastic staff who serve as role models for other teachers.

This team's responsibilities include:

a)   identification of school goals and priorities related to the learning climate;

b)   conducting an audit of instructional needs and resources, including the status of textbooks and supplemental materials, student health and safety considerations, and extracurricular enrichment programs;

c)   preliminary planning for conducting the project; and

d)   setting up a program for assessing staff progress.

Matters of general planning, leadership, goal setting, and establishing priorities can then occur before the staff orientation. Following the initial staff orientation, the BLT meets monthly for planning, coordination and evaluation. A successful BLT normally meets two weeks prior to the principal's whole staff meeting to prepare for the climate topic and activities to be acted upon that month.

Research on Effective Schools

"Administrators and teachers develop mission statements . . that underscore the school's academic goals."

Cotton, K. *Effective Schooling Practice: A Research Synthesis, 1995 Update,*
Northwest Regional Education Laboratory.

Initial Orientation

Purposes

- Familiarize the staff with the concept of the *School Learning Climate Program*.

- Present an overview of the program modules.

- Assess the current level of school learning climate.

- Establish and reach acceptance on a working agreement for conducting the *School Learning Climate Program*.

Key Considerations

The initial orientation should focus on presenting the ideology on which the *School Learning Climate Program* is based. All staff need to have a full understanding of the program. It is also important to provide a brief overview of each of the modules within the program. The next step for the Building Leadership Team is to conduct an overview assessment of the current strength and weaknesses of the existing school learning climate. This will be followed by in-depth study as each month the staff works with one module at a time.

Finally, a working agreement should be developed and accepted by all staff participants. This agreement needs to identify expectations from the principal and teachers who are to conduct the *School Learning Climate Program*.

Principal's Staff Meeting

Purposes

- Provide a forum for discussing issues of the *School Learning Climate Program.*

- Develop targets for examining modules.

- Set the direction for staff activities.

Key Considerations

Each month, the principal meets with the entire professional staff in her or his building to discuss topics related to the *School Learning Climate Program.* According to the implementation calendar established by the BLT, one topic or module is targeted for study and action each month. At this staff meeting, the principal reviews the selected topic or module and sets the tone and direction for the staff activities that month.

Maintenance Meetings

Purposes

- Provide for small group study and discussion.
- Consider implications from each module.
- Help ensure broad involvement and active participation.
- Facilitate staff in sharing their successes and difficulties in implementing the program.

Key Considerations

The purpose of the maintenance meeting is to provide for small group study or discussion related to topics or concerns of the *School Learning Climate Program.* These are intended as regular biweekly meetings to consider the practicality or implications of suggestions from the modules.

Maintenance meetings should focus on application of the suggestions from the modules or from the building staff.

Teachers need to decide the best way to form maintenance groups. Usually this is done according to a common interest, such as by subject or grade level. For example, teachers might meet according to grade level in the elementary school while secondary teachers may wish to group by department or subject. Once a maintenance group is formed, a chairperson should be selected and agreement should be reached on the dates and times for the biweekly meetings. Members of the BLT *should not* act as chairpersons of maintenance groups. While BLT members should participate in these groups, they should not attempt to run or dominate group discussions.

Assistance Dyads

Purposes

- Provide for staff support.

- Assess regular program outcomes.

- Offer suggestions on a more informal basis for program improvement.

Key Considerations

Throughout the modules, teachers are encouraged to assist one another in following through with suggested activities, techniques or tasks. One of the easiest ways to accomplish this is for teachers to form assistance dyads. For example, two teachers from the same maintenance group might agree to work together for the year on activities from the *School Learning Climate Program*. This arrangement facilitates communication and also can develop into a valued support system. Teachers may be uncomfortable working closely with other teachers at first, but sharing and problem-solving should stimulate full cooperation toward common goals.

Research on Effective Schools

"In effective schools the staff engage in ongoing professional development and collegial learning activities."

Effective Schooling Practice: A Research Synthesis (1990),
Northwest Regional Education Laboratory.

Time Commitments

Purposes

- Assist with regular participation of all staff.
- Maintain commitment to the *School Learning Climate Program*.

Key Considerations

Following the initial orientation the implementation model identifies four project functions. Each require monthly staff time. Each participant should expect to devote approximately one hour each week to activities of the *School Learning Climate Program*. The actual time may be more or less; however, it is essential that all teachers and the principal commit time for these project activities:

Project Implementation Schedule

The suggested schedule for implementing the *School Learning Climate Program* illustrated in *Figure 1-1* and identifies monthly topics and activities for:

1. Building Leadership Team;
2. Whole Staff Meetings;
3. Maintenance Meetings; and
4. Staff In-service.

Figure 1-1
A MODEL FOR SCHOOL LEARNING
CLIMATE PROGRAM IMPLEMENTATION

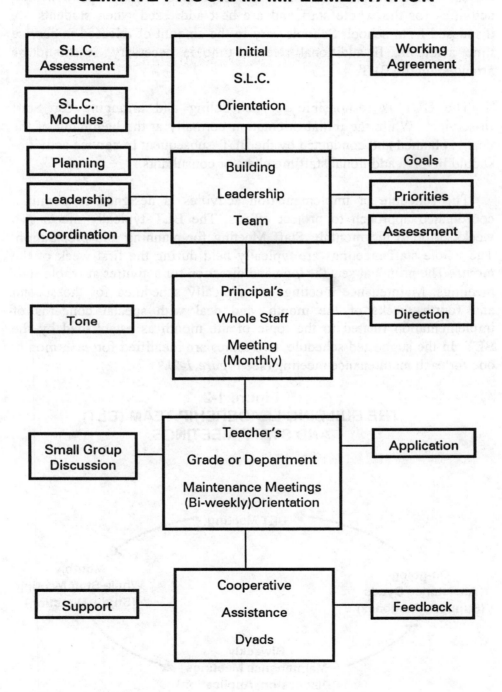

The activities of the Building Leadership Team, Staff Meetings, and Maintenance Meetings should occur on a regular schedule each month. The released-time Staff In-service, however, is scheduled as time and funds permit and involves either a half-day or full-day of staff time. The topics identified for Staff In-service represent major implementation activities for the whole staff and are best addressed when students are dismissed from school. Schools vary in the amount of released in-service time available. If additional released-time is necessary, it should be arranged by the BLT.

The BLT is responsible for scheduling and arranging for Staff In-service. While the initial orientation normally at the beginning of the year is planned and conducted by the BLT, subsequent in-service activities should involve additional staff members or consultants.

The schedule of implementation activities is designed to permit a coordinated approach to project efforts. The BLT typically meets two weeks prior to the monthly Staff Meeting for planning and preparation. The whole staff meetings are typically held during the first week of the month. The principal sets the tone and direction for activities at whole staff meetings. Maintenance meetings are typically scheduled for the second and fourth weeks of the month, and deal with special concerns of implementation related to the topic of the month as established by the BLT. In the suggested schedule, two topics are identified for each month, one for each maintenance meeting (see *Figure 1-2)*.

Figure 1-2
THE BUILDING LEADERSHIP TEAM (BLT)
AND STAFF MEETINGS

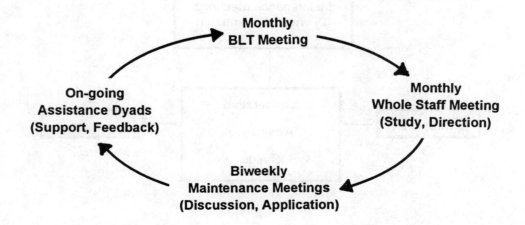

**Monthly
BLT Meeting**

**Monthly
Whole Staff Meeting
(Study, Direction)**

**On-going
Assistance Dyads
(Support, Feedback)**

**Biweekly
Maintenance Meetings
(Discussion, Application)**

Presenting Learning Climate Modules

As stated earlier, the concept of the *School Learning Climate Program* as described in the modules must be treated with unity for maximum benefits. The module presentation and discussion schedule may be organized as follows:

Initial Orientation (2 days in August)

First Day:

Module 2 – An Effective School Learning Climate

Module 3 – Expectations for Learning

Module 4 – Organization, Role Definitions and Rewards

Module 5 – Grouping and Tracking

Second Day:

Module 7 – Academic Engaged Time

Module 10 – Reinforcing Achievement

Module 11 – Use of Assessment Data

Module 12 – Parent Support and Involvement

September:

Module 6 – Effective Instruction

October:

Module 8 – School Discipline and Classroom Management

November:

Module 9 – Student Team Learning

Each project participant should receive a full set of School Learning Climate Modules several weeks prior to the initial staff orientation. In particular, *Modules 2–5, 7,* and *10-12* should be read by each participant before the orientation, as those modules will be presented during the two days of in-service. Because *Modules 6, 8* and *9* will be considered in detail in months subsequent to the orientation, reading should be done just prior to the month each topic is targeted for study.

The activities which appear at the end of each module are suggested ways to put into practice the content of the module. These activities are only some of the possible ways to follow through on the ideas presented. Each staff is encouraged to develop additional activities that may better meet their needs.

Beginning in September and extending through the school year one module should be targeted for study and discussion each month by the staff. Obviously, some modules deal with topics or activities that cannot be concluded in a month. However, it is recommended that the staff move on to the next topic as scheduled, initiating as many activities as possible and temporarily postponing remaining activities until a later date. In some cases, incomplete work on a module can be continued while a new module is being investigated. If not, return to the unfinished activities as soon as possible. Studying modules and initiating activities according to a fixed schedule usually presents problems only during the first year in the *School Learning Climate Program*. Once an understanding of the modules has been achieved, the need to schedule so tightly is lessened. Especially during the second year, less time will be needed for covering modules and more time should be available for follow-through activities.

Since limitations of time in the initial orientation prevent full consideration of the modules presented, it is necessary that general understanding of each module be achieved. Beginning in December, the remainder of the year should be divided between follow-up activities associated with the modules presented in the Initial Orientation and evaluation of project implementation. The Building Leadership Team should develop a schedule of module topics for further staff investigation beginning in December and extending through the school year. (See Suggested Implementation Schedule.)

We are confident that this program will result in increased achievement if properly implemented and followed. However, staff members must agree that they want and are willing to work for positive change. Improving the school learning climate will not be easy, since it requires change in people, which is difficult at best. But a staff that is committed to raising achievement can do it. A thorough study of these modules will provide the understanding and guidance needed to begin that change.

Research on Effective Schools:

- "Administrators and teachers base curriculum planning on clear goals and objectives."

- "A school-based management team [BLT] makes many of the decisions regarding school operations."

- "Strong leaderships guides the program. "The principal and other administrators continually express expectations for the improvement of other instructional programs."

Cotton, K. *Effective Schooling Practice: A Research Synthesis, 1995 Update,* Northwest Regional Education Laboratory.

Selected Bibliography

Andrews, R. L., and R. Soder. Principal Leadership and Student Achievement. *Educational Leadership* 44 (1987): 9-11.

Cotton, K. *School Improvement Research Series: Research You Can Use.* Portland, OR: Northwest Regional Education Laboratory, 1994-95.

Cotton, K. *Effective Schooling Practices: A Research Synthesis, 1995 Update.* Portland, OR: Northwest Regional Education Laboratory, 1995.

Deal, T. E. and K. D. Peterson. *The Principal's Role in Change: Technical and Symbolic Aspects of School Improvement.* Madison, WI: University of Wisconsin, Wisconsin Center for Education Research, National Center for Effective Schools, 1993.

Effective Schooling Practice: A Research Synthesis. Portland, OR: Northwest Regional Education Laboratory, 1990.

Fullan, M. "Coordinating School and District Development in Restructuring," In *Restructuring Schooling: Learning from Ongoing Efforts,* edited by J. Murphy and P. Hallinger, Newbury Park, CA: Corwin Press, Inc., 1993, 143-164.

Lezotte, L. W. and B. C. Jacoby. *Effective Schools: Practices that Work.* Okemos, MI: Effective Schools Products, 1991.

Murphy, J. and P. Hallinger. "Characteristics of Instructionally Effective School Districts." *Journal of Educational Research* 81 (1988): 175-181.

Pavan, B. N., and N. A. Reid. "Effective Urban Elementary Schools and their Women Administrators," *Urban Education,* 28/4 (January 1994): 425-438.

Peng, S. "Effective High Schools: What Are Their Attributes?" In *Effective School Leadership: Policy and Process*, edited by J. J. Lane and H. J. Walberg. Berkeley, CA: McCutchan Publishing Corp., 1987, 89-107.

Rosenholtz, S. J. *Teachers' Workplace: The Social Organization of Schools.* New York: Longman, 1989.

Rosenholtz, S. J. "Workplace Conditions that Affect Teacher Quality and Commitment: Implications for Teacher Induction Programs." *The Elementary School Journal* 89 (1989):422-439.

Sammons, P., Hillman, J. and P. Mortimore. *Key Characteristics of Effective Schools: A Review of School Effectiveness Research.* London: International School Effectiveness and Improvement Centre, University of London, November 1994.

Module 2
An Effective School Learning Climate

Key Concepts and Considerations

- The Relevance of School Learning Climates
- Measuring School Learning Climate
- Improving School Learning Climate

Success

In some of our most economically destitute communities we find a few schools with large numbers of its students graduating and going on to college, or they are entering the world of work with strong academic backgrounds. However, too few schools in predominantly low income, urban communities are doing as well as they should. Often these schools are beset with discipline problems, violence and poor attendance. Regrettably, they also exhibit low achievement levels in that a large portion of their students fail to attain important academic skills and knowledge. There are, of course, middle and upper income schools across the social spectrum that also experience these problems. But in low income urban areas, the problems are so concentrated that many educators and the public mistakenly believe that these public schools cannot provide effective learning climates.

This assumption is both misleading and harmful to attempts at helping low-achieving schools to become effective teaching and learning centers. Even if conditions in the home or community provide impediments to learning, schools *can* create effective learning climates that produce high achievement levels in their student bodies. High achieving, low income, minority schools do exist, and they have been extensively studied. These exemplary schools in poverty areas reflect the early extensive studies by Bloom (1976) and his associates who concluded: ". . . what any person in the world can learn, almost all persons can learn if provided with appropriate prior and current conditions of learning" (p. 7). These "appropriate conditions for learning" are what we identify as an effective school learning climate.

What is it that low achieving schools can do to succeed? They can do what high achieving schools do wherever they are found, be they in low or high income settings. This module describes and explains effective school learning climates and certain of the conditions that must occur for their implementation. Subsequent modules further expand on the attitudes, beliefs, structures, and instructional programs that characterize effective learning climates — the prerequisite for an effective school.

School Learning Climate

The term *climate* is a sensitizing concept in social science. It is used like it is used in the study of weather. Climate refers to a condition that generally characterizes or permeates an area. The temperature in the shade may be less than in the direct sunlight, but it is still considered helpful to know the overall heat-cold index. Moreover, the general climate temperature has a great deal to do with how hot it is in the shade. Restated, the heat in an area may vary but it is useful to know the general temperature, be it in Tampa, Montreal, Los Angeles, Seattle, or elsewhere.

In social science the term climate similarly refers to a general social condition that characterizes a group, organization or community, such as the general opinion in a community on the "innate educability" of lower income, African-American children. In one community the climate of opinion may be that black children are no more innately impaired than other children, while in another community the climate may favor presumed biological differences. This does not mean that everyone in each community believes the same thing. Rather climate refers to a *social tendency.* The importance of the concept is that even though related, climate is a social force that is a distinct influence from the influence of particular individuals on students. In this sense, climate constitutes the background conditions (e.g., expectations, norms, values) which together shape interaction.

In a school, for example, the climate of expectations for students in how they should dress can reinforce or counter the influence of particular peers or teachers. If the overall climate in a school is that all students can learn to master reading skills, then a teacher who tells a student that he or she is too impaired to learn will have less relevance than if the climate of opinion is that only a small portion of the students can learn. On the other hand, a teacher who holds a high expectation for a low income student will be more effective if supported by a school climate of high expectations for all students. Many teachers have held high expectations for certain of their students and have been disappointed. One reason for this is the counter force of an antagonistic climate of expectations in the school at large.

It is important to recognize that the term *social climate* can refer to any of several different social characteristics in a community. Organizational climate most often refers to the nature of human relations among adult members of the organization. Climate also has been used to refer to the degree of order or violence within a school. Although both these, and other types of climate, have some relevance, they do not adequately describe the climate that is most relevant to learning academic skills and knowledge. In other words, there are many school climates, and some are not as useful as others in explaining the academic achievement levels of schools. We are concerned with the academic *learning climates* of schools, which hereafter we shall refer to as *learning climates.*

The *learning climate* of a school takes into account certain forces in the school's social system. The social system we are most interested in is the set of relationships between and among students, teachers, principals, parents, and others which are most relevant to the academic learning that takes place in a school.

School Learning Climate

- A school's learning climate, as used here, refers to a collective set of factors within a school that affect academic subject matter learning among students.

- A school's learning climate is the collective set of attitudes, beliefs, and behaviors within a building. It goes beyond the individual to the group norms of a school. These norms tend to be maintained over time with new members being socialized into the prevailing sets of expected behaviors.

- Since schools share a common function in society, there is some similarity in learning climates from school to school. On the other hand, there is a uniqueness among schools. Different schools stress different philosophies, instructional practices, methodologies, beliefs and expectations about students' abilities to learn. This variation produces different levels of student achievement.

- A school's learning climate can be changed, and the people who are members of the school are the main change agents. Outsiders will have little impact on the norms within a school building unless the adults in a school desire or are willing to change.

In summary *school learning climate* refers to the normative attitudinal and behavioral patterns in a school which impact on the level of academic achievement of the student body as a whole, including:

- teachers' expectations for and evaluations of students,

- academic norms,

- students' sense of futility with respect to learning,

- role definitions,

- grouping patterns, and

- instructional practices.

When the learning climate of a school produces high academic performance levels, the school is in our terms, an *effective school*. Effective schools are those which produce a mastery at relatively high levels of critical academic skills and knowledge in nearly all of their students, regardless of their ethnic, racial or socio-economic status, or the economic level of the community. As such, effective schools have learning climates that involve the interaction of certain patterns of attitudes, beliefs, norms, role definitions, structure, and instructional behaviors.

We group these factors into three clusters: *school ideology, organization,* and *instructional practices.* This is based on a wide range of research in the United States, Canada, United Kingdom, and elsewhere. Although we have identified the characteristics of effective schools in these three clusters for convenience of discussion, no one cluster, or any combination of two clusters, can adequately explain the degree to which a school is effective. Rather, the total complex of these three categories of factors interact to produce learning outcomes. In other words, these clusters are not separate and independent; they have an interactive relationship. Changes in one cluster are likely to produce changes in the other two. (Perhaps these clusters are more useful for purposes of description than as distinct characteristics since there is considerable overlap between them.)

School Ideology

School ideology refers to the general beliefs, norms, expectations, and feelings that characterize the school social system. The beliefs that nearly all students can learn and that teachers can teach, is one critical characteristic in producing a large portion of the student body with high academic skills. The performance expectations for students and staff are generalized school-wide norms, or standards of achievement. It is the internalization of these norms by students, parents, and staff which most directly affects their achievement levels. Research indicates that when a school's staff tends to believe that many of its students are slow or unable to learn, there will be a high sense of futility among students regarding their ability to achieve. Many students simply give up trying to succeed.

When the school is characterized by such feelings, it is almost inevitable that the school's level of achievement will be low.

Schools organized on the basis of an ideology where many students are identified as non-learners, slow, needing special attention, poorly motivated, or unable to learn complex concepts, are those schools that are most ineffective. A school that differentiates between students who are expected to learn and those who are not expected to learn at high levels will never be a high achieving school. In a sense, the school may be creating the very condition it wishes to avoid by reinforcing a climate of failure rather than success. After all, as documented in the subsequent modules of this manual, if the staff in a school acts as if students will fail, they are designing their school to produce this failure. The school's staff thus unintentionally creates and reinforces the very conditions of low achievement it seeks to avoid. Regrettably, many students are the brunt of schools systematically designed for failure. They are not given a true opportunity to succeed.

Organizational Structure

Students must believe they can and will learn in school. Unfortunately, this belief alone is not enough. Even high teacher expectations and high levels of student confidence are not sufficient to produce effective schools. A positive ideology of beliefs, norms, and expectations must be accompanied by an organization that fosters academic mastery among all pupils and rewards both effective teaching and successful learning. It is not uncommon to find in failing schools that students who learn at low levels are rewarded with less homework and fewer demands. Seldom in failing schools are teachers rewarded for raising the achievement level of the entire school. The standards are low in low-achieving schools.

Even with good intentions, all too often schools organize to differentiate students by presumed abilities to learn — not by what they have learned but by what they presume the students can learn. One of the most common methods of differentiation by presumed abilities occurs when schools organize students into different tracks, different sections, or different groups based on staff perceptions of students' learning abilities.

As documented in *Module 5* and elsewhere, college prep *verses* low level vocational education, algebra *verses* low level business math, and the top reading groups *verses* bottom and middle reading level groups, are only a few examples of how some students are grouped for failure, and others for success.

When students are grouped in such a fashion the outcome is clear — large numbers of students are defined as unable to learn, and they live up to this low standard of achievement. Students in accelerated groups receive reinforcement for fulfilling the high expectations associated with their group membership; and similarly, students in the low groups are recognized and rewarded for failing to learn at high levels. These rewards for failure may include less homework, reduced accountability for their behaviors, and encouragement to pursue non-academic endeavors. It is no wonder that students in low achieving groups fulfill the low expectations held for them. These groups also become convenient scapegoats for school officials and others to explain away the persistence of disciplinary and other problems.

As long as the organizational characteristics of a school provide a system of rewards for failure, failure will continue to occur. In order to have an effective school, nearly all students must be expected to achieve at a high level and not be separated on the basis of presumed ability to learn. To accomplish this, all teachers must accept the responsibility of guiding students to high achievement. It is also true that principals must provide the leadership for organizing schools in such a way that all students and teachers are rewarded for effective teaching and learning. In addition, students and teachers must be given reasonable opportunities to succeed.

Instructional Practices

There is a pervasive belief that the main thing teachers and principals need in order to be successful is to have students with a desire to learn. While student desires are important and are shaped to a considerable extent by both the ideology and organization of their schools, desire is not enough. Student desire must be supported with opportunities for success, i.e., effective instructional practices.

Students often have the desire to learn a subject but are inhibited by inappropriate instructional practices. Simply stated, their desire to learn is undermined by inflexible or ineffective teaching methods.

While *student self-concept of academic ability* is important, students do not learn most academic subjects simply because they believe they can learn. Students learn when they receive instruction that is in accord with their belief that they can and should learn.

The modules in this book will help in this regard. They provide ways for engaging in effective reinforcement, student-team learning, assessment, and time-on-task, to mention a few key elements, when designing instructional programs. Taken together, these modules on instructional techniques provide a framework for transforming high expectations for students into high student achievement throughout a school. These modules for creating effective school learning climates are built upon a key assumption:

> **Effective teachers engage in direct instruction which involves students in learning tasks.**

Effective Schools

Until recently, research seemed to indicate that schools make little difference in the achievement outcomes of students beyond the influence of family background characteristics. Race and economic status, used in some studies as an index of family background, seemed to account for differences in achievement from school to school (Coleman et al., 1966; Jencks et al., 1972). However, more recent research indicates that schools can and do make a difference in student outcomes beyond family socio-economic and racial characteristics.

In addition to overcoming family background characteristics, the preponderance of the research literature indicates that schools can be effective regardless of the community in which the school resides. It is what goes on *inside* a school that is most relevant in determining success or failure for nearly all students. If it were true that schools in the most impoverished areas were doomed to failure, why are there are so many success stories (e.g., Payzant and Gardner, 1994; Dickinson and Smith, 1994; Oxley, 1994; Odgen and Germinario, 1994; Louis, Rosenblum, and Miles, 1990; Phi Delta Kappa, 1980; Brookover et al., 1979)? It is now clear that effective schools do exist in all types of communities. Schools can produce achievement in low income areas. The question is how?

A Profile of an Effective School

In describing the school learning climate for effective schools, we are virtually profiling an "ideal" school. Though this is an ideal model, some schools closely approximate this profile and produce high achievement levels, despite the kinds of communities where they are located. The goal of this manual is to help create schools that match this profile as closely as possible.

A.   The Ideology of an Effective School

1.   **The professional staff holds the following beliefs and attitudes:**

 a. All students can learn the school's objectives.

 b. All students are expected to reach high standards of achievement.

 c. Teachers can successfully instruct all students in the school's objectives.

 d. Individual and school-wide achievement tests and performance measures are appropriate measures of school success.

 e. There are norms of high achievement for staff in working with students and counteracting apathy, negative attitudes, ineffective practices, and low performance.

 f. The staff is committed to producing high achievement for all students, no matter what it takes.

Research on Effective Schools

"No one is complacent about student achievement; there is an expectation that educational programs will be changed so that they work better.

Effective Schooling Practices: A Research Synthesis 1990,
Northwest Regional Educational Laboratory.

2. **Students' perceptions of the school learning climate:**

   a. Students perceive and reinforce norms that high achievement is expected of all students.

   b. Students have a high self-concept of academic ability. This is the student's self-assessment of his or her ability to learn. (Self-concept functions as a threshold variable: high self-concept of ability does not guarantee high achievement but lack of an adequate self-concept of ability may preclude high academic performance.)

   c. Students have a low sense of academic futility. Sense of futility is a perception by the student that nothing one does will make a difference in school, and that trying to learn or succeed is hopeless because of the system. (Students with high futility are low achieving and poorly motivated.)

B. **The Organizational Structure of an Effective School**

1. **Role expectations for appropriate behavior are defined in terms of achievement**

   a. The "effective teacher" role is defined as instructing all students to attain high achievement.

   b. The "good student" role is defined as a high achiever.

c. The "effective principal" role is an instructional leader who acts as a coach and cheerleader for effective instruction by all teachers and high achievement for all students.

d. Leadership is shared with the staff so as to create a common goal for all.

Research on Effective Schools

"In effective schools the power to effect change is multiplied rather than reduced because it is shared."

Odgen, E. H. and V. Germinario. *The Nation's Best Schools: Blueprints for Excellence, Volume I: Elementary and Middle Schools,* Technomic Publishing Co., Lancaster, PA, 1994.

---

2. Reward structures in the school are centered on achievement

a. Teachers are recognized and rewarded for producing high achievements for all students.

b. Students are recognized and rewarded for high achievement and improved performance.

c. The principal is rewarded for promoting a high achieving school in which all students master objectives.

Research on Effective Schools

"Research . . . indicates that actions are motivated by what an individual perceives are the outcomes of those actions . . . students will not be highly motivated in school unless they believe that what they are learning will be of value to them and that effort will help them learn."

Koossterman, P. and M. C. Cougan. "Students' Beliefs About Learning School Mathematics." *The Elementary School Journal,* 94/4 (March 1994): 357-388.

3.   Stratification of students is minimal

   a.   Flexible heterogeneous grouping is used rather than homogeneous grouping of students by presumed ability to learn, by race, or by socio-economic status.

   b.   Testing programs and performance observations are used for diagnosis of learning and instruction needs rather than sorting and selecting between levels of students.

   c.   Remediation of problems is based upon diagnostic uses of tests and performance observations. Remediation implies child advocacy based on academic needs, not homogeneous grouping for the sake of convenience.

   d.   Compensatory education and special education programs are designed to help students "catch-up" to grade level and are conducted in and coordinated with the regular classroom.

Research on Effective Schools

"Teachers in effective schools make use of heterogeneous cooperative learning groups, structuring these so that there are both group rewards and individual accountability."

Cotton, K. *Effective Schooling Practices: A Research Synthesis 1995 Update*, Northwest Regional Educational Laboratory.

---

4.   Differentiation of the instructional program is minimal

   a.   Common high minimal instructional objectives and achievement expectations are established for all students.

   b.   Common instructional materials are used for all students.

   c.   Common role definitions (which involve a mastery of the skills and knowledge that are prerequisites for higher levels of learning) are stated for all students.

d. When some differentiation is necessary in order to provide "catch up" to grade level, it is limited in scope and duration.

C. The Instructional Practices of an Effective School

1. School goals and instructional objectives are defined and shared

    a. School goals, of which first priority is attaining mastery of instructional objectives by all students, are clearly stated.

    b. Standards for mastery of instructional objectives for all students, and procedures for certifying attainment of those standards, are clearly stated.

    c. Instructional objectives for each grade level are clearly stated and reflect the school's goal of basic skill achievement.

    d. Professional staff recognize and accept the priority of mastery of instructional objectives for all students.

2. An effective program of structured, direct instruction is incorporated into a mastery learning strategy for achievement of objectives by all students (see *Module 6).*

3. An orderly, relatively quiet, work-oriented atmosphere reflects effective school and classroom discipline (see *Module 8).*

4. Use of instructional program results in high percentage of the total school day as "academic engaged time" for all students (see *Module 7).*

5. Use of academic competition and cooperation to promote peer learning and motivation (see *Module 9).*

6. Effective use of reinforcement principles, contingent upon expected learning conduct (see *Module 10).*

7. Effective use of assessment data (see *Modules 6 & 11).*

    a. Ongoing monitoring of student progress, including diagnosis and regular feedback to pupils, is carried out.

b. Accurate record keeping of mastery of objectives by all students is required.

c. Diagnostic information is used in planning corrective instruction.

d. School-wide data is used for evaluating and improving the school's instructional program.

Research on Effective Schools

"Test results, grade reports, attendance records, and other methods are used to spot potential problems. Changes are made in instructional programs and school procedures to meet identified needs."

Effective Schooling Practices: A Research Synthesis 1990,
Northwest Regional Educational Laboratory.

Illustrations of School Learning Climates*

The following cases represent different aspects of both effective and ineffective school learning climates. Research strongly indicates that teachers' expectations of students' academic achievement are a major facet in the learning climate. The following vignettes illustrate this and other aspects of the school learning climate.

"We Are All In This Together"

The Mid-town Elementary School is composed predominantly of African-American, working class children who are achieving well above the state average. On a recent visit, the staff was asked, "How do you account for your success? Mrs. Johns, an experienced teacher, answered for the staff, "We are all in this together. We have a job to do. If Johnny doesn't learn to read today, we will see to it that he learns to read tomorrow.

---

*These vignettes are true examples, but names and places are fictitious.

This simple explanation of their effective program summarizes one important aspect of an effective school learning climate. The staff assumes that all their students can learn. The staff has accepted the responsibility for teaching them. No one person is responsible; they are all committed to do the job. To modify a well-known African proverb: "It takes a whole school to educate a child."

"Don't Make Us Look Bad"

A black fifth grade teacher, separated from her husband, moved herself and her three children from Louisiana to Illinois. Her job in a low income, inner city school with mostly African-American students had gone well. She had called or visited every parent of her students. Eighty percent of the parents responded that she was the first teacher to communicate positively with them. After a time she began hearing subtle hints about being a "do-gooder" and "apple polisher" from her fellow teachers. When these hints became less subtle, she was forced to start having lunch by herself in her room. It was not long before she was told that "the way it is here is not to make waves, keep the kids quiet with busywork, and read your paper while they copy out of the encyclopedia." She continued her remedial reading work, cooperation with parents and high quality teaching. Results began to show, even though most of her students were far below grade level. Remarks about a woman alone with three children being in a precarious situation really shook her up, but she persevered with her teaching efforts. Finally, she was told outright to conform or to expect physical consequences to herself, her family, car, or home. She returned to Louisiana. The negative learning climate of the school remains unchanged and the achievement level remains extremely low.

This case history portrays starkly the negative sanctions and the power of the social group to set standards and norms for the school. Often if these norms are unprofessional, a good teacher must become a social isolate or eventually conform to the negative standards.

"The Lounge is for Working"

A low income, suburban high school composed mainly of Appalachian white students has unusually high achievement and it has an effective learning climate — it is an effective high school. Observation of the teachers' lounge reveals that this school does not have a socially oriented atmosphere among the staff during school hours. The teachers use the lounge as a serious work place. Conversations revolve around how to help a student improve in math, how to overcome a problem, or how to implement a new idea. Students are not put down, compared to siblings, or "tagged" with a bad image that precedes them to the next grade. Teachers believe their pupils can learn and are visibly proud of their achievements. The students in the school seem industrious, eager and well-behaved.

This school is another example of the power of the social group to set positive standards. This building also illustrates that behavior in the lounge is often reflective of the overall school learning climate. The true feelings and beliefs about the students and the school typically surface in informal atmosphere settings of the staff.

"The Grass is Greener on the Other Side"

An industrial city in Illinois is split by a river. The east side is low income and minority. A large elementary school is overcrowded (the old mansions of the rich are now subdivided into multiple apartments) and has gone from ninety percent white students to eighty percent minority in six years. Many members of the staff are older and have experienced the turnover of student population. The school, formerly a model school, is now a low achieving school. Comments such as "If I had a class like those kids on the west side of town, I'd really teach them," or "I've got the top ability class this year; maybe if I'm lucky I'll have average achievement," and "These kids' parents just don't care about them so how can you expect them to learn?" are common. The low expectations of the staff are reflected in the school's low achievement level with students.

This last example is a classic case of "blaming the victim." The staff has set up a defense that projects the cause of failure onto the students and parents, rather than looking at how their low expectations impact on their students' performance levels.

These vignettes are extreme but true examples. Not all schools have school learning climates as extreme as those reported here. The learning climate unique to each school, however, does explain much of the achievement outcome. Because of this relationship, we need to know how to change the learning climate if we are to raise achievement.

Research on Effective Schools

"Effective schools provide students with an understanding of basic academic skills and parents with regular communications about their child's achievement. An effective school will provide students with an opportunity to be involved in the decision-making processes with the school."

Townsend, T. "Goals for Effective Schools: The View from the Field," *School Effectiveness and School Improvement,* 5/2 (June 1994): 127-148.

Improving School Learning Climate

We have said that the nature of the learning climate that characterizes a school includes many factors, but the administrators, teachers, aides and other staff personnel are the major forces in that climate. Although the "peer culture" is important, it is the adult staff that sets the tone for academic achievement in school. The adult members of a school social system are the primary agents in developing the learning climate which defines the appropriate behavior for themselves and their students. In addition, the staff and the principal in a school, not the district administration or others outside the building, have the greatest impact on the school's learning environment.

It is precisely because of these facts that the achievement levels in a school can be improved or made worse. What is created by the staff can be changed by the staff. However, habits of belief and behavior do not change easily. The professional staff, nonetheless, must assume the burden of initiating the change process if the school is to raise its academic performance level. This requires a commitment on the part of the staff to produce high levels of student achievement in the student body and to develop and implement the attitudes, beliefs, and behaviors that will result in such high performance.

If the staff is to be successful in changing the school learning climate by changing themselves, several concerns need attention. First, the principal and staff must learn how schools have brought about high achievement. This knowledge must then progress to application. The school learning climate program offered here, and its framework for implementing an in-service program, provide a way to do this. However, all proposed changes contemplated should be based on actual needs. This requires assessing the current school learning climate. The results of this assessment can then give a realistic picture of needs, resistance to change, or other factors before a program is undertaken.

Addressing Negative Attitudes and Behaviors

If the school learning climate is to improve, faculty and staff must become more aware of the subtle relationship between what on its face may seem as innocuous acts, and how these acts influence the student body's level of academic achievement. For example, many school faculties are, unfortunately, characterized by negative and disparaging remarks about Mary's ability, Billy's family, or Joe's behavior. This tendency varies from school to school but is definitely a reflection of differing school learning climates. Some teachers may defend this behavior as merely "blowing off steam" or expressing frustration, with no harm intended. Intended or not, this type of atmosphere leads to lower expectations and evaluations of student ability. It reinforces a belief that some students and their parents constitute obstacles to education, rather than being partners in the learning program. Additionally, the very fact that there is need to "blow off steam" in one school, while another school does not evidence the same frustration, is itself a reflection of the differing school learning climates. Of course, these examples could be expanded to include extended breaks, leaving the classroom excessively, inadequately preparing for class, and the like. Certainly, the vast majority of teachers are caring and committed educators. Yet, if a staff wishes to improve the academic achievement level of its student body, it will need to reduce any subtle behaviors or expressions that retard student achievement.

There are other, equally subtle characteristics of school staffs that also impact on its student body's performance level. For example, teachers may unconsciously behave in ways that, when dealing with students who come to them unprepared, mistakenly respond to their background. There is a mistaken but pervasive belief that low income and some minority pupils do not learn in our educational system. Many myths, stereotypes, and personal experiences reinforce this belief system. Such factors as personal frustrations in schools, socialization of new teachers by "experienced" staff, teacher education that emphasizes individual differences in ability, research reports that mistakenly conclude that family background is the primary determinant of pupil performance, and certain racial and ethnic stereotypes, have contributed to this belief. This belief system in turn has had the effect of absolving educators of their professional responsibilities to be instructionally effective.

Even when informed about high-achieving, low income schools, some faculty will be resistant to suggestions for change. Fear of failure, unfamiliarity with new programs, insecurity about personal competency, and rejection of research findings will be some of the reasons they will give for their resistance.

This is why it is helpful to approach the process of improving a school's learning climate on a collective basis. If the entire staff engages in the change program, the process is less threatening to individuals. Thus, full discussion by the staff should precede any monitoring of the learning climate.

There is another important reason for involving the entire staff in the program for change. If members of the staff are empowered to create a school program which they find to be interesting and exciting, such interest and excitement over school transfers to the students. In schools where teachers and staff are engaged as interested professionals, so too will the students be engaged as interested learners.

We should have learned by now that no superintendent or principal can be effective by simply ordering her or his staff to accept responsibility for assuring that all students learn; unless, that is, the staff accepts such direction. Improving the learning climate on a collective basis means a sharing of leadership. It also may help to relieve tension among the staff and the reluctance of some to participate, if staff self-monitoring is done as light-hearted bantering. The object is not to be harsh and critical and thereby cause some to become even more resistant to change. This is where effective leadership and social skills are so important.

The school's responsibility for high achievement for all students raises other problems with respect to changing a school's norms. What is the individual teacher's responsibility with reference to the building norms and commitment to student achievement? Can a teacher be allowed to sit back and refuse to join or support others in establishing the collective norm for high achievement? Does a teacher have a responsibility to be a catalyst for improving the building norms? How much risk, in terms of being called a "rate-buster," must the teacher take? Does the responsibility of a teacher end with his or her own class? These are not easy questions but they require appropriate answers.

Given research on the strength of school norms in affecting student body achievement levels, it becomes very difficult to accept an individualist or isolationist stance. If there are staff "holdouts" — complacent, noncommitted, or highly skeptical staff members — the rest of the staff may have to ask them to: 1) refrain from interfering; 2) keep an open mind on results of the change process; and 3) apply peer pressure to get them to participate. Again, effective leadership and social skills will be needed to work with "holdouts."

Nonetheless, regardless of how well changes are implemented in school norms, there will be some conflict. This is illustrated by feedback from an educator who assisted in the preparation of the first edition of these modules:

> *"If the analogy of 'rate busting' is used, the question would be more understandable to teachers, particularly teachers in this city. It really needs to be out on the table, so that all parties to the change process know what's coming and can anticipate their roles in "creative conflict." The example given in this module of the new teacher being forced out because she or he worked too hard is in no way extreme: it is the "norm," in fact.*

Probably every teacher could come up with a similar story. We are just more polite about it than blue collar workers. Principals get heat, too, for rate busting on achievement."

In terms of authority, a primary legal responsibility for a school's academic achievement level is with the principal. However, while a principal may have the authority, the majority of the power or ability to affect outcomes in the classrooms rest in the end with the teachers and other staff. Thus, while the principal should take a role as a change agent in improving the school learning climate, he or she must do so in a way that elicits the cooperation of the staff when they enter their classrooms. One way of doing this is through sharing leadership with the staff.

Yet since the senior administrator is publicly responsible for the ongoing academic program, there is the very real possibility of role conflict and stress. An ineffective principal may have difficulties choosing between what seems as a stable, happy, but low achieving school and the path of change and improvement with its attendant conflict.

Any effort to improve schools, no matter how skilled the principal and other staff leaders, will lead to some conflict. This potential for conflict should be recognized in advance and put "on the table." Personal threat and hostile reactions will thereby be minimized. Although raising the achievement of a school is often characterized by staff dissension, schools with declining achievement levels are often marked by a complacent staff and tensions as well. In the long run, tension and conflict tend to decline when the achievement level of the school improves. Knowing that the students are achieving much better will do wonders at reducing stress. In addition, the perils of boredom, teacher burn-out and resistance often are overcome by their involvement as co-leaders for change. The principal, even though she or he shares leadership, has the most resources to reinforce the staff with rewards, including eliciting from the district and community additional support for staff initiative and participation.

Research on Effective Schools

"Change is not fully predictable and not without pain. However, change can also be rewarding if everyone is given the opportunity to participate."

Fullan, M. G. (with Stiegelbauer, S.), *The New Meaning of Educational Change.* Teachers College Press, Columbia University, New York, 1991.

The Climate Watchers Process

Even when a teacher or other staff person wants to change, it is often difficult to dispense with old habits. Yet change that is difficult for the individual can often be accomplished with the active support of a group of peers. Various cooperative self-help groups are based on this concept.

The support for this approach to change goes back to the World War II experiments of Kurt Lewin (1952) involving efforts to change the eating and cooking habits of housewives. With the need for prime cuts of meat overseas, groups of women were encouraged to use less traditional parts of the animal (e.g., brains, kidneys, tongue, etc.). Various methods were tried including using university experts, providing demonstrations and lectures, and making visits to individual homes. *In the end, the only system that worked well was the institution of a group decision process among women who mutually supported one another, followed by check-ups and monitoring to see if they achieved their goal.* The belief that attitudes and behaviors are common to the group functions to shape the attitudes and behaviors of the group's individual members.

The norms and beliefs about students that are a part of an ineffective school learning climate, therefore, should be scrutinized and extinguished by the group, particularly beliefs that minority and poor students cannot learn well. Practices such as ability grouping and individualized instruction that result in the sorting and differentiation of students should also be questioned by the group. This is because attempts by *individuals* to alter their beliefs and behaviors without social support often fail. Suggestions or efforts at change are more likely to succeed if they are part of a *group* effort of watching or monitoring each other and reinforcing positive improvements. This is a process of supportive interaction to accomplish a common goal of creating effective norms that support high achievement for all students. The following are essential aspects of this climate watchers process:

1. Identifying both ineffective and effective attitudes and behaviors with respect to achievement.

2. Explaining why and how these factors relate to achievement.

3. Creating awareness of the existence of these ineffective behaviors in day-to-day routines and instructional practices.

4. Setting up a regular forum for discussion of these behaviors.

5. Instituting a checking-up procedure among the group to report progress (or lack of it) in changing ineffective behavior.

6. Establishing a process for recognizing and rewarding those who are successful in improving achievement levels.

This type of group process provides the basis for the cooperative peer forces which can yield powerful results in changing behaviors. However, if the *Climate Watchers* process is to be effective, it must also operate at an informal level among the staff members. The informal monitoring of conversations and behavior takes place continuously as the staff meet each other in the lounge, the corridor, the office or at lunch. Aspects of this informal part of the process include:

1. Climate monitoring becomes a part of the ongoing, daily discussion among members of the school staff.

2. The group becomes aware of the consequences of their beliefs, statements and actions on school achievement.

3. The group members mutually discourage undesirable or ineffective attitudes, comments, and behavior, and reward effective behavior as it occurs throughout the building.

4. This informal, ongoing monitoring of conversation and behavior also is a part of scheduled gatherings, such as faculty or grade level meetings or mutual assistance dyads.

The combination of formal meetings for check-in and informal mutual monitoring of the group's behavior is more effective than either one by itself. However, getting the informal group dynamics to function on an ongoing basis may be difficult. While the process can be explained and encouraged in the regular formal setting, the actual informal monitoring has a spontaneity that must somehow spark to life by itself. The first step is commitment of the staff to develop an improved learning climate, coupled with agreement to criticize or reward one another spontaneously. Again social skill is required so that criticism is not done in a way that makes the object of attention even more resistant to change. To imply that another is dumb or evil is not an effective way to elicit change.

A key question now becomes "What specific attitudes and behaviors should be changed?" What kinds of questions should the group ask of one another during check-in times, and what activities should be monitored informally? Teachers, the principal, and others on the staff should discuss such questions as: "What have you done this week to maximize learning for all students?" "What have you done today that might influence the way pupils evaluate themselves?" "Have you said anything that might prejudice another teacher toward a student's performance next year?" "What do remarks in this school indicate about expectations for students' achievement and evaluations of their ability?"

A more adequate answer to these questions is further spelled out in this entire set of modules. In general, however, it may be noted that behavior and attitudes that are consistent with an effective school learning climate and effective instruction should be publicly acknowledged. Conversely, behavior which impedes high achievement or reflects negatively on students' ability to learn should be rebuked in a fashion that does not result in more resistance. For example, if a teacher is publicly embarrassed her or his peer teachers may raise to his or her defense and scuttle the program. There is likely to be far less of a problem in giving praise. The staff should ensure, however, that praise is contingent on actual improved performance and changes in behavior; a mutual admiration society for continued low achievement or negative attitudes will hinder improvement.

Although a properly conducted climate watching process can produce powerful incentives for change, it will be most effective if all the members of the group participate. Unfortunately, the tradition of the autonomous teacher deciding alone upon instructional matters, leaves many teachers and other staff as unwilling to engage in activities which may be perceived as critical of another. This is reinforced by the general reluctance to publicly criticize another person no matter how sensitive and careful one might be. If one is to be effective in honest evaluations of others one must embed such criticisms in extensive reinforcement of the value of the object of that attention. David Johnson in *Reaching Out* (1995) provides excellent advice on how to confront others with whom one disagrees, even superiors, in a way that is accepted as help rather than as a threat.

Measuring the Effects of Learning Climates

A useful assessment process that includes testing and performance evaluation is necessary to assure an effective school learning climate. The primary outcome to consider when measuring the effects of a school's learning climate is the student body's achievement level. If the achievement level is low, the learning climate is not what it should be. However, outcome results provide only a general indication of the level of the effectiveness of the learning climate, and not what it is about the climate that needs improvements. What is needed is more formative evaluation in order to know why a school learning climate is functioning as it is.

We should not downplay the amount of information that can be obtained from various test data. *Module 11* discusses the use of assessment data to improve classroom instruction and the overall building program. However, other kinds of data should also be acquired. Effective instruction often involves students in performing and not just in passively receiving information. As such, data on student performances assembled in portfolios can sometimes give a more accurate picture of what has been learned — especially with higher order skills — than can paper and pencil tests. Student standardized achievement test results, however, may be the only available source of information about the effectiveness of a school's learning climate. This is particularly true if an individual or a small group of teachers is attempting to implement this program independently.

Summary

Studies provide strong evidence that the academic failures common among low income, minority schools need not occur. Unfortunately, the social system of most low achieving schools is designed to not only accept but to continue failure. Collectively, we should discard a belief in the inevitability of the normal or bell-shaped curve, which is used to justify differentiating and sorting students so that many fail. Instead, if we substituted the concept of the "J" curve (Allport, 1934), with its assumptions that nearly all can and will learn, we could then develop a mastery model of instruction in which the results would conform to higher expectations for students. We would foster an effective school learning climate that ensures, or at least makes highly probable, mastery of certain minimal academic competencies. Adoption of this position does not mean we must ignore some hard realities of education. In fact, there may be some community and peer group norms and some economic facts of life that impede high academic achievement in some low income, minority urban areas. However, there also is the fact that some low income, minority urban schools produce higher academic achievements than some middle and higher income schools in all-white communities. Furthermore, there is no evidence to show that negative community factors, where they exist, must inevitably result in low achievement in school.

As professionals, we should not use a student's home environment or social status as an excuse for inappropriate instruction or poor academic achievement. Instead, we should help our students, our peers and our public to understand the real importance of the school social system, the classroom environment and our teaching activities. We must recognize that high achieving, economically disadvantaged schools are living proof that poor children can be educated to high levels of achievement. We should get on with the business of creating classroom environments and school learning climates that promote high achievement.

Suggested Activities

Develop two written statements for your school: one, a statement of purposes and beliefs and two, a school achievement plan.

As these documents should represent the position of the school staff, involvement of both teachers and the principal in developing them is essential. Both documents should be consistent with the concepts of effective school learning climate outlined in this module; and they should reflect the major position of the staff on the mission of the school in maximizing the achievement of all students in the school. The School Achievement Plan identifies the building approach to instruction for staff and students.

It is suggested that a format of short, capsule statements be used instead of a lengthy narrative style. They should be informative, but concise, as they are working guidelines for making educational decisions. Examples of such documents follow:

Suggested Statement of Purpose and Beliefs

- The purpose of the school is to educate all students to high levels of academic performance.
- To fulfill this purpose, the members of this school staff believe:
  - All students should have a challenging academic program.
  - All students should master their grade level objectives.
  - Teachers are obligated to prepare all students to perform at mastery level on the objectives for the grade.

- Parents should understand the academic goals of the school and support their child and the teacher's efforts to reach those goals.

Suggested School Achievement Plan

Identify and Assess Achievement Objectives

- Learning objectives to be mastered will be identified for each grade level.

- A standard for mastery performance for the school will be set by the staff each year and explained to students and parents (see *Module 3*).

- Assessment of academic progress for all students will be continuous and conducted as follows:

  - Formal pre-test: gather information on students;

  - Informal: at the beginning of the course — including test and performance evaluation data;

  - Formal: quarterly assessment to evaluate progress and weaknesses;

  - Informal: continue monitoring and recording;

  - Formal: post-test evaluation at the end of the course;

  - Progress reports will be sent to parents following each formal assessment of student learning;

  - The teacher will certify at the end of the course that each student has or has not achieved according to the established standard for mastery. A copy of the certification will be sent to each student's parent(s) or guardian(s);

  - To meet the school standard for mastery, it is expected that:

    - teachers will organize and conduct instruction so that mastery performance is possible for all students;

    - students will exert whatever effort is necessary to learn their objective; and

    - parents will support and assist their child's efforts to learn the objectives of the grade.

Document Student Achievement

The practice of certifying student achievement is consistent with the expectation that students will achieve at high levels. This is the logical consequence of setting performance standards. The purpose of performance certification is to officially establish that a student has, or has not, achieved according to the expected standard for the grade.

The following guidelines are suggested:

- The course post-test or comprehensive test is the primary instrument for certification as it requires the student to demonstrate understanding of the entire course. These tasks may be very complex and require performance not amenable to simple right-and-wrong objective tests, such as those involved in developing mastery of certain writing skills.

- When students achieve the standard of mastery established for their grade level, the teacher can indicate this on a Certificate of Academic Performance. Conversely, if the standard of mastery is not attained, the teacher can indicate this as well.

- If the teacher feels that certain test or performance results do not accurately reflect the student's understanding of the objectives for the grade, the teacher can use other data for certification — if it is objective and verifiable. The idea is to objectively verify the level of student mastery of subjects.

- The teacher should make a genuine effort to inform parents about the student's success, or lack of success, in meeting the standard for mastery in the subjects specified. A copy of the Certificate of Academic Performance should be sent home.

- Records of certification should be available when a student goes to a new teacher or to a new school. A copy of the Certificate of Academic Performance should be included in the student's cumulative file.

Records of Certification

- Teachers and administrators of the school should complete their respective school learning climate assessment forms. This is designed to produce a profile of strengths and deficiencies of the school's learning climate. The results of the learning climate assessment should be compiled focusing on the areas that need improvement, then discussed with the whole staff. The deficiencies identified in the school profile represent the areas of greatest concern and should be targeted for special emphasis.

Set Priorities

Changing too many things at once as this can be overwhelming and defeating. Instead, list the areas requiring change or attention and then prioritize them according to the following:

- What needs immediate attention?
- What should be completed by the end of this year?
- What should be worked on next year?
- What needs further study or clarification?

Reach consensus on a realistic, but challenging, program of change for the building.

Climate Watchers

Create a Climate Watchers' process. Essentially, this is a way to encourage the total building staff to publicly monitor itself so the beliefs, attitudes, and behavior associated with effective school learning climate can become standard operating procedure. The climate watchers should operate at both the formal meetings and informal levels of school organization. A single topic/concern that has been identified by the group should be discussed. It is recommended that a discussion topic for the following meeting be identified at the current session. This allows time for staff consideration, preparation, or a trio of new practices. It is also recommended that one person in the group assume responsibility for overseeing the climate watchers function at each meeting. This involves leading the discussion and seeing that a topic is established for the next meeting's agenda.

An important feature of each climate watcher session is the "check in" time where all members of the group report their success or lack of success in adopting or dealing with the topic of the last meeting. Establish the expectation that all members will report at each meeting — not just those who volunteer. Positive reinforcement should be expressed to encourage individual efforts. Also, negative sanctions should occur naturally as called for.

The staff must also spontaneously develop the mutual monitoring of daily behavior on an informal basis. Informal, continuous checking-up will increase awareness of unconscious remarks and practices that are contrary to an effective school learning climate. In order to help institute and support this informal climate watching, the staff should also discuss at the formal climate watchers sessions the extent to which the staff is monitoring one another on an ongoing basis, with the goal of increasing the extent of this informal process. Only when the informal process has become an accepted and regular part of the group norms will the climate watchers reach maximum effectiveness.

Generate Lots of Discussion

- At meetings, use the vignettes from the module to generate staff discussion about factors that contribute to good or poor school learning climate. Encourage faculty to identify not only deficiencies or problems, but also suggestions for improvements. Also, sharing individual experiences involving the learning climate from working in other schools will add meaning to the discussion.

Selected Bibliography

Allport, F. "J-curve Hypothesis of Conforming Behavior." *Journal of Social Psychology* 5/1 (1934): 141-181.

📖 Austin, G. R. and H. Garber. (editors). *Research on Exemplary Schools.* Orlando, FL: Academic Press, 1985.

📖 Avviam, O. "The Impact of School as a Social System on the Formation of Student Intergroup Attitudes and Behavior." *Journal of Educational Equity and Leadership,* 7/2 (Summer, 1987): 92-108.

📖 Block, A. W. *Effective Schools: A Summary of Research.* Research Brief. Arlington, VA: Educational Research Services, Inc., 1983.

📖 Bloom, B. S. *Human Characteristics and School Learning.* New York: McGraw-Hill, 1976.

📖 Borger, J. B., Lo, E., and H. J. Walberg. "Effective Schools: A Qualitative Synthesis of Constructs." *Journal of Classroom Interaction,* 20/2 (Summer 1985): 12-17.

📖 Bossert, S. T. "School Effects." in *Handbook of Research on Educational Administration,* edited by N. J. Boyan, New York: Longman, 1988, 341-352.

📖 Brookover, W., Beady, C., Flood, P., Schweitzer, J., and J. Wisenbaker. *School Social Systems and Student achievement: Schools Can Make a Difference.* South Hadley, MA: J. F. Bergin Co., distributed by Praeger Publishers, New York, 1979.

📖 Brookover, W. B., and L. W. Lezotte. *Changes in School Characteristics Coincident with Changes in Student Achievement.* East Lansing: Institute For Research on Teaching, Michigan State University, 1977.

📖 Clark, D. L., Lotto, L. S. and T. A. Asuto. "Effective Schools and School Improvement: A Comparative Analysis of Two Lines of Inquiry." *Educational Administration Quarterly,* 20/3 (Summer 1984): 41-68.

📖 Coleman, J., Campbell, E., Hobson, C., McPartland, J., Mood, A., Weinfeld, F., and R. York. *Equality of Educational Opportunity.* Washington, DC: U.S. Government Printing Office, 1966.

📖 Cororan, T.B. "Effective Secondary Schools." In *Reaching for Excellence: An Effective Schools Sourcebook.* Washington, DC: National Institute of Education, May 1985, 71-97.

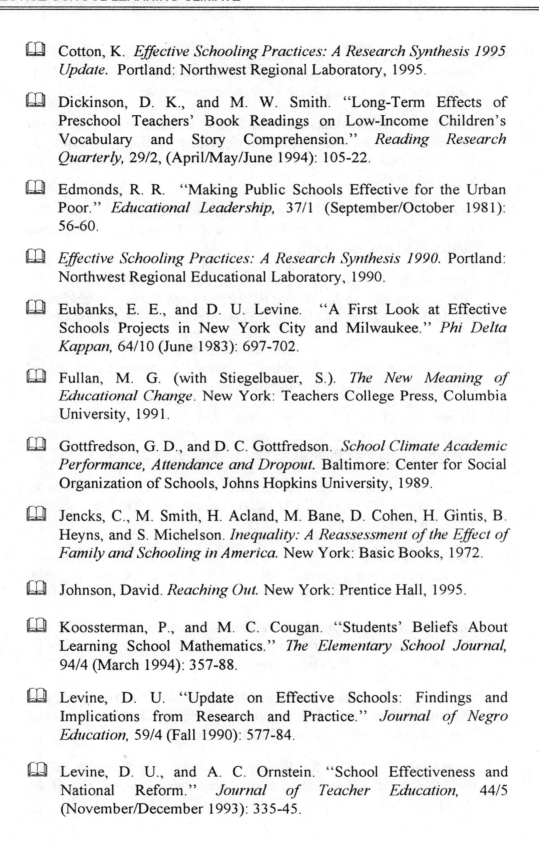

Cotton, K. *Effective Schooling Practices: A Research Synthesis 1995 Update.* Portland: Northwest Regional Laboratory, 1995.

Dickinson, D. K., and M. W. Smith. "Long-Term Effects of Preschool Teachers' Book Readings on Low-Income Children's Vocabulary and Story Comprehension." *Reading Research Quarterly,* 29/2, (April/May/June 1994): 105-22.

Edmonds, R. R. "Making Public Schools Effective for the Urban Poor." *Educational Leadership,* 37/1 (September/October 1981): 56-60.

Effective Schooling Practices: A Research Synthesis 1990. Portland: Northwest Regional Educational Laboratory, 1990.

Eubanks, E. E., and D. U. Levine. "A First Look at Effective Schools Projects in New York City and Milwaukee." *Phi Delta Kappan,* 64/10 (June 1983): 697-702.

Fullan, M. G. (with Stiegelbauer, S.). *The New Meaning of Educational Change.* New York: Teachers College Press, Columbia University, 1991.

Gottfredson, G. D., and D. C. Gottfredson. *School Climate Academic Performance, Attendance and Dropout.* Baltimore: Center for Social Organization of Schools, Johns Hopkins University, 1989.

Jencks, C., M. Smith, H. Acland, M. Bane, D. Cohen, H. Gintis, B. Heyns, and S. Michelson. *Inequality: A Reassessment of the Effect of Family and Schooling in America.* New York: Basic Books, 1972.

Johnson, David. *Reaching Out.* New York: Prentice Hall, 1995.

Koossterman, P., and M. C. Cougan. "Students' Beliefs About Learning School Mathematics." *The Elementary School Journal,* 94/4 (March 1994): 357-88.

Levine, D. U. "Update on Effective Schools: Findings and Implications from Research and Practice." *Journal of Negro Education,* 59/4 (Fall 1990): 577-84.

Levine, D. U., and A. C. Ornstein. "School Effectiveness and National Reform." *Journal of Teacher Education,* 44/5 (November/December 1993): 335-45.

📖 Levine, D. U. and L. W. Lezotte. "Effective Schools Research," in *Handbook of Research on Multicultural Education*, edited by J. A. Banks and C. A. Banks, New York: Macmillan, 1995.

📖 Lewin, K. "Group Decision and Social Change" in *Readings in Social Psychology*, (Revised Edition), edited by G. E. Swanson, T. M. Newcomb, and E. L. Hartley. New York: Henry Holt and Company, 1952.

📖 Lezotte, L. W. and B. C. Jacoby. *Sustainable School Reform: The District Context of School Improvement.* Okemos, MI: Effective School Products, Inc., 1992.

📖 Louis, K. S., Rosenblum, S., and M. B. Miles. "On the Move: Two Success Stories," in *Improving the Urban High School: What Really Works*, Lous, K.S and Miles, M.B. Teachers College Press, 1990.

📖 Mortimore, P. "School Effectiveness and the Management of Effective Learning and Teaching." *School Effectiveness and School Improvement*, 4/4 (1993): 290-310.

📖 Odgen, E. H. and V. Germinario. *The Nation's Best Schools: Blueprints for Excellence: Volume I: Elementary and Middle Schools.* Technomic Publishing Co., Lancaster, PA, 1994.

📖 Oxley, D. "Organizing Schools Into Small Units: Alternatives to Homogeneous Grouping." *Phi Delta Kappan.* Vol. 75., No. 7, March 1994, pp. 521-526.

📖 Payzant, Thomas W. and M. Gardner. "Changing Roles and Responsibilities in a restructuring School District." *NASSP Bulletin.* Vol. 78., No. 560, 1994, pp. 8-17.

📖 Phi Delta Kappa. *Why do some urban schools succeed? The Phi Delta Kappa study of exceptional urban elementary schools.* Bloomington, Ind.: Phi Delta Kappa, 1980.

📖 Sammons, P., Hillman, J. and P. Mortimore. *Key Characteristics of Effective Schools.* London: International School Effectiveness and Improvement Centre, University of London, 1994.

📖 Townsend, T. "Goals for Effective Schools: The View from the Field." *School Effectiveness and School Improvement*, 5/2 (June 1994): 127-148.

Module 3
Expectations For Learning

Key Concepts and Considerations

- High Expectations – High Achievement
- Teacher Expectations and School Learning Climate
- The Self-Fulfilling Prophecy
- Transmission of Expectations
- Improving Expectations and Student Learning Climate
- Criterion and Normative Based Expectations
- Avoiding Illusions of High Expectations

High Expectations – High Achievement

What teachers expect of their students, their students are likely to learn. That is the essence of the *self-fulfilling prophecy*. When students perceive high standards from their teachers, and believe that other educators in the school also expect them to act and perform at high levels, they tend to achieve at high levels. When these perceptions of high expectations are the norm — a climate of high expectations — the likelihood of an effective school learning climate is enhanced. On the other hand, when students believe that their own teachers and teachers in general, think they are incapable, that no matter what they do they will fail, then they will perform at low levels. If the pervasive belief in the school is failure, then failure is what the school produces. In short, students tend to rise or fall to the level of expectations held by educators. They fulfill prophecies. In this sense, schools create "smart" or "dumb" students, depending upon the demand level for achievement placed upon those students.

While many educators are aware of the role of self-fulfilling prophecies, seldom do they realize the magnitude of influence that their attitudes and behaviors have on their students. This is, in part, because the process by which influence is formed and transmitted is largely of an unconscious or latent nature. The reason for the relevance of teachers' expectations is expressed in the *affect/effect theory of mediation* (Rosenthal, 1989). This theory states that:

> *A change in the level of expectations held by a teacher for the intellectual performance of a student is translated into a change in affect shown by the teacher toward the student and the degree of effort shown by that teacher in teaching that student (Rosenthal, 1989).*

This module explores the relationship between teachers' expectations for themselves, other teachers, their students, their students' peers, and others (see *Figure 3-1)*. The sources of these expectations also are examined. The first part of this module focuses on interactions between the adult staff and the student body. The second part addresses the process by which teacher expectations become self-fulfilling prophecies. By understanding these processes, teachers and other educators should be able to avoid negative self-fulfilling prophecies that damage students. Finally, suggestions are made for improving how students perceive their learning climate.

Figure 3-1
SCHOOL LEARNING CLIMATE FACTORS

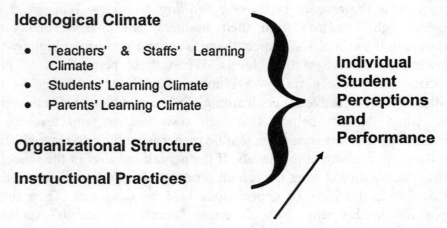

Ideological Climate

- Teachers' & Staffs' Learning Climate
- Students' Learning Climate
- Parents' Learning Climate

Organizational Structure

Instructional Practices

Individual Student Perceptions and Performance

Other Factors:

- Perceptions and actions of significant others
- Personal characteristics

Expectations and Student Perceptions

As was the focus of the second module of this book, the adult staff of the school provides the primary ideological force in the school learning climate. The key to this statement is in the influence of teacher expectations — not only on themselves and their students — but also on how other teachers, staff, parents and students respond toward one another.

Teachers have extensive and direct influence on students with regard to student norms for learning. This includes time to be spent on studying, work to be completed, how many students are thought capable of learning well, students' behavior and the help students seek from their teachers. One important consideration in assessing the value teachers place on academics, is how much priority they place on such interests as sports, boy-girl relations, faculty parties, and even gossip among teachers. Another strong influence is the percent of students that teachers expect to finish high school or are capable of going to college. Such expectations set the tone for the character of learning that occurs in school.

The expectations of the teaching staff tend to become, even if not explicitly expressed, the functioning goals of the school. If the purpose of teachers is primarily social control, academic achievement will be secondary and low — as well as academic excellence on the part of the school as a whole. Again it should be noted, student performance is more than simply the result of student competencies and attitudes toward learning. Student academic performance is related to the standards for performance held by the teaching staff, and the priority teachers give to these standards. By setting a demand level for achieving mastery, a norm is created which the students eventually internalize. Simply stated, if achievement is demanded of them by their teachers, students soon come to demand it of themselves.

Students also are influenced by other adults in school, their peers, and their parents who may take into account many things besides academics. Popularity, athletics, music, dating, cars, and even drugs and violence are important criteria that peers typically use to evaluate one another. Nonetheless, academic success or failure as a student is still important with most peer groups, although this peer influence is often misunderstood

(Vandell and Hembree, 1994). As academic success declines, the relevance of academic achievement is downgraded by students. In other words, students are aware of the reason they go to school. It is to learn academic skills and knowledge. How much priority they give to academic achievement obviously varies. When students' friends are not academically successful, or when their academic work seems unrelated to current and future goals, they turn to other pursuits to meet their need for recognition. Yet in effective schools, the agenda of academic mastery for all sets the tone of the social agenda, rather than vice versa.

In some school settings, high achievement is discouraged by friendship groups. Often these influential peers are the very ones who have been allowed to fail or to "get by" with minimal achievement. In a sense, the success of one becomes a source of conflict among peers who have been denied success. For example, Clasen (1992) found that in some urban settings "high-achieving African-American students run the risk of both physical and verbal abuse from peers." On the other hand, Clasen (1992) fortunately found that with the help of teachers and principals, this excellence-alienation link can be removed or extensively weakened. It is clear, therefore, that teachers are linked to student achievement in multiple ways, including *via* peer group pressures.

Teacher expectations and evaluations are directly linked to the achievements of their students through differing amounts of instruction, time spent interacting with students, quality of materials, and the use of rewards and punishments for certain kinds of behavior. In short, high expectations by teachers produce more and better instruction; low teacher expectations result in less instruction and attention. This difference among teachers and the relevance of this difference for student achievement has been well-documented by many researchers over many years (e.g., Cotton, 1995; Brookover, et al., 1979; Brophy & Good, 1974; Finn, 1972; Rist, 1970).

What is more recently documented is that teachers are important not only individually, but collectively as a climate force. The teaching climate often shapes what the individual teacher teaches as a significant other in the lives of students (Brookover et al., 1979; Cotton, 1995). An analysis of how these expectations of teachers individually and collectively as a climate force, impact on students is the essence of the self-fulfilling prophecy — *the affect/effect mediation theory* — which is addressed later in this module.

Teachers also are indirectly linked to student achievement. The norms, expectations, and attitudes that the student body holds come from student perceptions of others, particularly their perceptions of teachers (see *Figure 3-2)*. Student perceptions of individual teachers, and teachers as a group, linked to student academic norms, student sense of academic futility and student self-concept of academic ability — all critical factors in student performance. In an early study, Brookover and associates (1979) found that one aspect of the student learning climate — student sense of academic futility — accounts for more than half of the variation in a school's achievement level. And teachers directly influence students' sense of academic futility. This sense of futility has a lasting effect long after contact between particular teachers and students have ended.

Figure 3-2
DIRECTION OF TEACHER INFLUENCE

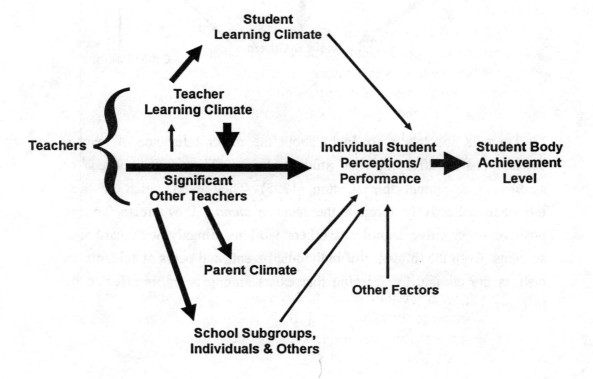

As illustrated in *Figure 3-3,* prior teacher expectations (collectively and individually) influence how teachers evaluate, which in turn impacts on peers; and also indirectly on student evaluations through their influence on parents and others in the lives of students. Expectations in the causal chain are critical in the sense that they influence so many other outcomes in school.

Figure 3-3
TEACHER EXPECTATIONS AND EVALUATIONS

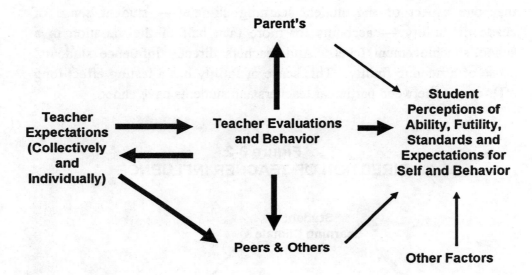

There is absolutely no doubt about the major relevance of teacher expectations in affecting what students learn. There are hundreds of studies to document this (Cotton, 1995). They exert much of their influence collectively through the *teacher climate* they create, and as positive or negative significant others working directly with particular students. Even the influence of individual parents and peers of students, as well as the climate for learning that exists among peers, is affected by teachers' expectations.

Student Climate and Achievement

The three most important subvariables of the student learning climate in a school are: 1) the general level of academic standards or expectations held by the student body (i.e., academic norms); 2) the general level of the student body's self evaluations of competencies pertinent to their academic roles; and 3) the general level of the students' sense of academic futility or efficacy.

While there is variation between and among schools, there also is variation in climate variables within schools for various students. For example, some variation in overall school norms will occur among various student friendship and teacher friendship circles. Restated, acceptable standards for grades, amount of time devoted to homework, and the importance of academic work compared to non-academic activities, will vary by the "crowd" of a student (Brown and Steinberg, 1991). Each crowd, however, will be affected by the general student learning climate and the other learning climate variables in the school.

Research on Effective Schools

"No students are expected to fall below the level of learning needed to be successful at the next level of education."

"Teachers let students know that there are high standards for behavior in the classroom."

Effective Schooling Practices: A Research Synthesis 1990,
Northwest Regional Educational Laboratory, 1990.

The Personal Attributes of Students

Self-conception of Ability

Evidence shows that the self-concepts of academic ability of students are associated with their achievement levels. This association, however, is not well understood. Perhaps this is because the association is not linear in the sense that the higher the self-concept, the higher the achievement. Rather, self-concept of academic ability functions as a necessary, but *not* as a sufficient factor in the personal decisions of students about whether to learn something. A certain amount of confidence in one's ability to learn is necessary to facilitate intentional learning, but is no guarantee that learning will occur. This is illustrated by the fact that most students with low academic self-concepts are low achievers. Not all students with high academic self-concepts, however, achieve at high levels. Students may believe that they can learn something, but choose not to do so. Restated, an adequate self-concept of academic ability is a critical condition for most academic learning to occur, but self-concept of ability alone will not assure such learning. Other factors must be present as well.

In general, student self-conceptions of ability are like certain other personal attributes related to learning in school. They are the consequences of teachers' expectations, evaluations and actions. Teachers are an especially strong factor in influencing student beliefs in their ability to be academically successful, because, as illustrated in *Figure 3-3,* even parental and peer evaluations of a students' academic learning abilities are a function of the assessments and actions of teachers.

Student Perceptions of Futility or Efficacy

Another characteristic of students which impacts on what and how much students learn in school is their sense of academic futility (or efficacy). Futility reflects a sense of hopelessness; futility means a student experiences strong feelings that the school system is stacked against him or her, that no one cares, that he or she has to be lucky to succeed, that no matter what she or he does, only failure in school is possible, or that one might just "get by" and pass. The student may attribute this feeling of futility to racism, poverty or some other condition which is beyond his or her control. Sadly, feelings of victimization by "the system" are often reinforced by groups in such a way as to make the individual feel even more powerless. Even when opportunities for success are presented, the individual's perception of the situation is so warped by group definitions of victimization that legitimate opportunities are overlooked.

It should be recognized that a sense of hopelessness may be held at the same time as holding a high academic self-concept of ability (as has been observed among certain categories of minority students). This apparent contradiction may be explained by the rationale: "I know I've got low grades and don't do well in school, but it's not my fault; I could do it, but the system keeps me down."

In summary, both a low sense of futility and a high self-concept of ability are prerequisite conditions for high achievement. Students have to not only believe in themselves, but also believe that the school system, of which they are a part, will help them. Students must believe that any effort they make to learn will make a difference in what they learn in school and later in life.

Student Standards and Expectations

Each of us have standards for how satisfied we are with what we do in our various roles. Along with these standards we have *expectations* for self. The academic expectations and standards that a student holds for self are extremely relevant personal characteristics. What are the major sources of these student expectations and standards?

Like student evaluations of academic ability and feelings of academic efficacy or futility, their standards and expectations for academic performance are largely influenced by others. They are influenced by the climate of values and expectations held for them, and the values and expectations of particular others, especially their teachers.

Research on Effective Schools

High expectations must be accompanied with a demand that students exhibit strong work habits. As research documents, teachers who hold strong beliefs about the importance of work habits and classroom behavior also appear to practice better instructional methods and to effect better achievement.

Fuchs, L. et al. "The Relation Between Teachers' Beliefs about the Importance of Good Student Work Habits, Teacher Planning, and Student Achievement." *The Elementary School Journal* 94/3 (January 1994): 131-345.

Criterion *vs.* Normative Based Expectations

A critical issue concerns the criteria used in evaluating student competencies in academic tasks. Are their attempts to learn successful or futile? Should we judge their performance based upon objective criteria, or by comparing their efforts with the performance of others? As discussed in *Module 6,* students who are expected to master certain academic skills as determined by objective assessments, and who are taught by mastery learning methods, tend to view their intelligence and ability as *modifiable.* They have objective evidence that they can become smarter and more skilled. They are also more willing to attempt progressively more challenging learning tasks — becoming academic risk takers — because they have proof of their success in prior efforts.

The picture is very different for students who learn to judge their competencies based on how well they do compared to others. When achievement is measured relative to the group, skill mastery may not occur. A student's performance may exceed the group norm, yet still result in failure to achieve mastery.

For example, if the group norm of a 6th grade class is to perform at the 3rd grade level, the individual who exceeds the group norm and performs at the 4th grade level is still not achieving an adequate level of mastery in an absolute sense. This helps to explain why so many students manage to finish their schooling while never having achieved mastery of even the most rudimentary skills necessary to function in society. Evaluating a student on the basis of group norms of achievement alone — especially if the group norms are low — inevitably produces students whose level of mastery in language, mathematics, writing and other critical skills is inadequate.

Mastery learning, based upon objective standards of achievement, can serve to raise group norms to the point where they reinforce rather than hinder the learning climate. This has important implications for the role of teachers. While it is important for teachers to hold high expectations for students, *high expectations alone are not enough.* Teachers need to communicate specific and objective criteria for students to use in judging the merits of their performance. When such objective standards are communicated, students feel a true sense of mastery; their positive self-conceptions of ability are reinforced by a proven set of skills. *Therefore high learning expectations, coupled with specific objective criteria for assessment, together form the basis of an effective school learning climate.*

Avoiding the Illusion of High Expectations

There is a danger in having performance expectations based on the group norms of a school, rather than an objective referenced criteria. This danger is apparent when you have a class graduating from a failing school, where the average performance level of many graduates is so low that they lack the basic skills for college or even for low-tech jobs. They lack the functional competencies required in society, yet they have graduated from school!

These students and their parents falsely believe that they have learned what they need because their apparent performance matches that of graduating peers. It is only when they attempt college or seek employment that they realize a harsh truth . . . they require remedial instruction. Perhaps that is why the charge of "educational malpractice" rings true when employers, parents, teachers and others encounter people with diplomas who lack necessary competencies. Indeed, the essence of educational malpractice is to "cool out" students and their parents by getting them to falsely believe they have succeeded when they have not.

When high expectations are held, they should be honest, based upon objective assessments of performance. This means there should be no rewards for false mastery. Achievement expectations must be tied to specific outcomes that everyone can understand.

The Relative Influences of Others

Research shows that the school environment affects student academic achievement independent of parental influence (Coon et al., 1993); that high expectations from parents are not enough to overcome any negative effects from school (Voelki, 1993); and that teacher expectations show significantly higher correlation with childrens' reading and mathematics achievement than do the expectations of parents (Reynolds, 1992). Although teacher influences on student outcomes are greater than those of parents, parents have important bearings on student experience (Stiller and Ryan, 1992). Just because parents have a role to play, no one should excuse a school for failing to educate students by blaming parents. Even where there is little or no support from parents, children can still be taught to master the subject matter. Teachers can teach them providing, they hold the right expectations for themselves and their students; and they follow through by providing appropriate educational experiences. Thereby, a lack of parental support can be overcome.

Recognizing the relevance of teacher expectations for students does not mean, however, that the magnitude of teacher influence fails to vary. For example, teacher expectations are an especially powerful force with elementary students, whereas secondary and post-secondary students tend to rely somewhat more on a wider range of significant others to provide them with feedback. In addition, teachers' expectations for low achievement have greater influence with low income students than on middle class students (Brookover et al., 1979). Low income, Native American students typically need much more support from their teachers if they are to go to college, than do middle or upper socio-economic status white students. Perhaps many well-meaning teachers "cool out" lower class parents' into accepting the presumed "reality" of a low status future for their children. Thus, teachers may sometimes have the effect of reducing disadvantaged parents' expectations and evaluations of their children.

The Self-fulfilling Prophecy

In the study three decades ago of *Pygmalion in the Classroom,* Rosenthal and Jacobson (1968) concluded that the IQ scores of certain students, who had been labeled as academic "bloomers," went up more than scores of other students in the class. These students actually were not know to be "bloomers," but had been randomly selected. Their IQ's apparently went up because their teachers thought they were brighter and treated them as special.

Although the original *Pygmalion* study has been criticized on methodological grounds, massive amounts of evidence have since been compiled testing this question: Does the level of teacher expectations really influence the level of student achievement (i.e., do high teacher expectations actually foster high achievement, and low expectations produce low achievement)? The answer, based on extensive research, is a clear-cut "yes." (There are many reviews of the extensive research literature on the relevance of teacher expectations. See for example Cotton, 1995 and the *Effective Schools Research Abstracts).* Thus, educators need to be aware of the specific mechanisms by which their expectations can result in self-fulfilling prophecies. Knowing this, teachers and staff can work to avoid transmitting low achievement expectations.

Research on Effective Schools

"Taken as a whole, the research literature on teacher efficacy shows that teachers who believe they can make a difference do make a difference."

Weber, B. J. and L. M. Omotani. "The Power of Believing."
The Executive Educator 16/9 (Sept. 1994): 35-38.

A Definition

Self-fulfilling prophecy is defined as a process which begins with an unsubstantiated expected outcome for a person that is treated as though it were true. Subsequent actions are then conducted that assure the prophecy comes true. The outcome, in turn, convinces the person making the judgment that his or her original expectation was correct. In education, an example of this process is a teacher's mistaken expectation that Native American children are innately poor learners in school. Because of this evaluation, a Native American student is given lower level instruction in mathematics than other students. The student then performs poorly on subsequent mathematics testing compared to students taught at a higher level. This low performance is then used to confirm the original false expectation for Native American students. In essence, the educator is creating the very condition he or she is attempting to find.

Several generalizations regarding the self-fulfilling prophecy follow. In any given case, some or all of the following may apply:

1. Both the prophecy and the mechanism by which it is brought about are done unconsciously. Because of this, self-fulfilling prophecies can be difficult to discover or to end.

2. Expectations often are based on cultural prejudices or stereotypes (usually of such a subtle nature that the person is not aware of them).

3. Self-fulfilling prophecies can operate at both the group and the individual level. In education, the individual, a whole class, whole tracks, or an entire school may be a victim of self-fulfilling prophecies.

4. Self-fulfilling prophecies usually result from small but consistent effects, leading to cumulative results. Thus over time, the effects build up with later distorted judgments based on earlier ones. This is especially true when the process starts in infancy. In other words, what we perceive and measure as ability or aptitude may be a cumulative, long-term effect of self-fulfilling prophecies.

5. Masses of students are being prophesied to only be able to learn at low levels — well below their abilities (Pool and Page, 1995).

6. Beliefs that support a negative self-fulfilling prophecy for individuals in one group may be judged as positive for another group. For example, in some quarters high-achieving recent immigrant children from Asia are viewed as "over achievers." On the other hand, some

people view high achievement among certain other minority youth as being "uppity." In other words, double standards are rather common place. False self-fulfilling prophecies may come to an individual from one's own ethnic group as well as from other groups.

Sources of Teacher Expectations

Teachers take into account a great many things other than actual performance levels when they assign grades to students. While grades and grade-point averages correlate with performance, as measured by external observations and test scores, more than half of the variation in one is not typically explained by variation in the other.

There are many reasons for this. A teacher, for example, may include in a student's grade reactions to the disruptive behaviors on the playground. Grades can be given for deportment, as they can for academic performance (Brophy and Good, 1986). There also is the question of the reliability and validity of tests that teachers use to assess performance.

One key to understanding the evaluations or grades teachers give for performance, is whether students' responses enhance or hinder a teacher's sense of competence. Student behavior which is achievement oriented, dependent, and compliant is rewarding to teachers. This type of behavior meets the needs of teachers for classroom control, and is consistent with most teachers' ideal student. On the other hand, independent, creative, or unruly students do not meet most teachers' needs for success. Teachers often have low achievement expectations for these "different" students.

There is, of course, much more to the question about why teachers, school administrators, and other staff respond as they do to various categories of students. In answering this question it is important not to ignore two vital conditions: the traditions and the beliefs that characterize society at large. No matter how much research data is gathered, if a research finding runs counter to a commonly held cultural belief or value, the research will be rejected by many; and this is without regard to how well the research has been conducted.

Educators as a group are more objective than many others. Yet most educators reflect many of the stereotypes in the culture at large. It wasn't too long ago that teachers did not give African-American youth an opportunity to play basketball because they were deemed physically or mentally incapable of being effective athletes. Today that stereotype is gone, but there are other misconceptions; some of which are even more socially and personally harmful to our youth.

One mistaken misconception which harms students concerns beliefs about the nature of intelligence. Some mistakenly believe that intelligence is one dimensional rather than multidimensional; that it is genetically fixed rather than subject to modification; and that intelligence tests measure capacity to learn rather than selected problem-solving abilities at a given time. While one may use current ability to estimate capacity to learn new skills and knowledge, there is no assurance beyond the obvious that such estimation is correct. For example, if one observes someone swimming, one may reasonably state that the swimmer is able to swim. However, if one cannot swim at a given time one should not conclude that the person will never learn to be able to swim. Yet that is what has been done to many young people. Some students show up at school and are not able to perform at grade level, and some psychologists and educators presume these children to be of less intelligence. When educators and their communities believe such prejudicial views, they preclude a desirable learning climate for many students.

Educators and others can arrive at inaccurate assessments of an individual's or a group's presumed capacity to learn by other than IQ or achievement tests. These cues may be appearance and cultural identity that have no relation to learning potential. For example, they may use such cues as dress, grooming, weight, language or family identification as indicators of students' learning capacity. All educators need to be aware of the possible biasing and effects of such cues.

The following is a list of cues which have been identified by researchers as typical sources of bias among educators. They were first taken from reviews of research over two decades ago (Brophy & Good, 1974 and Persell, 1977). Today, to the dismay of many, they are still used.

We need to guard against using them to impose lower expectations on undeserving students:

Sex. Young boys and older girls are sometimes the recipients of prejudicial low academic expectations. This often is a function of mistaken beliefs about the relevance of boys' maturation and sex role discrimination which harms females.

Socio-economic status level. Low expectations are typically held for children of families with low level income and education. Status based on the jobs held and the place of residence of the parents often are used to prejudge students.

Race and ethnic identifiers. African-American, Hispanic and Native American students receive lower expectations than other students. Asian students receive high expectations.

Negative comments about students. Negative comments by other teachers or principals often result in lower expectations.

The status of the school. Rural and inner city schools often are associated with lower expectations than suburban schools. The racial, ethnic and income level of the school is often a factor in such prejudice.

Appearance. Lower expectations are associated with clothes and grooming that are out of style, made of cheaper material, not brand name or purchased at thrift or discount stores.

Oral language patterns. Nonstandard English often is the basis for holding lower expectations for students.

Neatness. Lower expectations are associated with general disorganization, poor handwriting or other indicators.

Halo effect. There is a tendency to label a student's current achievement based upon past performance evaluations of a child.

Readiness. There are negative effects when teachers assume that maturation rates or prior lack of knowledge or experience are unchanging phenomena, thus precluding improvement.

Seating position. Lower expectations are typically transmitted to students who sit on the sides and in the back of a classroom.

Socialization by experienced teachers. Experienced teachers have a tendency to stress the limitations of certain students for new teachers rather than the need to work on improving the performances of students.

Student behavior. Students with poor non-academic behavior also tend to receive lower academic expectations from teachers.

Teacher training institutions. Some faculty within colleges of education perpetuate myths and ideologies of individual limitations of students. This results in prejudicially low expectations for large numbers of students.

Teacher education textbooks. Some textbooks also perpetuate myths and ideologies that individual students have limitations which reinforce prejudicially low expectations for students.

Tracking or grouping. Students in a lower academic track are mistakenly presumed to have been placed there for good reason (i.e., they have limited capacities and can never be expected to learn critical knowledge and skills).

Transmission of Expectations in the Classroom

Earlier we asserted that a self-fulfilling prophecy is transmitted by providing instruction and evaluations in accord with the prophesied expectations. We also pointed out that a double standard of judging the same behavior may occur depending on who exhibits the behavior. This section examines specific classroom behaviors teachers use to communicate certain expectations to classes or to particular students. Unless otherwise indicated, the following are instances of decreased amount of instruction (i.e., fewer opportunities, less time-on-task) associated with lower expectations. In many cases, teachers are unaware of the differences in how they react to various students or classes, or how they are affected by different norms from school to school.

Expectations influence the:

- Amount and quality of praise for correct answers.

- Actual amount of teaching students receive.

- Content covered.

- Response opportunity factors such as:

  - number of times students are called upon,

  - extent to which the question is challenging, and

  - degree of cognitive demands.

- Academic and non-academic content of teacher-student interaction.

- Verbal and non-verbal warmth and acceptance.

- Non-verbal cues, including:

  - eye contact,

  - forward lean,

  - affirmative head nods,

  - smiles, and

  - physical contact (e.g., pat on shoulder, hugs).

- General encouragement and support.

- Teacher assistance and willingness to help.

- Wait time (such as the amount of time a student is given to respond to a question before the teacher gives the answer or moves on to another student).

- High academic evaluations – reflected by percent of students expected to master skills sufficient for success in the next level class, complete high school or attend college, or be well prepared for employment opportunities.

- Reinstruction of students in failure situations (i.e., probing, restating questions, giving hints, etc., until student learns the desired knowledge or skill).

- Evaluative feedback and constructive criticism of school work.

- Orientation toward goals (lower expectations are associated with the belief that non-academic goals are the most appropriate objectives for students).

Lower expectations tend to result in increased:

- Negative comments or negative expressions.

- Harshness and punitiveness of discipline techniques.

- Rewarding or praising incorrect or inappropriate answers or behavior.

- A belief that the student is unable to respond correctly or appropriately and so must be praised.

Not all students are equally susceptible to self-fulfilling prophecies. The extent to which students are influenced by teachers is related to the importance of teachers as significant others. Other factors such as the student's age, parents, and the extent and character of peer affiliation, and community values all affect the degree of influence of a particular teacher. Yet lowered teacher expectations tend to result in less instruction and low levels of academic achievement. As such, the need for examining individual teaching and teaching climates for possible biasing actions is great.

Teacher Climate Impacts Student Climates

Throughout the first three modules we have stressed the negative effects of lowered expectations, and by implication, the positive effects of high expectations for student performance. We also emphasized that there is a multiple link between teachers' expectations and student achievement. A direct link focuses on the teachers' role in "creating" poor or excellent student performance through a series of behaviors which reflect their expectations of students. Indirect links also occur when teachers teach to make self-fulfilling prophecies a reality. Some students perceive not only that teachers expect less of them, they also believe that success in their school is not likely for students "like them." When there is a consensus where the student body generally expects the same poor achievement from themselves as do their teachers, and that the teachers won't help them to do better, the odds are further increased that the students will do poorly.

The most effective way of reducing student feelings of futility in their school is for teachers collectively, as well as individually, to establish a positive self-fulfilling prophecy. This involves expecting all students to master those skills and knowledge, based upon objective performance standards, necessary to be successful in the class. The staff — principals, teachers, coaches, counselors and others — need to communicate, "You can learn and we'll see that you do learn." This means ensuring that the various sources of negative bias and the transmission of false judgments are not allowed to operate. Successfully implementing a school learning climate means an increase in the actual amount and quality of teaching for all students.

High expectations alone, however, will not produce mastery learning on the part of all students. Skills and knowledge are acquired through a teaching-learning process. As the students acquire desired skills and knowledge this will demonstrate to them that it is possible for them to learn, and that the school is committed to teaching them.

Summary

Teacher expectations as a climate factor is part of a web of interacting relationships among the staff and students within the overall school learning climate. The particular importance of teacher expectations and evaluations for their students has a multiple link to achievement: directly through the phenomenon of self-fulfilling prophecy and indirectly through students' self-concepts of their academic ability, their senses of academic futility or efficacy and the standards and expectations they hold for themselves as students.

The self-fulfilling prophecy is an unconscious process in which an estimate of ability is acted upon as though it were true. Differing instruction which corresponds to teacher prophecies is the primary means by which self-fulfilling prophecies are carried out. Educators holding negative prophecies for students are often unaware of the degree to which false, harmful assessments are made, of sources of bias, and of the ways in which negative expectations are transmitted to students.

Suggested Activities

1. View the film *Eye of the Storm* which depicts the blue eye, brown eye experiment on discrimination among third graders. Where and how do students pick up on differences? While this film is over 25 years old, it is pertinent to events in schools at this time? The faculty should discuss the effects of discrimination in terms of expectations for learning: What are the effects over time? What factors are the focus of discrimination in real life? How do teachers and other adults transmit these cues to students? How do other students transmit cues?

2. Use group problem solving to deal with issues of poor or negative expectations related to students, staff, parents, or the community. Topics of this kind should be brought up at whole staff or biweekly grade/departmental meeting. Dealing with the problem or issue, not the individual, is generally the best approach. However, in some cases, identifying the person(s) is appropriate and effective for solving a problem, provided the discussion, remarks, and suggestions are kept objective and constructive.

    For example, a teacher may need help in understanding what can be done to counteract examples of negative self-concept displayed by students in his/her class. Try to suggest specific actions or strategies for attacking the problem. One suggestion might be for the teacher to try to eliminate negative cues that pupils receive from teachers, parents, and other students. Further suggestions for how to do this should come from the group. In this instance, increasing the academic proficiency of students through frequent success experiences would be a good start. Building self-esteem without effective instruction and remediation of skill deficits is not the answer.

3. Teachers are encouraged to get feedback on their classroom behavior to see if they are unconsciously communicating different levels of expectations to students. This can be done by an individual teacher using a tape recorder to record classroom remarks. Replaying the tape

will be informative and can be done privately. Also, having another teacher observe your class for this purpose is encouraged.

4. The faculty should attempt to implement the strategies to improve student learning climate described in this module. If possible, some measure of the student learning climate (e.g., tardiness, absenteeism, attendance on the day of a test, informal surveys of student attitudes, levels of motivation, amount of scapegoating, etc.) should be taken before and after the program to assess its effectiveness. This is especially appropriate for middle school and senior high school students.

Selected Bibliography

ABC News (Producer). *The Eye of the Storm.* New York: ABC Merchandising, Inc., Film Library, 1970. (This is an older film but still valuable. It illustrates with Iowa 3rd graders how discriminatory behavior towards groups can be created in a classroom).

Bempechat, J. "Fostering High Achievement in African-American Children: Home, School and Public Policy Influences," *Trends and Issues* No. 16, ERIC Clearinghouse on Urban Education, New York, 1992.

Bonetari, D. "The Effects of Teachers' Expectations on Mexican-American Students." Paper presented at the Annual Meeting of the American Psychological Association, New Orleans, April 1994.

Brookover, W., Beady, C., Flood, P., Schweitzer, J., and J. Wisenbaker. *School Social Systems and Student Achievement: Schools Can Make a Difference.* So. Hadley, Mass.: J. F. Bergin Co., distributed by Praeger Publishers, New York, 1979.

Brophy, J. E. and T. L. Good. *Teacher-Student Relationships: Causes and Consequences.* New York: Holt, Rinehart and Winston, 1974.

Brophy, J. E. and T. L. Good. "Teacher Behavior and Student Achievement" in *Handbook on Research on Teaching,* Third Edition, edited by M. C. Wittrock. New York: Macmillan Publishing Co., 1986: 328-377.

📖 Brown, B. and L. Steinberg. *Non-instructional Influences on Adolescent Engagement and Achievement, Final Report: Project 2.* Washington, DC: U.S. Department of Education, Office of Educational Research and Improvement, 1991.

📖 CBS (Producer). "Marva." From *60 Minutes.* New York: Carousel Films, Inc., 1979. This is another older but still valuable film. It is a stark portrayal of an African-American woman's private school in which her students in a poverty area of Chicago master Chaucer, Shakespeare, and other advanced work.

📖 Clasen, D. "Changing Peer Stereotypes of High-achieving Adolescents," *NASSP Bulletin* 76/543 (April 1992): 95-102.

📖 Coon, H. et al. "Influence of School Environment on the Academic Achievement," *Intelligence* 17/1, (January-March, 1993): 79-104.

📖 Cotton, K. *Effective Schooling Practices: A Research Synthesis 1995 Update.* Portland, OR: Northwest Educational Research Laboratories, 1995.

📖 Dryden, S. *The Impact of Instrumental Music Instruction on the Academic Achievement of Fifth Grade Students.* M.S. Thesis, Fort Hays, KS: Fort Hays State University, 1992.

📖 *Effective Schooling Practices: A Research Synthesis 1990.* Portland, OR: Northwest Regional Educational Laboratory, 1990.

📖 Fennema, E. et al. "Teacher Attributions and Beliefs about Girls, Boys and Mathematics." *Educational Studies in Mathematics* 21/1 (February 1991): 55-69.

📖 Finn, J. D. "Expectations and the Educational Environment." *Review of Educational Research* 42/3 (1972): 387-410.

📖 Ford, D. Y. "Black Students' Achievement Orientation as a Function of Perceived Family Achievement Orientation and Demographic Variables," *Journal of Negro Education* 621 (Winter 1993).

📖 Fuchs, L. et al. "The Relation Between Teachers' Beliefs about the Importance of Good Student Work Habits, Teacher Planning, and Student Achievement." *The Elementary School Journal* 94/3 (January 1994): 131-345.

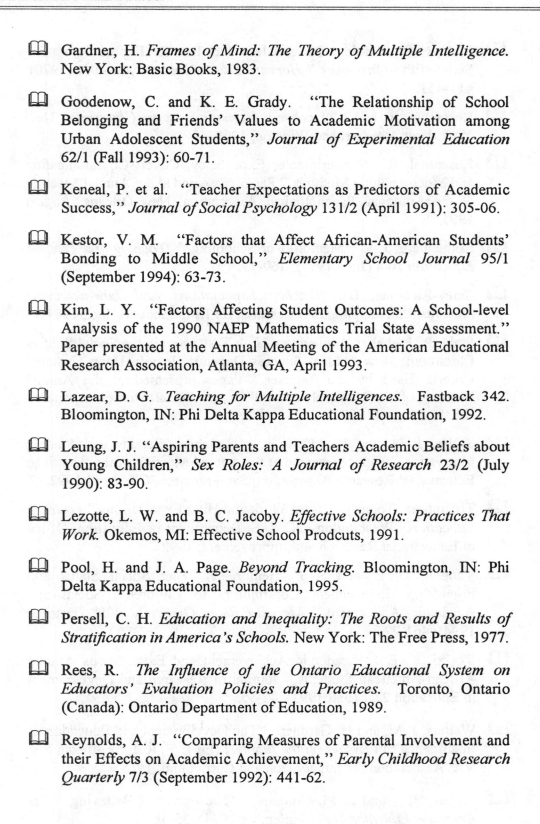

Gardner, H. *Frames of Mind: The Theory of Multiple Intelligence.* New York: Basic Books, 1983.

Goodenow, C. and K. E. Grady. "The Relationship of School Belonging and Friends' Values to Academic Motivation among Urban Adolescent Students," *Journal of Experimental Education* 62/1 (Fall 1993): 60-71.

Keneal, P. et al. "Teacher Expectations as Predictors of Academic Success," *Journal of Social Psychology* 131/2 (April 1991): 305-06.

Kestor, V. M. "Factors that Affect African-American Students' Bonding to Middle School," *Elementary School Journal* 95/1 (September 1994): 63-73.

Kim, L. Y. "Factors Affecting Student Outcomes: A School-level Analysis of the 1990 NAEP Mathematics Trial State Assessment." Paper presented at the Annual Meeting of the American Educational Research Association, Atlanta, GA, April 1993.

Lazear, D. G. *Teaching for Multiple Intelligences.* Fastback 342. Bloomington, IN: Phi Delta Kappa Educational Foundation, 1992.

Leung, J. J. "Aspiring Parents and Teachers Academic Beliefs about Young Children," *Sex Roles: A Journal of Research* 23/2 (July 1990): 83-90.

Lezotte, L. W. and B. C. Jacoby. *Effective Schools: Practices That Work.* Okemos, MI: Effective School Prodcuts, 1991.

Pool, H. and J. A. Page. *Beyond Tracking.* Bloomington, IN: Phi Delta Kappa Educational Foundation, 1995.

Persell, C. H. *Education and Inequality: The Roots and Results of Stratification in America's Schools.* New York: The Free Press, 1977.

Rees, R. *The Influence of the Ontario Educational System on Educators' Evaluation Policies and Practices.* Toronto, Ontario (Canada): Ontario Department of Education, 1989.

Reynolds, A. J. "Comparing Measures of Parental Involvement and their Effects on Academic Achievement," *Early Childhood Research Quarterly* 7/3 (September 1992): 441-62.

📖 Rist, R. C. "Student Social Class and Teacher Expectations: The Self-fulfilling Prophecy." *Harvard Educational Review* 40/4 (1970): 411-451.

📖 Rosenthal, R. and L. Jacobson. *Pygmalion in the Classroom.* New York: Holt, Rinehart and Winston, 1968.

📖 Rosenthal, R. "Experimenter Expectancy, Covert Communication and Meta-Analytic Methods." Paper presented at the Annual Meeting of the American Psychological Association, New Orleans, August 1995.

📖 Rothenberg, J. J. "Memories of Schooling," *Teaching and Teacher Education* 10/4 (June 1994): 369-79.

📖 Smey-Richman, B. *Teacher Expectations and Low-achieving Students.* Philadelphia, PA: Research for Ritter Schools, Inc., 1989.

📖 Stahl, R. J. et al. "Achieving a High Test Score in the Social Studies Classroom: How Student Success Depends Heavily Upon Unstated Criteria Used by the Teacher." Paper presented at the Annual Meeting of the National Council for the Social Studies, Anaheim, CA, November 1990.

📖 Stiller, J. D. and R. M. Ryan. "Teachers, Parents and Student Motivation." Paper presented at the Annual Meeting of the American Educational Research Association, San Francisco, CA, April 1992.

📖 Tominloon, Tommy. "Hard Work and High Expectations," *Issues in Education.* Washington, DC: U.S. Department of Education, Office of Educational Research and Improvement, 1992.

📖 Vandell, D. L. and S. E. Hembree. "Peer Social Status and Friendship: Independent Contributors to Children's Social and Academic Adjustment," *Merrill-Palmer Quarterly* 40/4 (October 1994): 461-77.

📖 Voelki, K. E. "Academic Achievement and Expectations Among African-American Students," Journal of Research and Development in Education 27/1 (Fall 1993): 42-55.

📖 Walters, J. M. and H. Gardner. "The Development and Education of Intelligence" in *Essays on the Intellect* (Ed.). F. R. Link Alexandria, VA: Association for Supervision and Curriculum, 1985.

📖 Weber, B. J. and L. M. Omotani. "The Power of Believing." *The Executive Educator* 16/9 (September 1994): 35-38.

Module 4
Changing the Organization

Key Concepts and Considerations

- School Structure and Goal Attainment
- Leadership Among the Staff
- Counselors
- Teachers
- Remedial Education Staff
- Special Education Staff
- Non-instructional Support Staff

Each school — and every principal, teacher, or other staff member — is influenced somewhat by community sentiment for what it is expected to teach students. How much influence the community has is the question. If a community believes that its school should produce a large proportion of its students who will be ready to attend college, then it will presume that the school will work toward that goal. Similarly, if a community accepts the idea that most students will fail, it will believe that the school will not be of help to most students. However, it is wrong to presume that local community sentiment is the overwhelming force behind school operations — that it controls the day to day school's operation. This is only partially true.

True, there is often a statistical correlation between community expectations and student achievement. Thus, it is easy to blame the community for student failure. Blaming the community, however, is much too simple. There are situations where community expectations for students are low, yet their schools produce high achieving student bodies. This is because a local community seldom has all that much control over what is taught and learned at school. As with any organization, schools can have their community's intent displaced by other, sometimes unintended forces.

The staff of a school is an intervening force between the community and students who may not have the same beliefs and values as the community they represent. Also the community may hold contradictory sentiments. As a consequence, when the staff goes along with one public desire, it negates another. For example, if the community expresses both a desire for respecting social class differences in the advantages given to students, and equality of opportunity, these are incompatible goals. Also, it is important to recognize that educators often shape community expectations for what is possible, and for what the schools should be doing. Educators are not impotent in regard to school goals or how a school operates.

Research on Effective Schools

Clark and Astuto point out that school reform movements fail when reforms focus on competition rather than collaboration. Successful schools are those where teachers, administrators, parents, and students work together toward common goals instead of "pitting" one group within a school against another as is the case with competitive models.

Clark, D. L. and T. Astuto. "Redirecting Reform: Challenges to Popular Assumptions about Teachers and Students." *Phi Delta Kappan.* Vol. 75, No. 7, September 1994, 513-530.

Some problems occur, however, when a school's staff is not clear about what they should be doing. The school staff may have so many goals that their efforts to achieve academic goals are watered down. Similar to the effects of contradictory community goals, it is easy to have goals that are laudable, but to achieve one goal the staff may have to sacrifice another. Arguably, goals such as self-esteem enhancement, reducing disciplinary problems, better relations with parents, drug education, reduced ethnic conflict, driver training, health and recreation, and many others are important. Nonetheless, it is important to prioritize and subordinate goals. Even though worthy, subordinate goals should only be attempted in ways that do not interfere with the primary mission of the school. Schools that have as their prime purpose the creation of an effective school learning climate should make sure that no goal is displacing that prime purpose. Fortunately, when schools produce student bodies with mastery of critical academic skills and knowledge, other goals such as delinquency reduction and higher self-esteem also are achieved.

This should not be interpreted to mean that subordinate goals are irrelevant. For example, desirable personal outcomes, such as self-conceptions of academic ability, and beliefs that teachers will be of help are critical, but not sufficient vehicles to help students attain mastery of basic academic skills and knowledge.

Another instance of displacement away from a high level of academic performance by the student body occurs if the teaching method used is valued without regard for its actual outcomes. Some methods of instruction do not produce outcomes for which they are intended. Individualized teaching methods, for example, tend not to be positively associated with high-achieving schools. Often a method is proposed on a mistaken assumption that academic skills and knowledge are an inevitable by-product of the method without regard for hard data on outcomes. No matter how much a particular method of instruction is valued, spending time on it at the expense of developing academic skills and knowledge for all will result in a lower academic achievement level for the student body.

Research on Effective Schools

"Student disincentives to students' effort include: (1) a large number of non-academic activities which students are encouraged to pursue and which compete for their time; (2) public policies that reward students for making minimal efforts; (3) ambivalent messages when athletes are given privileged status; and (4) classroom practices by teachers who, although well-intentioned, give students unchallenging work, or convey to students their low expectations."

Tomlinson, T. "Hard Work and High Expectations: Motivating Students to Learn." *Issues in Education*, U.S. Department of Education, Office of Educational Research and Improvement, 1992.

The task in the development of high-achieving student bodies is to have a clear understanding that the primary goal and supporting activities must center on helping all students — the entire student body to master mathematics, science, social studies, and language skills and knowledge. We must make sure that at a minimum, each student in a class learns all that is necessary to do well in the next higher level class. In other words, it is important that essentially all students attain minimal mastery, at a relatively high level, of basic skills and knowledge. All other goals and activities must be accepted or rejected on the basis of whether they contribute to or interfere with developing a high achievement level by the school as a whole.

There should be no fear that the activities suggested in this manual will raise the level of students at the lower end at the expense of students who are already achieving well in school. An effective learning climate will not "dumb down" schooling. Rather, it will reduce the many "dumbing down" structures that already exist in many schools, particularly where the overall school achievement level is low.

School Structure and Goal Attainment

There is a phenomenon occurring in all organizations that can interfere with the attainment of organizational goals. This includes the goals of each unit within the organization, and the personal goals of each participant. Every principal, teacher, coach, counselor, aide, parent, bus driver, or other person who is affiliated with a school has personal goals or desires that at times will conflict with the goals of the organization. These personal desires may be the result of felt power needs, or of health, religious, economic, or social values. For example, there may be a teacher or principal who does not believe in equality of opportunity for females, African-Americans, or others. In such a case, that person may not act to facilitate the attainment of the goals for which this manual was designed.

On the other hand, there is reason to believe that many educators, especially those in low-achieving schools, are not happy with their situations. They would suppress their personal needs if they thought there was any chance of helping all of their students. Most educators work hard and make many sacrifices for their students. They willingly accept any help they think will realistically make a difference in moving their students forward — the goal of this manual. Unfortunately, educators have been the subject of misguided reform. Teachers have "seen it all" and been forced into "new" teaching methods that often fail. Hence, many teachers are cynical about ever being able to help all students to succeed at a high level in school. Because of the failings of misguided reform, it is easy to see why teacher attitudes and behaviors are not easily changed.

Research on Effective Schools

"Administrators and other instructional leaders . . . believe that all students can learn and that the school makes the difference between success and failure."

Cotton, K. *Effective Schooling Practices: A Research Synthesis 1995 Update,*
Portland, OR: Northwest Regional Educational Laboratory, 1995.

Changing Staff Perceptions and Behavior

Changing how a staff structures its behavior (i.e., how principals, teachers, counselors, coaches and others react toward students) is not an easy task. Yet staff perceptions and behavior must be changed if we wish to enhance the achievement level of low-achieving schools. This can be done if the staff is helped to recognize that any proposed changes are realistic, rest on sound research, and other educators in like situations have had success in implementing the proposed changes. Nonetheless, there will be problems because all peoples' beliefs are anchored in tradition, ideology and social support systems; but these systems can be changed if there is a focus on the sources of staff beliefs.

New teachers and other staff first enter school with a set of beliefs and attitudes about students they learned in their youth, from their families, and in college. School memories are clearly salient to teacher development and practice (Rothenberg, 1994). As teachers, however, they learn more about how they should label and respond to students. Teachers learn to expect certain behaviors and attitudes from their pupils.

One powerful force in the socialization of teachers is the character of stratification in school, particularly as expressed through practices such as ability grouping of students (see *Module 5)*. When schools group students — be it by sex, race, social status, or presumed intelligence — the grouping will be accompanied by differing teacher expectations and different teaching. This difference in expectations and teaching, of course, results in differences in what the students learn. Perhaps more than any other organizational feature of schools, ability grouping of students shapes the expectations and behavioral patterns of teachers and students alike. And it is this organizational structure which most needs to be altered if we are to create an effective learning climate for all students.

Not all grouping into higher and lower intellectual competency strata occurs on purpose. Often it is unintended. Whatever the reason, grouping on the basis of presumed intellectual capacity is extremely dangerous except in cases of severe mental impairment. It is a condition that produces failure. And the failures we create in school cause a burden to all of us, as well for those who failed to learn.

Socio-economic status is not the only criterion that many teachers have learned to use in making an assessment of student capacities. In some areas of the United States some teachers do not expect Mexican-American children whose native tongue is not English to excel in school (Bonetatic, 1994). In other instances, teachers were observed to tend toward relating the academic success of boys to intellectual capacity, and in the case of academic success of girls to their efforts (Fennema et al., 1991). The point is there are many sources of problematic teacher expectations which impact on what happens in school and which need to change.

Research on Effective Schools

"Schools can make a difference in enhancing the achievement of students from ethnically diverse, low-income families . . . "

Chrispeels, J. *Purposeful Restructuring: Creating a Culture for Learning and Achievement in Elementary Schools.* The Falmer Press, Washington, DC, 1992.

Reward Systems

Sometimes teachers learn their expectations because of the formal and informal reward systems of their schools. Even teacher ratings of student attractiveness is associated with teacher expectations of intellectual capacity (Keneal, 1991). The consequence is that these differences in teacher expectations are, for those labeled less able, accompanied by fewer opportunities to interact and participate in higher level classroom activities. In turn, these students make less effort to receive teacher attention and help, gradually withdrawing from learning in the classroom (Smey-Richman, 1989). However, culture stereotypes can be overcome. There are many examples where girls, Hispanics, African-American and poor white students have done well in school in spite of negative intellectual stereotypes. For example, Bempechat (1992) found that African-American children achieve well when they are in welcoming schools with high academic standards, regardless of poverty or single parent status. Whatever intellectual stereotype is applied to a group, a reward system is likely to develop that matches the stereotype and reinforces the stereotypical expectations. Educators must resist these cultural stereotypes.

We must reverse situations where we reward teachers for teaching some students much less than they are capable of learning; as is the case with some special education classes. There are also cases where staff members are positively recognized by principals for not bothering the principal, or for doing other desirable things, such as having an attractive room, being well-dressed, or being the life of a faculty party. If the activities for which the staff are rewarded do not assure high student achievement, or if the rewards become a means of displacing emphasis on achievement, then the staff is likely to devote its time and energy to these nonproductive activities.

Rewards should be given when staff contribute to high levels of mastery among all students, rather than when they provide for only a select number to attain high levels of achievement. The staff should be recognized and rewarded for the school's **overall** accomplishments. No staff member should be rewarded for continuing a pattern of low achievement, even if it is unintended.

Research on Effective Schools

"The culture of a school correlates strongly with how teachers perceive the effectiveness of the school. When principals actively engage in providing inspiration, teachers are more enthusiastic about teaching and develop higher levels of commitment to the school."

Cheng, Y.C. "Profiles of School Culture and Effective Schools."
School Effectiveness and School Improvement 4/2 (May 1993): 85-110.

The Principal's Role

Nearly all of the literature on effective schools emphasizes the importance of the school principal in bringing about high levels of student achievement. While we do not doubt this, we wish to make three observations:

First, there are effective schools in which someone other than the person occupying the principal's position provides the leadership necessary for change. This person may be an assistant principal, an instructional leader, or an influential teacher who fulfills the leadership role with the approval of the principal. Although it is usually easier for the principal to assume an instructional leadership role, other members of the school organization can and should be effective in facilitating leadership. Their talents should be used to assume some of the leadership responsibilities under the coordination and direction of the principal.

Second, because many demands are placed on them, principals can be distracted from their primary purpose of enhancing the learning of their student bodies. Not all demands can be avoided, however. Catastrophes can occur to which only the principal can respond. When this happens, another influential person in school should be prepared to take on the responsibility of conducting the instructional leader's role. This is another reason for principals to share leadership.

Third, it is impossible to specify all of the ways a principal should act to be effective in every school. There is one common feature, however, of effective leaders. Regardless of who fulfills the leadership role, the principal must act as the primary change agent. When a school is not as effective as it should be, many changes will be required in how the school operates, and only those who have been in charge will know what needs to be done to cause those changes to occur.

An Instructional Leader

The leadership role must be foremost if an effective school learning climate is to be created. The particular style of leadership, however, is less important than successfully carrying out necessary tasks. An effective leader must work to see that *specific learning objectives for each grade level and for each course are established.* Unless all members of the organization understand what is to be achieved at each age level and with each course, the teachers and other staff are likely to go in a variety of directions. The leader must provide incentives for arriving at a consensus on objectives. It is unlikely, however, that even the most knowledgeable leader can identify all of the important objectives. Nonetheless, someone needs to provide the leadership to see that this specification of goals and consensus is achieved. In addition, agreement on course and class objectives among the staff is essential for implementing and then evaluating the school's effectiveness.

Closely associated with identifying the instructional objectives at each level are the standards for asserting mastery by the students of the achievement objectives. We believe that criterion-based standards associated with mastery learning (see *Module 6)* must be the basis for evaluation. The goal should be that 100% of the students master all of the skills and knowledge necessary to proceed to the next level of instruction. Regardless of how much else is taught or learned, these objectives should be held for all students in a grade level. This means that the criteria or standards for evaluating student achievement should be clearly established and communicated to all teachers and students. Furthermore, all teachers must have the necessary instructional materials and resources to carry on the instructional program. The principal has a major responsibility for seeing that such materials are available.

The staff must agree on these standards of achievement and then adopt an instructional program, consistent with an effective school learning climate, to assure that all students attain the standards of mastery.

Because effective schools have common objectives for all students at each grade level and for each course, the tests and procedures that are used, both diagnostic and mastery, should be conveniently located in a central file. Teachers and other personnel in the school system may contribute to the development of such tests and procedures, but someone (generally the principal) should make certain that appropriate evaluation materials are available that are pertinent to the learning objectives. Department heads or other instructional leaders should assist in developing or supplying all testing and assessment materials.

The accumulation of summative test records and periodic objective referenced tests, along with performance observation procedures, are important resources in the evaluation of an instructional program. This involves the maintenance of records for each classroom, each grade level, and the school as a whole. The purposes of evaluation are to assess the degree to which all of the students master the objectives set for them and to determine what must still be done to maximize effectiveness. The principal should take primary responsibility for this activity.

Research on Effective Schools

"Administrators and other leaders . . . check student progress frequently, relying on explicit performance data. They make results public, and work with staff to set standards, use them as points of comparison, and address discrepancies."

Cotton, K. *Effective Schooling Practices: A Research Synthesis 1995 Update,* Portland, OR: Northwest Regional Educational Laboratory, 1995.

In order to assure that students master their learning objectives, the principal or designated leader should plan the school day so that adequate time is available for instruction in each of the areas. Teachers should participate in this planning, but there must be a commitment on the part of the leadership, the teachers and other staff that instruction and time on task will not be disrupted or invaded by other activities.

A Change Agent

There are eight important conditions that will facilitate a principal or other leader in seeking to be a change agent. The person:

1. believes he or she can be an effective change agent;

2. seeks to be a change agent;

3. receives the support of a core of his or her staff;

4. provides a planned and focused inservice program for effecting change;

5. obtains the support of the central administration and public;

6. reinforces the achievements of these staff who positively contribute to an effective school learning climate;

7. makes sure that the staff fully understands what is to be changed and why; and

8. receives recognition and reward for acting as a change agent.

Developing a working agreement. Since changing the learning climate requires commitments from the principal, teachers, and other staff, the building leadership team should identify the basic responsibilities of each staff position for conducting the program. This can be described in a working agreement that sets expectations for staff involvement. A clear statement of and a mutual commitment to the contents of the working agreement should be accomplished before attempting to carry out this program.

Each School Requires its Own Plan. If a large portion of the students in school are failing to achieve at high levels, major changes in the school's operation will be required. The process of making the necessary changes for creating a desirable learning climate, however, cannot be stated as a simple formula. Each school is different. Nonetheless, in every school that is not already achieving at the highest levels, the principal must be a strong agent for planned change. Thus it is essential that the principal foster the creation of a plan and then help make those changes necessary to implement the plan. The first step is for the principal to seek help in identifying what needs to be in the plan for a change in the school.

Involve the BLT. Identifying needed changes can be facilitated by the formation and operation of a *Building Leadership Team* (BLT), which includes teachers and the principal (see the discussion of the BLT in *Module 1).* The BLT must, of course, have a clear understanding of what it is trying to accomplish and then coordinate its efforts with the entire staff.

In the Beginning Involve the Leadership. Many people think that change in a school system necessitates the early involvement of the entire staff in the process of deciding the changes that are desirable. This is not necessarily true. If everyone agrees that certain changes are necessary, broad support would be helpful. There is evidence, however, that seeking agreement from everyone in the early stages of planning frequently results in little or no change. Some may favor current practice and they, therefore, should be involved at a later time in an inservice setting where their questions and concerns can be addressed.

If a major change in how the school operates is necessary — and it will be necessary if the school is a low-achieving school — then change is most likely to occur if the leader first involves a cross-section of other informal leaders from among the faculty. Then the principal should follow through with any appropriate compromises that might be necessary to elicit greater support.

Total Consensus is Not Necessary. It will be difficult for an entire school staff to reach consensus on both the need for change and the type of change needed. Furthermore, if consensus is reached in the early stages, it may be more on increasing salaries or doing things to increase job satisfaction than on fostering high achievement among all students. While job satisfaction is desirable, such satisfaction does not necessarily facilitate students' learning. A major problem occurs when a significant portion of the faculty is pleased with the way things are at the time. However, this is seldom the case in most low-achieving schools. Thus activities such as those suggested in this manual are likely to be welcomed.

Conduct Inservice Education. If it is feasible, and the principal or other leadership persons in the school are effective in conducting inservice education, it probably will be more efficient to use them rather than bringing in outside consultants. Whatever the case, effective inservice directed toward achieving mastery learning objectives must be provided to the staff.

Make Sure Everyone Understands. All the members of the school organization should have a clear understanding of the attitudes, beliefs, and practices essential for becoming a high-achieving school. It is not sufficient to give the staff members the modules in this book, or any other inservice training materials, and assume that all will become knowledgeable about them. To determine the extent to which all members of the school staff know and understand how the school learning climate should be changed, follow-up is necessary. Just because a staff understands how a particular program should be conducted, however, does not assure that it will implement the program.

Obtain District Support. Once the needed changes in a school's operation are decided upon, the principal needs to obtain the central administration's support. The school as a whole must be supported and rewarded for seeking to create a desirable school learning climate. In providing this support, the central administration should recognize the building principal and the individual staff members who are working for the necessary changes in school organization. The balance of the staff also should be recognized and rewarded for participation in the change process.

Recognize and Reward Staff. Similarly, the staff who have developed effective instructional practices should be recognized for their success in raising the performance level of the student body. Their greatest reward, however, should come from seeing the improved results: higher achievement for the entire student body. Such achievement, in turn, will result in higher job satisfaction among the staff.

Plan on enough time. Because innovative educational programs are often discussed, but not conducted over a period long enough to obtain a fair assessment of their impact, it is important that the principal develop a system of following through to assure that the intended changes in operation are being continued. There should be a check on the extent to which the desired changes occur. These checks should be continued for a two- to three-year period.

Evaluate regularly. Assessments should be done to determine the extent to which the beliefs, attitudes, expectations, and instructional practices of the program are in play. Program leaders can, by observation and other methods, also evaluate the extent to which a desirable school learning climate is implemented.

Make all expectations for the staff explicit. Staff expectations for the high achievement of all students should be made explicit in formal statements about the mission of the school (see *Module 2)*. In more informal settings these expectations should also be communicated. They should be set forth in inservice meetings and through a variety of social contacts. However, both formal and informal norms can be highly resistant to change unless there is appropriate reinforcement of desired expectations (see Lezotte et al. 1980). Before informal role expectations and behavior by the staff as a whole will change, the reward system will need to be altered to reinforce teaching for mastery of basic skills and knowledge by all students.

Leadership among the Staff

It is important not to forget that the school functions as a system. The individual roles of teachers, counselors, administrators, coaches, secretaries, students, and others combine to create the school learning climate. And while individuals have responsibility to perform their own roles effectively, there remains a collective responsibility on the part of the staff as a whole to create the total learning climate.

Most secondary schools have department heads who are administratively charged with responsibilities for budgeting, scheduling, curriculum planning for their units. In most elementary and some secondary schools, instead of department heads there are special positions of instructional leaders or coordinators (e.g., building coordinator of reading instruction). Department heads and instructional leaders should act to assist the building leadership to develop and maintain an effective instructional program. For department heads and other leaders, all functions and duties should be considered as a means to the end of raising the school's achievement level. Some key responsibilities for department heads and instructional leaders include:

Setting and Planning Objectives. The department head or instructional leader should ensure that there is a common set of grade level and course objectives which all students are to master.

Implementing instructional policy. Many instructionally related duties are delegated by the principal. They may include:

- *Maintenance or departmental meetings.* These should focus on activities and problems in getting all students to master instructional objectives. Discussion of strategies and suggestions from these modules must occur on a regular basis.

- *Monitoring.* The leadership positions can have positive input in seeing that expectations and evaluations of students are maintained at a high level.

- *Improving instructional programs.* The department head or instructional leader will have major responsibility for successfully carrying out and improving instruction so as to raise achievement levels (e.g., mastery learning, more time on task, group learning games).

Setting reward structures. The department head or instructional leader should have primary responsibility for seeing that the types of academically oriented reward structures (listed in this module under "Creating Reward Structures") are carried out for students.

Counselors

Counselors often have the responsibility for placing and advising students regarding curriculum choices and vocational planning. This responsibility involves both the choice of electives and when placement of students in courses. These responsibilities are especially relevant to the achievement level of the school as a whole.

Counselors should see that all students have equal opportunity to choose whatever further schooling or career they want upon graduation from high school. The implication of this position is related to our position on ability grouping. If students are being tracked, the counselors should lend their weight of influence to doing away with the tracking system. In the next module, discussion will treat the problems of eliminating tracking. Although problems associated with ability grouping are described in *Module 5,* the following considerations regarding the advisement and placement functions of the counselor are noteworthy.

Maximize opportunities. Counselors should be rewarded for maximizing the number of students who qualify for college or technical schools.

Communicate opportunities. Communicating to students about possibilities for college and other advanced employment opportunities is essential. (See "Communicating to Parents and Students" at the end of this module.) For example, a decision by a student to avoid a foreign language class in junior high can be an irreversible obstacle to acquiring the prerequisites for a particular college. The implications of a decision of that magnitude must be known by both students and their parents.

Do Not Let Students Track Themselves Downward. Students, like adults, often take the path of least resistance. Students may informally track themselves because of a desire to avoid work, especially if they are unaware of the consequences of such actions. Their parents, however, may not wish to let their child's reluctance to take a more difficult class preclude their later options, especially if the parents are aware of the consequences. "Easy" or "bone-head" classes in the curriculum that may be used as substitutes for mastering basic academic skills and knowledge should be abolished.

Encourage Positive Placements. Counselors should require positive student placements. Counselors sometimes contribute to informal tracking within a school by advising students to avoid certain "difficult" classes, or by making placements based on mistaken values placed on test scores or teacher recommendations. This should not happen. Any communication to students such as "You aren't capable of doing better," should never occur. Instead of limiting student options, counselors need to work to open up the system and concentrate on counseling that helps students to master academic competencies. Such counseling helps foster opportunity for success in college or in employment.

Teachers

Despite the influence of the principal and other staff members, the final responsibility for delivery of an effective school learning climate rests with teachers. And the particular way in which instructional programs are carried out — regardless of who proposes it — is strongly influenced by what teachers believe about themselves and their students. Considerable evidence indicates that there are differences in the way teachers view their roles — and that these differences result in differing levels of student achievement.

When teachers fail to emphasize the mastery of instructional objectives by all of their students, the school's achievement level will be lower than necessary. The implications are obvious. What is not taught is not learned. Teachers who spend time on tasks other than striving for high cognitive achievement by all of their students, are not as effective as teachers who have that goal and teach to attain it.

To achieve mastery by all students of basic skills and knowledge, there will be a need for considerable diagnostic testing by teachers, and then reteaching to assure that students who do not learn the material on their first exposure will be given additional opportunity to attain success. When this is done, it increases the likelihood that all students learn the common core of knowledge and skills.

Finally, the teacher who is effective in enhancing the achievement level of the school is one who is good at the teaching techniques explained in this set of modules. Teachers who wish to raise the level of their students' achievement can use these modules as a guideline for improving their effectiveness. Again, the achievement orientation advocated here is not likely to occur unless teachers are appropriately rewarded.

Remedial Education Staff

State and federally funded compensatory education programs are usually designed to provide extra help to students at risk of failure in school. While many of these programs have not been successful in that endeavor, a few have been very successful. The following characteristics are those of effective compensatory education programs.

Criteria of Success

The successful program is one in which students enrolled are able to progress to age-grade level achievement. This means "catching up." Regrettably, in many programs, students are expected to attain only a portion of a normal year's growth, or at best, the equivalent of a year's growth level. Consequently, students in these programs never catch up and usually fall further behind. This is particularly true where ability grouping is practiced. The success of the program should be measured by the percent of students who gain on or catch up to age-grade level performance.

Reward System

Rewards and recognition are given to teachers and administrators whose students gain on the norms for achievement for their age level. Rewards are not for continued below grade level performances or for simply increasing the numbers in special education.

Supplementary Instruction

Compensatory instruction in effective programs is supplemental to the regular instruction. Students do not miss what is taught in their regular classes.

Reinstruction

Compensatory instruction in effective programs concentrates on helping students master the objectives of the regular program. For students who are behind, this means either reinstruction over the objectives, work on deficient prerequisite skills, or both.

Coordination

The need for reinstruction to achieve the objectives of the regular program requires the coordination of a compensatory teacher's instruction with the regular classroom teacher. This requires communication on objectives, as well as student progress over specific objectives.

Responsibility for Student Achievement

In many ineffective programs the responsibility for student achievement is shuffled between the regular teacher and the compensatory teacher. We recommend that the regular classroom teacher maintain responsibility for the child's learning. The compensatory program is to help the regular teacher; it should not relieve the regular teacher of responsibility.

Place of Instruction

Most ineffective compensatory instruction occurs with "pullout" programs where students are removed from their regular classes for special instruction. Immediately, a problem with labeling affects results. Students often believe that the "dummies" go to special reading or math classes. This perception may be reinforced by the expectations of the regular classroom teacher. There are also problems of time lost to and from class and of scheduling around regular reading and math. In-class programming, in which the compensatory teacher joins with the regular teacher to provide extra reinstruction, is recommended for compensating programs. This format reduces problems caused by labeling.

State and Federal Guidelines

Some state and federal programs contain provisions to ensure that monies are spent only on eligible students. Eligibility is largely a matter of local definition, with considerable discretion in determining eligibility residing with those educators who administer the programs at the local level. This policy often results in rules that conflict with the effective program outlined here. But the conflict is usually more perceived than real. Effective compensatory education programs that do not violate policy guidelines and that achieve success are possible and do exist.

Paraprofessional Aides

Research shows that aides often hold low expectations for the achievement of certain students, and perceive their role as "cooling out" students (i.e., convincing the students to accept their lower status in school because of less ability, Brookover et al., 1981). Paraprofessional aids in effective programs are given training which stresses high achievement for all. Their activities should center on reinstructing students who have not yet mastered objectives, and in doing tasks for teachers that otherwise take away from instructional time. Rewards and recognition for aides should be dependent on achieving success in helping all students to catch up to grade level.

Special Education Staff

Special education programs are designed to give instruction to students considered physically, mentally or socially impaired. These students are considered to have impairments which restrict their learning or require special methods, such as for those profoundly hearing impaired. Unfortunately, special education programs often serve as a rationale for not teaching skills and knowledge appropriate for others. While not all special education programs are governed by low expectations, the danger of this occurrence must be guarded against. We are especially concerned for students who are labeled mildly attention deficited, learning disabled, emotionally impaired, or mentally impaired, rather than for the more severely impaired students. With such students, the tendency to teach them less is a real danger. Some of the ways this occurs are listed below.

- *Inappropriately low expectations due to low program goals.*

- *Negative labeling effects of peers* toward students who are in "special education."

- *Permanent enrollment as special education student* rather than receiving special help and then returning to regular student status.

- *The "difference" syndrome,* in which impaired students are viewed as so different from regular students that all the usual methods for working with students are considered ineffective, and completely different methods are presumed as necessary.

- *The "writing off" function,* in which regular education teachers are "relieved" of the responsibility for teaching students just because their students are identified as special education students.

- *The "expanding numbers" trend,* in which the number of identified special education students expands to fill the number of available slots. When this happens, more and more students are mistakenly identified as special education students. This often reflects pressures from regular classroom teachers to relieve themselves of "problem" students. State and Federal funding based on large numbers of probable special education students creates a strong pressure for school districts to increase the number of students in programs and thus, the amount of dollars coming into the district. This is a sham.

Effective special education teachers should counteract these negative trends by working to improve the total school learning climate. They can do this by helping set up a program that enables their students to gain on the norm group and thus function effectively in the regular program. Special education staff should serve as advocates for youth to make certain that they are not improperly placed in such classes. This will mean resisting pressure from some regular classroom teachers.

Non-instructional Support Staff

Schools require certain supportive services which facilitate the primary goals of the organization. Routines such as busing, lunchroom, maintenance, and secretarial-clerical procedures cannot be neglected. But these services must not detract students' time or effort from academic activities. Rather, these necessary routines must be planned and scheduled so that they facilitate the academic achievement of students.

The key to effective non-instructional staff behavior is consistent with our previous discussions of goal displacement. That is, daily routines of support staff must not be allowed to become an end in themselves, but a means to achieving high performance from all students.

The implications for non-academic staff are twofold. First, secretaries, bus drivers, custodians, and other personnel must perform their roles in a generally courteous and efficient manner. If a particular activity continually detracts from instructional time (e.g., discipline problems at lunch or on the bus), the principal and the staff must establish a new routine which does not create further discipline problems. A safe and well-ordered school is critical and will be discussed in *Module 8*. Second, support staff members must understand that their role is to support the instructional functions of the school. Their efficiency will allow the school to run smoothly and learning to continue with little interruption. Support personnel must be recognized and rewarded for this efficiency.

Summary

The role of the principal and other building leadership is critical to eliciting the support of staff in establishing an effective school learning climate. When the school staff stresses mastery of age-grade level objectives for all students that are prerequisite for the next level of learning in its programming, they will produce a high achievement level in the student body.

Principal's Responsibilities

We have alluded to several particulars for which the instructional leader must be responsible. The following outlines activities and functions for which the principal must take the lead. The principal or designated instructional leader must focus the planning, goal setting, and setting up of routines which effectively accomplish these tasks.

Instructional objectives. The goals of the school, particularly high achievement for all students, must be translated into grade level instructional objectives. This must be done first for reading, language arts, and mathematics. Other subject areas can follow, but emphasis should be first on acquisition of language arts and math objectives and skills. The grade level or departmental staff should develop a common calendar for teaching these objectives (see *Module 6).*

Student assessment. Yearly achievement data over the grade-level instructional objectives, with a criterion-referenced test, should be collected, analyzed, and discussed with the staff to pinpoint areas of strength and weakness (see *Module 11).*

School learning climate assessment. The principal should take the lead in utilizing and discussing with the staff both the formal instruments and the informal Climate Watchers Program (see *Module 2).*

Comprehensive planning. A comprehensive plan by which the staff will change and improve the school learning climate, consistent with the assessment results, must be articulated with staff cooperation.

Efficient use of faculty meetings. Faculty meetings are used for instructional issues. Administrative details should be handled through some form of written memoranda as much as possible.

Concentration on instructional problems. Departmental or grade level meetings should be organized around instructional problems. Sample topics include:

- Cooperation and sharing of teachers' ideas and materials, in connection with implementation of a mastery learning program (see *Module 6*).

- Monitoring academic progress of students.

- Discussing ways to increase time-on-task or improve classroom management (see *Modules 7* and *8*).

- Discussing ways to help students, who are below grade level or who are not mastering materials, "catch-up."

Establishing a file of objectives. A file of objectives, which indicates the district goals and grade level instructional objectives for the school and each class, should be developed. This should include instructional strategies, practice materials, and sample tests. The file should become the basis of the sharing of teacher materials for mastery instruction. This file should also be accessible to and contributed to by all staff. Finally, it should be under the direction of a staff member appointed by the principal, with responsibility to see that it is complete and is being used by the staff.

Creating Reward Structures

One of the most important aspects in creating an effective school learning climate is setting up a reward system that clearly "strokes" staff and students for academic success. In most schools, this will require a planned strategy to change the reward structure from informal, non-academic related norms to an ongoing, academically based norm. Some possible strategies include:

Praise and encouragement. The principal, for staff members, and teachers, for their students, must provide sincere praise for positive achievements that are related to the goals of the school (see *Module 9*).

Games, competitions. Group learning games within the classroom or between rooms foster a reward system based on cooperative, team-based academic achievement that results in highly visible trophies, banners, and public recognition (see *Module 8).* This can be extended to the area of attendance.

Formal recognition. Recognition in newsletters, bulletin boards, and school newspapers, for academically oriented activities adds incentive for achievement.

Academic displays. Creating room and school bulletin boards and overall decor around academic activities. Displays of student work that show excellence or improvement can be very effective.

Interscholastic teams. Establishing interscholastic "academic" teams with all of the usual hoopla of student assemblies and school spirit — but based now on cognitive competition.

Teacher rewards. Rewarding teachers with public recognition for having all students reach age-grade level goals or for displaying exceptional improvement through the year.

Student rewards. Providing picnics and game outings at the end of the year for all students who master grade level objectives or reach a set level of improvement through the year.

The above are merely suggestive of ways in which a faculty can change the reward structure in a school. Put simply, students must be rewarded for being good students and teachers must be rewarded for doing a good job of getting all students to achieve well. The principal should take the lead in this process of celebrating academic achievements.

Communicating to Parents and Students

For a social system to function effectively, all members of the organization must know the prescribed rules and regulations which define role expectations and appropriate behavior. Just as the principal is responsible for communicating goals and strategies to the staff, he or she also is responsible for the communication of policies, regulations, procedures, and expectations to both the students and their parents. This includes appropriate preparation for school, day-to-day rules and behavior, standards of excellence, goals and philosophy, and of course, procedures for sanctioning inappropriate behavior.

One means of communicating these general rules is through student and parent handbooks. Newsletters can provide updates on school events and problems throughout the year. Instruction-related topics, which are essential to be included are:

- The school discipline plan explained in detail;

- Attendance and tardiness policies;

- Explanation of grades, their implications, and methods of grade reporting. (Standards of excellence and school expectations for meeting these standards should be described.);

- What to expect at parent-teacher conferences;

- Explanation of the school's testing program; interpretation of scores in terms of grade level, percentiles, and national and local norms; and the specific score of their own child should all be described to parents.

An essential aspect of an effective school learning climate involves honest, accurate information on the likely consequences of student performance in school and decisions regarding curriculum. Clearly, for whatever reasons, many schools are now failing in this regard.

Role Definition for Paraprofessional Aides

The role of the paraprofessional aide is to assist the teacher to teach students. While the perceived role expectations for aides vary from school to school, some common positive role expectations concerning the use of aides include:

- Teachers are responsible for initial instruction of students and for monitoring the learning process.

- Aides help in the reinstruction of students who have not mastered objectives. Possible activities include:

- listening to students read;

- conducting drill for practice sessions;

- correcting practice exercises for students.

- Aides help students practice in areas where they are deficient and which are prerequisite to current instructional objectives.

- Aides relieve teachers of certain non-instructional duties for which they are authorized and trained.

Suggested Activities

Working agreement. The Principal or BLT should develop a working agreement that specifies the major expectation for staff involvement for implementing a school learning climate program (see *Module 1).* This set of expectations should be presented to the teachers for approval.

Goals and policies. Examine school and district goals and policies. Is high achievement for all students the number one priority of the district? If not, steps should be taken to formally amend the school and board policies. In addition, written procedures of the school or district which are inconsistent with the priority of high achievement for all students should be changed.

Public information. A public information program should be developed, emphasizing the goal of high achievement for all students. Public support from community groups — business, labor, churches, and community organizations — should be sought in addition to a direct appeal for help from parents. The section "Activities on Communicating to Parents and Students" indicates several essential points for inclusion in the program.

Reward structures. Both administration and staff should list the kinds of activities, attitudes, and behaviors that are currently rewarded, through both formal recognition and informal praise and encouragement. How these facilitate or hinder high achievement for all students should then be evaluated. For example, pep rallies are held before key athletic events. Are they held before major achievement testing? Does the school have intramural or interscholastic academic games and competitions? Why not?

(See the section on reward structures in these Activities.) Reward structure not consistent with high achievement for students and teachers must be changed.

A major problem in many if not most school districts is that the reward structure for principals, through both formal and informal channels, may not support high achievement for all students. This is particularly true when loyalty, team play, and keeping things quiet are most rewarded. Often there are implicit messages that these are "real" requirements of a good principal. Likewise, teachers may implicitly reward the supportive disciplinarian principal. Again, these explicit and implicit rewards must be reviewed, analyzed, and changed to be consistent with a desirable learning climate for students. This will require input and commitment from both the school and the district.

Role definitions. The school staff should examine the formal job descriptions of employees for discrepancies between job description and the staff responsibilities identified in this module. Those job descriptions which are inconsistent with the academic focus on high achievement for all students should be formally amended by the central office administration. (See respective role definitions in this module and for Paraprofessional Aides in the Activities.)

Changing informal norms. Informal norms and procedures for carrying out the routines of the school may also be inconsistent with the goal of high achievement for all students. The Climate Watchers Process described in *Module 1* is the best avenue for monitoring and changing informal norms that impede or hinder high achievement.

Logs of daily activities. The principal (and/or secretary) should keep a log of all activities and time spent for 2-3 days. This will provide basic information for improved planning and scheduling of work.

Plan of action. The principal should make sure the school has a "plan of action" that focuses all instructional responsibilities into a comprehensive set of activities. The principal must take the lead in seeing that this is done and that staff members know and are held responsible for their respective role behaviors. This plan of action should be consistent with the outline for an effective school learning climate described in *Module 1,* and the section of Principal's Instructional Responsibilities in this module.

Selected Bibliography

Bamburg, J. D. and R. L. Andrews. "School Goals, Principals and Achievement," *School Effectiveness and School Improvement* 2/3 (1991): 175-191.

Bempechat, J. "Fostering High Achievement in African-American Children: Home, School and Public Policy Influences," *Trends and Issues* No. 16, ERIC Clearinghouse on Urban Education, New York, 1992.

Bonetari, D. "The Effects of Teachers' Expectations on Mexican-American Students." Paper presented at the Annual Meeting of the American Psychological Association, New Orleans, (April 1994).

Brookover, W. B., Brady, N. M. and M. Warfield. "Educational Policies and Equitable Education" in R. L. Green (Ed.) *Procedures and Pilot Research to Develop an Agenda for Desegregation Studies.* East Lansing, MI: College of Urban Development, 1981.

Cheng, Y. C. "Profiles of School Culture and Effective Schools." *School Effectiveness and School Improvement* 4/2 (May 1993): 85-110.

Chrispeels, J. *Purposeful Restructuring: Creating a Culture for Learning and Achievement in Elementary Schools.* The Falmer Press, Washington, D.C., 1992.

Clark, D. L. and T. Astuto. "Redirecting Reform: Challenges to Popular Assumptions about Teachers and Students." *Phi Delta Kappan* 75/7 (September 1994): 513-530.

Cotton, K. *Effective Schooling Practices: A Research Synthesis 1995 Update.* Portland, OR: Northwest Regional Educational Laboratory, 1995.

Effective Schooling Practices: A Research Synthesis 1995 Update, Portland, OR: Northwest Regional Educational Laboratory, 1995.

Effective Schools Research Abstracts, Effective School Products, Ltd., Okemos, MI: Effective Schools (this is a series).

Fennema, E. et al. "Teacher Attributions and Beliefs about Girls, Boys and Mathematics," *Educational Studies in Mathematics* 21/1 (February 1991) 55-69.

Fullan, Michael G. with S. Stiegelbauer. *The New Meaning of Educational Change*. Teachers College Press, Columbia University, New York, 1991.

Fullan, M. "Coordinating School and District Development in Restructuring" in *Restructuring Schooling*, Editor J. Murphy and P. Hallinger. Newbury Park, CA: Corwin Press (1993): 143-164.

Hord, S. M. *Facilitative Leadership*. Austin, TX: Southwest Educational Development Laboratory, 1992.

Keneal, P. et al. "Teacher Expectations as Predictors of Academic Success," *Journal of Social Psychology* 131/2 (April 1991): 305-06.

Lezotte, L. W. et al. *School Learning Climate and Student Achievement: A Social Systems Approach to Increased Student Learning*. Tallahassee, FL: National Teacher Corps, Florida State University, 1980.

Rosenthal, R. "Experimenter Expectancy, Covert Communication and Meta-Analytic Methods." Paper presented at the Annual Meeting of the American Psychological Association, New Orleans, LA, 1989.

Rothenberg, J. J. "Memories of Schooling," *Teaching and Teacher Education* 10/4 (June 1994): 369-79.

Smey-Richman, B. *Teacher Expectations and Low-achieving Students*. Philadelphia, PA: Research for Ritter Schools, Inc., 1989.

Tomlinson, T. "Hard Work and High Expectations: Motivating Students to Learn." *Issues in Education*, Washington, DC: U.S. Department of Education, Office of Educational Research and Improvement, 1992.

Module 5
Grouping and Tracking

Key Concepts and Considerations

- Grouping Patterns
- Research and Grouping
- Grouping for Maximizing Achievement
- Untracking: Helping All Students Succeed
- How to Reach Common Goals at Grade Level
- Tracking: A Closer Examination

Grouping and tracking students on the basis of presumed intellectual capacities to learn is a common practice that has come under increasing attack. Pedagogical, political, and social traditions have fueled the practice of tracking, even though the evidence is clear that tracking has detrimental consequences.

Ability Grouping: A Failed Policy

At the pedagogical level — which is the focus of this book — our concern is over the kind of learning climate that is most likely to facilitate the development of skills and knowledge in the core areas of mathematics, social studies, language and science. Those who favor intellectual ability grouping (commonly referred to as homogeneous grouping) usually argue that such grouping is necessary to meet the needs of slower and faster learners. Further, they tend to argue that such grouping be made on a relatively permanent basis — referred to as "tracking." A match between presumed learning capacity and curricular tracks, it is argued, will reduce student frustration. Proponents also believe that low achievers slow down high achievers, and that each student will be more effectively taught with students of similar ability.

Proponents of untracking schools (the heterogeneous grouping of students) believe that tracking on the basis of presumed ability level harms students who are placed in the lower tracks, while failing to help those placed in higher tracks. Proponents of untracking students also assert that tracking results in a lack of equity, is a violation of democratic values, produces low self-conceptions of learning ability, and causes a devaluing of self by those placed in lower tracks. Many argue that tracking programs based on presumed ability result in two unfortunate consequences: more academic failure, and heightened racial and social class animosity. The proponents of heterogeneous grouping also contend that tracking students by ability level creates lower achieving schools — not just lower achieving individuals — than untracked schools.

Research on Effective Schools

". . . grouping students by ability worsens the academic prospects of low-achieving students while doing nothing for the high-achieving students. Moreover, ability grouping appears to lessen the chances that tracked students will relate well to children of different ethnic and racial groups."

Reported in "Ideas and Programs to Assist in the Untracking of American Schools" by Howard Hill in *Beyond Tracking* (eds.) Harbison Pool and Jane A. Page, Bloomington, IN: Phi Delta Kappa Educational Foundation, 1995.

Research data over many decades is clearly on the side of those who favor untracking. The vast majority of research literature leads us to conclude that tracking is an inappropriate educational practice which lacks both a pedagogical and an ethical basis for its continuation.

The research which tends to favor tracking is at best limited. In only a few small studies have researchers found even the slightest gain for higher tracked students, and then there were negative consequences in the core subjects of reading, mathematics, science and social studies for the lower tracked students.

There seems to be only one exception where there have been some gains in achievement reported for students grouped on the basis of high levels of achievement. This occurs on occasion in classes for students deemed "gifted." Students in gifted classes in the ninth grade in one study, for example, showed a slight advantage in Algebra but not on other math subjects when compared to equally high achieving students who were not grouped. We can only speculate as to the potential gains for lower track students if they too were given the same opportunities and resources as those in "gifted" programs.

Research on Effective Schools

Ability grouping of first grade students can impact students for several successive years.

Pallas, Aaron M. et al. "Ability-Group Effects: Instructional, Social, or Institutional?" *Sociology of Education*, 6/1, (January 1994) 27-46.

This pattern of a slight difference favoring the performance of high achievers placed in classrooms for the gifted, over heterogeneously grouped classrooms, has been explained by the added services provided in gifted programs. Many of those who have been guided by a desire to maximize the talents of gifted students, are now asking that these added services be provided to all students. The emphasis of their work has been to develop a wide variety of activities for assisting both students who are deemed gifted, and those they believe have more limited potentials for high achievements. The Schoolwide Enrichment Triad Model (Renzulli and Reis, 1985) is perhaps the most widely used of these programs that are applied to the gifted as well as to other students in heterogeneous classrooms.

The significance of this is that many of the proponents of providing special help to gifted students no longer support ability grouping and tracking. Yet, tracking continues in a large proportion of our schools. And tracking is still the dominant curriculum structure, even though during the past decade and longer, a number of former low-achieving schools have been untracked and have raised their achievement levels. Tracking is still extensive even though we have had court decisions ruling against tracking as long as three decades ago (Hobsen *vs.* Hansen, 1967; Berry *vs.* Benton Harbor, 1974).

Why do so many teachers, school administrators, and persons in the community still believe that ability grouping increases achievement? The answer does not lie in solid research or in a rational explanation of the data. Rather, one answer rests with commonly held, but mistaken assumptions about the nature of ability to learn. Other answers involve subtle and latent ideologies about how opportunity, influence and wealth should be distributed, emotional commitments to previously held views, and a faith that tradition is a valid measure of what is right.

While research on ability grouping does not support the merits of this practice in terms of improving achievement levels for all students, it does suggest something else. Ability grouping may be one of the most significant ways to maintain and increase social class distinctions between groups. Poor children are often grouped together, and likewise the economically advantaged are grouped together. In effect, tracking reinforces the tensions and conflicts between economic groups.

For those who seek to reduce group tensions and maximize the achievement level throughout their schools, the task, therefore, involves more than just a recitation of the research literature. It concerns how educators should go about the process of implementing an untracked school in ways that elicit the support of both the educational staff and the community.

Research on Effective Schools

While testing has been a primary vehicle for placing students in various tracks, the use of such tests as a means for placing students in ability groups is, in fact, a detriment to high educational standards, high educational goals, and a demanding curriculum.

Darling-Hammond, Linda. "Performance-Based Assessment and Equation Equity." *Harvard Educational Review* 4/1 (Spring 1994): 5-30.

Untracking: Helping All Students Succeed

Teachers' decisions regarding grouping have significant effects on student achievement. For example, how often have you heard the belief expressed that it is the *role of the teacher* to challenge the ability of high achievers while teaching to the lower ability of low achievers? This expression is often put into operation through the use of different workbook assignments and practice materials — generally as a result of establishing different learning objectives for "high" and "low" ability students. In addition, education resources are more favorably distributed to students in the advantaged groups. Different skills are taught to students through different instructional methods and by using materials deemed appropriate for the differing achievement levels of the students. In such a situation, if the teacher has three ability groups, he or she will typically prepare three curricula:

1. that establishes superior-inferior attitudes among students;

2. increases the achievement gap between the groups of students; and

3. legitimizes and makes acceptable below-grade level achievement for some students. It also functions to isolate and divide class members physically, mentally, emotionally, and socially. Achievement potential is reduced, conflict potential is increased.

Research on Effective Schools

". . . heterogeneous, inclusive classrooms offer a prime opportunity for many creative ideas and solutions to be developed and tried. Inclusive education and creative problem solving, therefore, are positive interdependent characteristics of effective schooling."

Giangreco, Michael F. et al. "Problem-Solving Methods to Facilitate Inclusive Education." In *Creativity and Collaborative Learning: A Practical Guide to Empowering Students and Teachers*, Jacqueline S. Thousand et al. (Eds.). Baltimore, MD: Paul H. Brookes Publishing Col, 1994, 321-346.

Grouping people together of differing skill levels or differing social status does not mean that invidious comparisons will not be made by students. However, any damage done by such comparisons will be far less than that which occurs from segregation by school or by classrooms in a school. Tracking is a form of segregation that produces serious social class and racial animosity in this culture, without substantive benefits. For lower track students, behavioral problems and school dropout also tend to emerge more frequently as a direct result of their relative track position. And as every teacher knows, misconduct by one group has negative educational consequences for all groups.

Individualized *vs.* Personalized Instruction

Schools often receive political capital from parents, educators, business leaders and concerned citizens by claiming that they offer an "individualized" instructional program to students. So-called individualized instruction suggests that the school is making special efforts to help some or all students achieve at elevated levels. It suggests that there is a degree of monitoring of each student's progress that virtually guarantees improvement for any student. This progress is presumed to occur because the curriculum is to be tailored to the academic strengths and limitations of each student.

Sometimes claims of individualized instruction are used to justify tracking in school. In particular, it is argued that students in the lower tracks will be given individualized help in order to ensure that they "catch up" to the more advanced groups. Similarly, it is suggested that those students at more advanced levels will receive individualized instruction so as not to be held back by slower students. Such promises have obvious appeal to parents of students at all performance levels because of the implication that their children will be singled out for special educational attention.

On the other hand, schools which sometimes claim they have done away with tracking also advertise that they offer individualized instruction. Such individualized instruction, it is argued, is the very thing which has replaced grouping by ability. Accordingly, achievement expectations for each student will vary rather than being defined by one's relative group position. This too has obvious appeal to many because individual uniqueness rather than group defined criteria will guide the school's instructional practices.

But what is the truth of such claims? Are schools which assert that they offer individualized instruction actually doing it? More importantly, is individualized instruction truly a sound pedagogical practice? When is it a good idea and when might individualized instruction hinder a school's efforts to create an effective school learning climate?

The troubling thing about such questions is that there is very little research examining what schools actually do under the auspices of individualized instruction. Moreover, it is our experience that many public and private schools claim to have a program of individualized instruction, yet such claims cannot be verified by observations in the classroom. An even more fundamental concern, however, is whether individualized instruction is desirable in the context of creating high-achieving schools.

In our review of the practice, we find little to support the supposed merits of individualized instruction. Indeed, individualized instruction is often a hindrance to creating an effective school learning climate. True, there are times when individualized remedial work is necessary and desirable, particularly if such help is temporary, is highly focused in nature, and is based upon principles of mastery learning. More often than not, however, so-called individualized instruction is based upon questionable educational assumptions. For individualized instruction to be useful, appropriate diagnostic testing must occur. Seldom is such testing done properly. More importantly, individualized instruction by its very nature conveys a range of achievement expectations to students and to their parents, rather than a consistent set of high expectations for all students. In essence, individualized instruction tends to reinforce the false belief that individual differences in ability are so disparate than only a select few are capable of high achievement. Such a premise is fundamentally antithetical to the core assumptions of an effective school learning climate.

On the other hand, effective schools promote a personalized approach to instruction. Personalized instruction differs from individual instruction in several important respects. Rather than holding highly disparate achievement expectations based upon presumed individual differences in ability to master learning objectives, personalized instruction assumes that all can and will learn what is required. These expectations are communicated to all students by creating a more intimate learning environment where mentoring relationships tend to flourish.

In such environments, all the teachers know all the students. Each student is assigned a faculty or staff advisor who regularly monitors the student's progress. Classes tend to be small, thus fostering more intimate connections between members of the learning community. Simply stated, there is an atmosphere where students not only know what is required, but are motivated to perform well because they do not want to "let down" those in the learning community whom they care about, and who care about them. Regular monitoring occurs, special help is available when needed, and mentor-student relationships prevail. Fellow students tend to help one another achieve learning objectives, rather than seeing their peers as competitors in a zero sum game. Finally, given the sense of belonging to a community in which one is a valued member, student behavioral problems tend to be minimal. There is no place to hide if a student acts out or is not performing up to expectations, and someone who cares is there to correct the problem before it becomes extreme.

To further facilitate such personalized instruction, frequent contact between the teachers and parents occurs. Calls and notes home regarding student progress, invitations to observe in class or participate in field trips, and other forms of involvement enhance the sense that this is a supportive community. Students, parents, and staff all have a greater sense of power over their lives in such a personalized environment. Feelings of alienation — derived from a sense of isolation and futility — are lessened among students, their parents, and among staff. Simply stated, a learning-rich *esprit de corps* emerges.

Even within large schools, it is possible and desirable to create a personalized approach to instruction. Schools within schools, where smaller groups are formed and stay together for more than the course of a term year, facilitates a personalized approach. This is further enhanced by cooperative learning (Johnson and Johnson, 1993). The point is that consistently high expectations, expressed through mentoring relationships and a shared sense of community, helps to sustain a powerful effective school learning climate.

It is important to note that we do not contend that teachers should refrain from all manner of grouping students based upon their skills. For example, students require mastery of certain algebra concepts before taking calculus. Rather, teachers should use the variety of techniques outlined in *Module 6* for appropriate instructional practices. The negative effects of homogeneous grouping and goal differentiation can be avoided by using the following grouping patterns for the instructional purposes shown.

1. Use whole class grouping for initial instruction on common objectives. Whole-class instruction* should be the primary type of grouping method, supplemented with other types of grouping as needed.

2. Use heterogeneous student learning groups for regular practice and reinforcement of skills.

3. Use temporary homogeneous performance grouping for corrective instruction or enrichment. This type of grouping should be used selectively, based on identified common student deficiencies, and it should be short-lived.

4. Use personalized instruction for corrective, enrichment, or extension learning and supplementing whole class instruction.

We do not contend or expect that all variations in achievement will disappear in heterogeneously grouped classrooms. We do expect, however,

---

*Whole-class instruction tends to be heterogeneous in approach in contrast to individualized instruction simply because of the number of students involved. This pattern works because new content can be provided to more students at the same time with economy of preparation. Many teachers feel that direct observation and management of student time and attention are facilitated. Some provision must usually be made for individual student needs, to assure that all students master the appropriate grade-level objectives. This process is outlined in *Module 6* on *Effective Instruction*. Particular attention should be paid to the section on feedback and corrective/enrichment instruction, as these are essential characteristics of effective whole-class instruction.

that nearly all students will master certain information and skills. Some will learn more than others, but all will learn what is critical for them to know in order to move to the next higher level.

The above grouping patterns sometimes overlap and can be adjusted to fit varying classroom needs. This is generally a useful framework for grouping decisions that maximize student achievement and address teacher's instructional and management concerns. By heterogeneous grouping we limit the negative effects of ability grouping while still making possible effective management of the classroom. Heterogeneous small groups and teams also facilitate the mobilization of peer culture in teaching through peer instruction, peer modeling or peer reinforcement. The methods of cooperative learning (Dishon and O'Leary, 1994) have proven especially successful in this regard.

While student learning teams *(Module 9)* may be kept together for considerable periods of time, it is important that instructional groups be flexible rather than permanent. In the initial stage of teaching a particular objective, the teacher may discover that some students are at or near mastery in an area, while other students require a great deal of instruction. The groups for this particular task may then be heterogeneously formed to include students at different levels of mastery so as to use peer positive norms in instruction.

Limited use of homogeneous groups is appropriate only for corrective or enrichment instruction. When a particular learning objective is completed, these performance groups should be dissolved and new groups formed for the next task. Research demonstrates that the same students will not always be the "fast" or "slow" learners. Thus it is essential that instructional groups be formed only for specific instructional objectives, contain a mixture of more advanced and less advanced performers, and then be dissolved when the class moves on to a new objective.

Research on Effective Schools

"Schools that have started the untracking journey have seen student achievement and self-esteem rise, especially among students formerly placed in low or average groups. Classroom and school climate are greatly improved as discipline problems decline."

Wheelock, A. *Alternative to Tracking and Ability Grouping.*
Arlington, VA: American Association of School Administrators, 1994.

How to Reach Common Goals at Grade Level

The research is clear: ability grouping and tracking in the early grades is the basis for much of the disparity in achievement that occurs at the secondary level. Thus, the early years of schooling should get priority treatment to make sure that ability grouping is no longer practiced. Although the past can't be undone, many secondary schools need to begin procedures for untracking now, even though much damage has occurred.

Since differences in student achievement tend to increase over time, the problem of coping with students who have wide differences in achievement is compounded in the upper elementary grades and in secondary schools. For example, there may be students in the fifth and sixth grades who are reading at the first and second grade levels.

How should teachers instruct students whose grade levels are below the "norm" to master the appropriate age-grade basic skills? Three suggested techniques are:

1. If the grade level skills are the type which do not require prior knowledge, heterogeneous grouping and practice is recommended.

2. Students functioning below grade level can be homogeneously grouped for corrective instruction, yet still be instructed in the same

grade level skills that all students are expected to master during heterogeneous or whole class instruction.

3. Teach selectively only the skills necessary for grade level mastery that will help students learn faster. A combination of both homogeneous and heterogeneous grouping patterns may be used. For example, two days per week use homogeneous groups for remediation or enrichment, and three days per week use heterogeneous groups or whole-class instruction for group learning on common objectives.

When grade level skills require prior knowledge, it may be necessary to group and instruct students temporarily on the basis of common prerequisite skills deficiencies. This form of grouping should be flexible, because it will not always be the same students who need remedial work. Further, it is only those essential prerequisite skills which need remediation. We should not assume that students must go page by page in the second, third, and fourth grade level basal readers and workbooks before being exposed to the fifth grade level objectives. The goal is age-grade level achievement, not total content coverage below grade level if there are deficiencies.

Research on Effective Schools

"Effective schools use whole-group instruction when introducing new concepts and skills."

Cotton, K. *Effective Schooling Practices: A Research Synthesis 1995 Update*, Northwest Regional Educational Laboratory, 1995.

We began this module by claiming that ability grouping has failed to produce acceptable levels of achievement in all students. Worse, ability grouping often creates academic failure for many, while heightening racial and class antagonisms between groups. Finally, tracking creates a climate which fosters relatively greater disciplinary problems among the groups defined as least capable. Such problems in turn have negative consequences throughout the entire school.

It is our view that so long as tracking persists, a school cannot achieve an effective learning climate where all students achieve at desired levels. Tracking by its very nature is a "zero sum" game in that it *always* creates academic winners and losers.

Under a tracking system, testing is used to screen and place students, rather than diagnose problems and remediate weaknesses. Under a tracking system, group norms of achievement are more relevant to setting performance standards than are the objective criteria which reflect mastery learning. Many students will perform at group level norms, even though those group norms are far below minimal competence requirements in society. Under a tracking system, large numbers of students will be "age promoted" (if they do not drop out first), only to find that the completion of secondary school has not helped them to master core skills necessary for employment or college. All of these aspects of tracking an antithetical to the principles of mastery learning associated with effective schools.

Summary

To reach common goals, flexibility in grouping is necessary. Teachers must have common grade-level learning expectations, and must use various forms of grouping to communicate these expectations and improve achievement. Certain basic skills should be expected of all students, including those currently functioning below grade level.

The ways in which students are grouped has a great influence on student achievement. Homogeneous grouping by ability, or tracking, is connected with differentiated goals and objectives, and this has a proven negative effect on overall student achievement. Heterogeneous grouping, however, with high achievement expectations for all students has a positive effect on student achievement. Therefore, grouping practices which have an inhibiting or limiting effect on students' learning basic skills should be re-examined and replaced with more appropriate and productive approaches. In summation, teachers should use grouping practices that are designed to:

- Communicate and model common expectations for student learning.

- Facilitate mastery of basic skill objectives by all students.

- Reduce prerequisite skill deficits as quickly as possible in order to facilitate current grade level instruction.

- Intellectually challenge all students.

- Eliminate any justification for below-grade level achievement.

- Facilitate an environment of cooperation rather than conflict between students.

Suggested Activities

1. Discuss current grouping practices at your school. Review the positive and negative effects of grouping practices from the module and try to arrive at a consensus as to the most productive grouping methods for all students.

2. Expect all students to master their grade level skills and communicate this clearly to both students and parents at the beginning of the year or the course.

3. Provide for "filling in the holes" for students below grade level, as well as teaching them current grade skills. Remedial education teachers should target prerequisite skills required of identified students. This obligates the regular classroom teacher to specify the critical skills needed by students to facilitate learning grade level skills. Regular, (at least weekly) ongoing communication should take place between the classroom teacher and a remedial education teacher about what should be taught and about student progress. Obviously instruction, both in and out of the regular classroom, must be coordinated and directly linked.

4. Identify the sex, race, and social class (if possible) compositions of your instructional groups. If strict homogeneous grouping by performance has been used, groups may be composed largely of one sex, racial, or economic group rather than being mixed. For example, tracking may result in mostly minority students or boys being in certain classes. This should be remedied by switching to heterogeneous performance groups for instruction. Using a whole-class approach for

basic skills, grade level instruction will eliminate the classes imbalanced by sex, race, class or ethnic identity.

Selected Bibliography

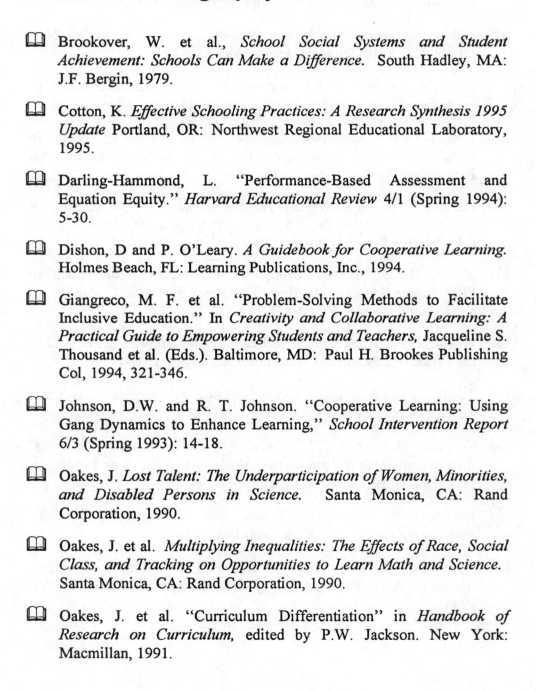

Brookover, W. et al., *School Social Systems and Student Achievement: Schools Can Make a Difference.* South Hadley, MA: J.F. Bergin, 1979.

Cotton, K. *Effective Schooling Practices: A Research Synthesis 1995 Update* Portland, OR: Northwest Regional Educational Laboratory, 1995.

Darling-Hammond, L. "Performance-Based Assessment and Equation Equity." *Harvard Educational Review* 4/1 (Spring 1994): 5-30.

Dishon, D and P. O'Leary. *A Guidebook for Cooperative Learning.* Holmes Beach, FL: Learning Publications, Inc., 1994.

Giangreco, M. F. et al. "Problem-Solving Methods to Facilitate Inclusive Education." In *Creativity and Collaborative Learning: A Practical Guide to Empowering Students and Teachers,* Jacqueline S. Thousand et al. (Eds.). Baltimore, MD: Paul H. Brookes Publishing Col, 1994, 321-346.

Johnson, D.W. and R. T. Johnson. "Cooperative Learning: Using Gang Dynamics to Enhance Learning," *School Intervention Report* 6/3 (Spring 1993): 14-18.

Oakes, J. *Lost Talent: The Underparticipation of Women, Minorities, and Disabled Persons in Science.* Santa Monica, CA: Rand Corporation, 1990.

Oakes, J. et al. *Multiplying Inequalities: The Effects of Race, Social Class, and Tracking on Opportunities to Learn Math and Science.* Santa Monica, CA: Rand Corporation, 1990.

Oakes, J. et al. "Curriculum Differentiation" in *Handbook of Research on Curriculum,* edited by P.W. Jackson. New York: Macmillan, 1991.

Oakes, J. "Can Tracking Research Inform Practice? Technical, Normative and Political Considerations," *Educational Researcher,* 21/4, (1992): 12-21.

Oakes, J. and M. Lipton. "Detracking Schools: Early Lessons from the Field," *Phi Delta Kappan* 73/6 (1992): 448-54.

Oakes, J. *Keeping Track: How Schools Structure Inequality.* New Haven, CT: Yale University Press, 1995.

Pallas, A. M. et al. "Ability-Group Effects: Instructional, Social, or Institutional?" *Sociology of Education,* 6/1, (January 1994): 27-46.

Pool, H. and J. Page (eds.). *Beyond Tracking: Finding Success in Inclusive Schools.* Bloomington, IN: Phi Delta Kappa Educational Foundation, 1995.

Renzulli, J. S. and S. M. Reis. *The Schoolwide Enrichment Model: A Comprehensive Plan for Educational Relevance.* Mansfield Center, CT: Creative Learning Press, 1985.

Slavin, R. E. "Ability Grouping and Student Achievement in Elementary Schools: A Best Evidence Synthesis." *Review of Education Research,* 57, (1987): 293-332.

Slavin, R. E. "Are Cooperative Learning and Untracking Harmful to the Gifted?" *Educational Leadership,* 48/6 (1991): 68-71.

Teddy, C. and S. Stringfield. *Schools Make a Difference,* New York: Teachers College Press.

Thousand, J. S. et al. (Eds). *Creativity and Collaborative Learning" A Practical Guide to Empowering Students and Teachers*, Baltimore, MD: Paul H. Brookes Publishing Col., 1994.

Wheelock, A. *Crossing the Tracks: How "Untracking" Can Save America's Schools.* New York: New Press, 1992.

Wheelock, A. *Alternative to Tracking and Ability Grouping.* American Association of School Administrators, Arlington, VA, 1994.

Module 6
Effective Instruction

Key Concepts and Considerations

- Alignment
- Teaching and Mastery Learning
- Effective Instruction
- Dealing with Prerequisite Skills and Corrective Instruction
- Feasibility
- Cooperative Mastery Learning

While the total school climate dramatically affects the academic achievement of students, the events that occur in each classroom also play an important role in that climate. What happens in classrooms can make or break any commitment the school or the district has in creating an effective school learning climate. Therefore, efforts to increase the academic achievement of all students should consider classroom instructional practices that will help all students learn. To do this requires that there be an alignment among the school's objectives, the content of what the teachers attempt to teach, the methods and processes of classroom instruction, and the way student assessment is conducted.

Alignment and Method

It should be obvious that what is taught in a course should match, or highly overlap, that which the school intends to be taught. No school will be effective if the course objectives, or the teachers' objectives, are out of alignment with the school's objectives. It also should be obvious that testing students should be based on school and course objectives. Yet such alignment between objectives, teaching and testing is seldom present. In fact, in many schools there is no clear statement about how curriculum, instruction, and testing relate to one another.

The objective of this module is to examine several instructional methods and teacher behaviors that studies have shown to be effective for increasing student achievement. What is presented here as effective instruction is actually a combination of six compatible instructional methods. Each method is a process shown to contribute to higher achievement when used alone. When used together, they form a comprehensive approach to instruction which multiplies the success of each. The components of effective instruction and their functions are:

Learning for Mastery. Learning for mastery is for general instructional organization, and for structure and goal-setting. It includes "mastery performance standards" and the "feedback corrective" process which is described in subsequent sections of this module.

Direct Instruction. Direct instructional techniques are for the whole-class instruction phase of mastery learning. Whole-class instruction includes initial presentation of content by the teacher and controlled practice opportunities.

Time-on-Task. One of the most important characteristics of an effective school is that it involves students for the time necessary to learn that which is intended. This is discussed in *Module 7.*

Appropriate Discipline and Classroom Management. The character of the discipline and management practices of a classroom is a critical feature of the process by which effective teaching takes place. This is described in *Module 8.*

Cooperative Mastery Learning. Cooperation among peers can provide a vehicle where all students succeed. This approach is often used as both a means of instruction and as a reinforcement tool. This is described more fully in *Module 9.*

Appropriate Reinforcement. A great deal of ineffective instruction occurs when there is an inappropriate application of rewards and punishment to the actions of students. This process is described in *Module 10*.

Teaching and Mastery Learning

In recent years, converging lines of research from various disciplines have begun to zero in on methods of teaching in effective schools. Some of this research includes a whole spectrum of instructional behaviors, and some is limited to one or two main factors, such as reinforcement and student time-on-task. This research on effective schools and on effective teaching is counter to earlier and weakly supported conclusions that schools were largely irrelevant. This earlier work discouraged the belief that teachers could help essentially all students to master critical academic skills and content. Now, however, improved research methods and far more research demonstrates the feasibility of successful teachers and effective schools. Coherent sets of instructional methods and behaviors, coupled with high achievement expectations, do increase student achievement. Teachers may try these methods with confidence and determine for themselves their practicality and degree of effectiveness. The methods that get the best results should replace those which so far have resulted in unsatisfactory student performance.

Mastery Learning and the "J" Curve

The concept of a "normal or bellshaped curve" distribution of ability has had a mistaken and a severely damaging effect on students and on teachers' sense of efficacy to be able to teach all students. If teachers assume that student achievement follows such a curve, they expect a large portion of students will be unable to learn except at low levels. They expect "winners" and "losers" from each group of students. Labeling and grading practices follow this set of expectations, so that students internalize the expectations. One result of this mistaken view is that many students of such teachers tend to internalize the negative labels imposed on them — often at an early age. Students come to think of themselves as A, B, C, D, or F students.

Mastery learning accurately assumes that ability to learn the critical academic skills and content reflects a "J" curve (Allport, 1934). See *Figure 6-1*. That is, nearly all students are capable of mastering what is now considered the high end of the "J" curve at the conclusion of a course. Learning for mastery is based on the notion that at least ninety-five percent of students can learn any given subject to a high degree of mastery, given sufficient time and appropriate instruction. "Aptitude" for a particular subject is seen not as a predictor of final achievement level, but as an indication of the amount of time required by the student to reach mastery on new material. There may be slower learners and faster learners in various subject areas, but these time differences tend to not be great. Students should not be labeled "poor" or "good" students based on differences in time required. Regardless of initial differences at the onset of instruction, the end of instruction is a high level of mastery shared by nearly all students (Bloom, 1976).

FIGURE 6-1
STUDENT ACHIEVEMENT UNDER TWO CONDITIONS:
Normal "Bell" and "J" Curve Distributions

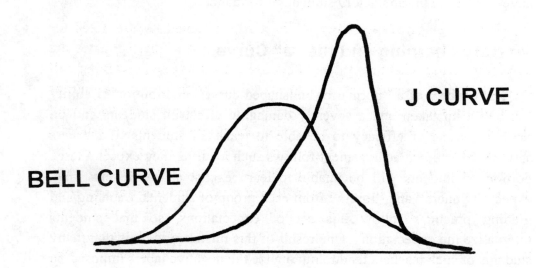

Under Assumption A, assume that 90 percent of the students learn Unit 1 adequately, while 10 percent do not; and that these 10 percent will not learn any of the later units (2-10) adequately because Unit level I is basic to all that follows. Assume further that while 90 percent master Unit I adequately, some of these will not learn Unit level 2 adequately. For each additional unit, more students fall by the wayside until by Unit level 10, only 10 percent learn it adequately while 90 percent do not. If these students are given a summative test in which all 10 units are equally represented, the curve of achievement is likely to approximate a normal distribution with considerable individual variation. To overcome this low level of achievement in level 10, one must increase the success rate at level 1.

Under Assumption B (mastery learning), however, assume also that 90 percent learn Unit level I adequately, while 10 percent do not; but these 10 percent are provided corrective instruction until at least 95 percent or more have adequately learned Unit level 1, before entering Unit level 2. This process is repeated on each unit. The goal is to have 95 percent or more of the students achieve mastery before moving on. Using the same summative test as in Assumption A, over 90 percent of the students in Assumption B reach about the same level of achievement as the top 10 percent of the students under Assumption A. The result is a J curve distribution.

Unlike "ability level," which is often assumed to be fixed or unalterable, the assumption behind mastery learning is that aptitudes are subject to change. If students learn how to learn, their rate of learning will increase. For example, students who take three or four times as long as other students to master a unit at the beginning of a course may take about the same time as the others to master the final unit of the course. Students in programs organized for mastery tend to become more similar to one another, both in terms of the amount learned and the time needed to learn. The effect is cumulative; learning skills are maintained and transferred to new courses or subject areas. In high-implementing mastery learning classrooms, eighty or ninety percent of students performed high level work based on objective criteria. In comparable classrooms based on a bell curve using the same basic materials, only twenty percent reached a high level under traditional teaching conditions (Bloom, 1978). Criterion referenced testing, reflecting mastery level learning objectives, thus changes the structuring of grading. Instead of a grading structure which always creates winners and losers (the bell curve), it is possible to have nearly all winners (the J curve) with a demonstrated mastery of learning objectives.

Learning for mastery has its most profound effect when used as a system, over time, by cooperating teachers with congruent objectives, materials, and tests. The achievement resulting from such a system is different qualitatively and quantitatively from that of other methods.

Research on Mastery Learning

Since Benjamin S. Bloom first presented his thesis on "Learning for Mastery" in 1968, there have been over 2000 studies done on the effectiveness of mastery learning as a teaching tool (Guskey, 1993). It is ". . . indeed, one of the most research generative works to appear in the educational psychology literature (Hymel and Dyck, 1993). Nearly all of this research supports the use of mastery learning at all educational levels (Kulik et al., 1990), and with a wide diversity of subjects such as: Spanish (Obando and Hymel, 1991), science (Guskey and Passaro, 1994), mathematics (Richies and Thorkildsen, 1995), computer literacy (Dafeldecker, 1987), and health education (Rehnberg and Barabasz, 1994).

Mastery learning has also been found to be an effective teaching method when used with a wide range of students, including high risk students (Parraro et al., 1994), students with disabilities (Schrag, 1993), multicultural students (Anderman and Midgley, 1992), and students who are achieving at the college level (Jackson, 1995). In other words, differing characteristics of students ultimately make little difference in achieving mastery of subject matter.

What is particularly appealing about mastery learning is that it enhances the effectiveness of a number of other teaching methods, including but not limited to cooperative learning (Lazarowitz, 1994), individualized instruction (Guskey, 1995), discovery learning (Guskey, 1994), peer teaching (Schrag, 1994), and whole language (Oran, 1993).

In *Module 4* we discussed how certain social psychological characteristics, such as student sense of futility (or efficacy) and student academic self-concept of ability, are important conditions relevant to developing high achievement among students. Mastery learning is reported to be an effective means for enhancing achievement, as well as effective at producing in students a sense of self-efficacy at being able to learn (Anderman and Midgley, 1992).

Research on Effective Schools

Students' self-efficacy is associated with three beliefs among students that are helpful for learning:

- the belief that intelligence is changeable;

- the personal adoption of learning-focused goals; and

- the use of cognitive strategies.

> Anderman, E. M. and Midgley, C. "Student Self-Efficacy as a Foundation of Classroom Goal Orientation." Paper presented at the Annual Meetings of the American Psychology Association (Washington, D.C. August 1992).

In spite of the research support for mastery learning, its use (while growing) is still relatively limited. Perhaps this is due to the presence of a large number of students who are far behind in grade level skills. The task of getting all students to achieve at grade level may seem overwhelming; yet here again, research demonstrates that master learning is effective at helping students to "catch-up" (Jenkins and Sileo, 1994). Nonetheless, mastery learning is not widely used.

One reason for this limited use of master learning may be a lack of understanding among many new teachers when they come out of college. In a study by Guskey (1993) of the effect of the development of mastery learning on preservice teacher education programs, he found that in nine education psychology textbooks published from 1990 to 1993, and three supplementary textbooks, that Bloom's *Learning for Mastery* was cited in only 5 of the 12 texts. The textbooks averaged 600 to 700 pages of which only 2.5 pages were allocated to the topic of mastery learning. These preservice teachers concluded that the textbooks' descriptions were limited and inaccurate.

On the other hand, Guskey (1993) found that master learning is generally well-received by teachers in inservice settings. The main reason for the limited use of mastery learning is the belief in a wide difference in fixed ability levels, plus the desire of some educators and powerful parents to keep the differentiated system (Brookover, 1995).

Stages of Mastery Learning

Master learning, as an instructional method, requires a variety of skills on the part of teachers, and a thorough understanding of the process. Master learning is a process of four stages on a continuum (see the following research box). This means that an effective teacher using master learning understands exactly what the student knows in regard to what is to be mastered. This is one reason why relatively sophisticated formative evaluation, as well as output assessment, (discussed in *Module 10)* are important skills for teachers.

Research on Effective Schools

Four Stages of Mastery Learning:

- Acquisition — the learner does not know the task

- Early Consolidation — the learner can perform part or all of the task

- Late Consolidation — the learner can demonstrate spontaneous mastery of the task

- Independent Mastery — the learner can perform independently and without prompting

Biemiller, A and D. Meichenbaum. "How Task-Directive Dialogue Changes with Mastery and Capacity." A paper presented at the Annual Meeting of the American Educational Research Association, San Francisco, CA (April 1992).

Implied in the mastery learning model is that there be small-step, sequential learning, with repeated evaluations and feedback to students on their performance. Constant and intermediate feedback may be a key for understanding the success of master learning. Frequent diagnostic or formative testing, in addition to summative testing for grading and course evaluation, is required in mastery learning. Regular feedback to students on their performance also is required to motivate students (Sherman, 1992). Mastery learning as a method of instruction involves formative evaluation before initial instruction, followed by further evaluation then corrective activities, and re-evaluation. To the four stages of master learning listed in the above box, we add a fifth: generalization. Generalization occurs when the student can apply what has been mastered to other tasks in other settings.

Effective Instruction

Effective instruction is based on teaching a common set of grade level skill and knowledge objectives to the whole class, with the expectation that all students will reach or exceed a stated mastery performance standard. Because of differences in entry levels, aptitudes (time necessary to learn), and the expectations of entering students, some will need extra time and corrective instruction to reach the mastery. Others will need enrichment instruction. This personalized help is given in practice, feedback, and reinstruction. It is generally given subsequent to initial instruction of the class. Initial instruction is carefully planned to establish and model expected outcomes for the entire class. Although outside help may be used if available — and, under conditions described here, students will help each other — it is the teacher who directs the process, who structures and paces the learning and who ensures continuity and maintains maximum time-on-task for the students.

To sustain and increase motivation, it is important for all class members to have frequent success experiences. Success is not accomplished, however, by lowering standards, by using objectives and materials below the age-grade of students in the class, or by allowing excessive off-task behavior. Rather, the objective to be learned is divided into small meaningful parts or "bites" for students experiencing difficulty. This process of identifying the prerequisite and component skills of an objective is called task analysis. Satisfaction for the students comes from mastering these small "bites" in succession.

Research on Effective Schools

"Teachers

- . . . at the beginning of the year or course . . . they review key concepts and skills thoroughly but quickly;

- use different materials and examples for reteaching than those used for initial instruction . . . more than a rehash;

- reteach priority lesson content until students show they've learned it;

- provide regular focused reviews of key concepts through-out the year;

- select computer-assisted instructional activities that in-clude review and reinforcing."

Cotton, K. *Effective Schooling Practices: A Research Synthesis 1995 Update,*
Northwest Regional Educational Laboratory, 1995.

Effective instruction has built-in mastery indicators. The teacher gets quick verbal feedback from all students, as well as frequent progress test results. This feedback helps to identify the students who need additional time and corrective instruction. Equally important, it also signals when practice is becoming excessive and the time has come for the class to move on to new tasks.

Planning for Effective Instruction

1. Identify a clear and measurable set of skill and knowledge objectives for the course. Planning, teaching and evaluating should all relate to these objectives. Some schools or districts already have well-established course objectives. If not, teachers cooperatively should establish them.

2. Establish a mastery performance standard for the course. For example, if it is believed that students must master at least 8 out of 10 of the skill objectives (or 16 out of 20) in order to function effectively at the next grade level, the mastery performance

standard is set at 80 percent. The teacher then aims for and anticipates that all students will reach or exceed the mastery performance standard of 80 percent.

3. Determine grades to be given for various levels of student mastery. For example, a student reaching or exceeding the mastery performance standard by the end of the course would get an automatic A or B, regardless of other factors such as level of participation in class or the amount of time spent. Students not reaching the mastery performance standard would receive grades below A or B, without regard to other factors. It is important here to make a direct connection between grades and the level of learning attained by the student on the stated objectives of the course.

4. Whenever possible, list the objectives of the course in a sequence, beginning with the easiest and working toward the most difficult. When listing the objectives in order, building in prerequisite skills for the next objective should always be considered so that a natural progression of learning takes place.

5. Using the school calendar, schedule the teaching of objectives for the semester or year. Be sure to allow extra time for the first objectives in order to bring students to mastery. Some students will have skill deficits to make up or will require more time to master the first objectives. If this extra time is planned for early in the course, the rest of the course will proceed more quickly and smoothly with less "backtracking."

6. Divide scheduled objectives into learning "units" of one or more week's duration. Each unit would focus on one or more main course objectives and would include initial whole-class instruction, practice, progress testing, and corrective/enrichment instruction. These units may include sub-objectives leading to mastery of a main objective, following the principle of breaking down complex tasks into simple, discrete steps which students master in succession. Units may be built around a theme or a certain body of knowledge which is appropriate for the age and grade level of the students. In this way the teacher can plan for maximum content coverage and add richness and variety as the group achieves mastery.

7. Plan initial whole-class instruction for each unit and gather the necessary instructional and practice materials. The teacher should model academic behavior for the students by being prepared for class and by having materials ready for use or distribution.

8. Develop or obtain a brief test or procedure which will measure only how students are progressing on the unit objectives. This is the progress or formative test. It is considered a part of student practice. Although it may be scored and recorded, it is not used to help determine grades.

9. Develop or obtain a test which measures final mastery of the unit objectives. This is the mastery or summative test used for grading students. Mastery tests may be given after each unit or after several units to conform to school marking periods. Test anxiety is reduced by having opportunities to take ungraded practice tests on the same objectives.

10. Identify alternative strategies for reteaching the unit objectives to students who did not reach mastery.

11. Identify enrichment or extension strategies for the unit objectives for those students who reach mastery earliest. It is important for advanced students to have opportunities to exceed mastery objectives for the group.

Note: Diagnostic or pretest information helps to focus planning, preparation, and time allotments on the greatest skill needs of students. It is possible, however, to proceed without such information and use the progress tests for adjustment and modification of instruction as the course proceeds.

Student Orientation

It is during student orientation that expectations are communicated to students for the first time. Teachers should plan in advance what to say to students, and plan subsequent behavior to convince the most dubious and discouraged among them. Teachers should . . .

1. present the objectives of the course to entering students. Put them in writing, post them on the classroom wall, send them to parents. This information is basic to students' senses of purpose, organization and self-management.

2. describe the mastery performance standard established for the course. Tell students that they are all expected to reach that standard, and describe the procedures to be followed which will help them to reach it. Stress individual and collective responsibility for learning, and the time and attention it will require.

3. inform students of the grades to be earned by reaching the mastery performance standard (A or B). Stress the direct connection between learning and grades. There will be students in most classes who have never been able to earn an A or B in their school careers because of "curve" grading, of being graded before adequate practice and corrective instruction, and because of behavior or other problems. Make a promise to these students that if they learn, they earn. Keep the promise.

Initial Instruction and Controlled Practice

Initial instruction on the common objectives is provided by the teacher to the whole class at the same time. Some successful techniques gained from studies of "Direct Instruction" are used here to keep all students participating at a high level.

1. The teacher determines lesson objectives, materials and methods. Student choices are limited and are made within the framework for learning established by the teacher.

2. Students know what to expect and are given complete and clear directions. The classroom is organized and businesslike. Disruptions are kept to a minimum through good planning and management on the part of the teacher and the building staff.

3. The teacher models task orientation by being prepared for class, having materials ready, and by maintaining active and continuous teaching behavior.

4. The teacher is directly responsible for initial teaching of content. Students at this point are not expected to learn independently through the use of worksheets, texts, or any other means. The teacher presents, illustrates, explains or demonstrates what is to be learned. Assignments for practice are made following the teacher's lesson, and are consistent with lesson content. Materials and activities reinforce and supplement instruction from the teacher.

5. The lessons proceed in small steps. Each step is built on the last, and builds toward the next. During initial presentation and during review, the teacher points out to students the logical sequence and the continuity of the lessons. Students are helped to see the meaning and the progression of their learning and to relate the skills they are learning to the larger objective.

6. Following instruction on content, the teacher conducts question-answer sessions with the class, making sure all students get chances to respond. Some practitioners suggest calling on students in order, so that students are not inadvertently or systematically left out. Hunter (1979) suggests posing questions to the class, waiting a few seconds so that all students must consider the correct response, and then calling on an individual to respond. The teacher uses a variety of group alerting techniques to keep all class members participating at a high level. The behavior to be avoided here is calling on a few consistent volunteers for responses and allowing the rest of the class to become spectators.

7. The teacher aims at a balance of high and medium success level in student responses by varying the level of difficulty of questions. For example, the teacher may wish to engage reluctant learners early in the session by starting with questions they can answer easily, and then moving them on to more challenging questions.

8. At the earliest grade levels easy, factual questions are asked at a fairly rapid pace. An occasional alternative to calling on individuals is asking for choral responses. With older students successful responses often require more time and thought. Recalling that the focus of this module is on sequenced skills, it is important to note that free-ranging discussion is not appropriate in this context, even with higher level skills as the objective. Student initiative should be encouraged at other times but not during focused language and math skills instruction.

9. Students are expected to respond. The teacher probes, restates or simplifies the question for those who do not answer or answer incorrectly, allowing them adequate time to respond. Modeling of correct thinking and responding is considered important for all the class members. An additional benefit of these planned interchanges is quick feedback to the teacher on the effectiveness of the initial instruction for the class and for individuals.

10. Students are provided immediate and objective feedback on their responses. Student errors are corrected in a matter-of-fact way before they can be practiced repeatedly. An error made by an individual may be treated as a group error, and the entire class corrected accordingly. Errors generally are treated as an inevitable part of new learning and no penalties are assessed during practice. This reduces student anxiety and encourages risk-taking.

11. Praise is used in moderation. The effective teacher praises *correct* thinking as well as *correct* response.

12. The teacher plans to make sure that students are firm in their mastery of each essential skill by extending practice slightly. Students are given two or three opportunities for errorless practice after they have learned the skill.

13. Independent seatwork, student learning teams or small study groups are the next opportunity for students to practice or apply new skills. The teacher should move around the classroom, check student work, and answer questions. The teacher continuously signals to the class that they should be on-task.

14. For students or groups of students needing more practice, special homework may be required, perhaps by contract for older students. Homework should reinforce lessons previously taught by the teacher, should be of a manageable amount so that low motivated students are not discouraged by it, and must always be checked and corrected.

15. Groups may be arranged for reinstruction and practice on particular skills or groups of skills. However, grouping should be flexible and arranged so that no students are permitted to be thought of as "low achievers." Also, no group should be excluded

from initial instruction. All should receive the teacher presentation, practice, feedback, and supervision.

16. Increasing skills of the class may be charted and posted on the wall to influence student effort and to increase motivation.

Feedback and Corrective/Enrichment Instruction

Corrective instruction is one of the most significant departures from conventional instruction. Teachers find it the most difficult, but the most rewarding part to implement. Many comment that their faster students seem to benefit as much as the slower ones because mastery is not assumed for anyone: it must be demonstrated concretely. Learning errors are caught before they are compounded and for students, education begins to be a self-correcting process. Success as a teacher and as a learner is increased.

1. After initial instruction and controlled practice opportunities, administer the progress or formative test to students. Remind them that the test is part of student practice.

2. Determine which students have mastered the unit objectives, and identify the learning errors of those who have not.

3. Inform students of their mastery level. Tests may be scored (but not used for grades) and returned to students, or discussed with them.

4. For students who have mastered the objective, provide enrichment or extension instruction and activities that will strengthen the learned skill and allow them to apply it in new ways or to new situations. An excellent reinforcement is to create conditions where mastery students can comfortably help others in the class to attain mastery (see *Module 9, Cooperative Mastery Learning).*

5. For students who have not yet mastered the objective, provide corrective instruction. Correctives always require additional time, practice, participation and alternative instructional strategies, whether they are for the whole class or for individual students.

Correction is done on a personalized basis. The teacher tries to determine the nature of the learning error (or the specific missing prerequisite skill), and applies corrective instruction in a mode different from that of the initial instruction, using knowledge of the student's particular needs.

Students react to cues in different ways; some grasp the meaning of a lesson more or less quickly from touch and manipulation, or from hearing and seeing a demonstration. In a classroom it is obviously not possible to use the precise best method for each child for each objective. However, it is possible to provide one or two well-selected alternative strategies for each objective. With practice and encouragement, students begin to see that they do have alternate ways of learning, that they will get help in finding and using these alternatives, and that they will get results if they put in the extra time they require to achieve mastery.

While there is a wealth of material available for planning alternative strategies, teachers are chronically short of time for finding and organizing such materials. Unless the materials are available in advance, they will not be used when needed. Here is where the value of cooperative effort by a building staff is greatest. A "stockpile" of successful strategies and materials should be maintained and increased annually to save time.

Ways of managing corrective instruction in the classroom include: small group study and practice, team study and practice, academic games, tutoring (including peer tutoring), assigned homework, and class exercise and drills.

6. Retest students after corrective instruction to determine mastery. Ideally the class moves as a unit after all students have mastered the objective. If handled correctly, this is a powerful motivator for class effort and student cooperation. In the best interests of the class, however, the teacher will have to decide when to move ahead. In making this decision, it should be recalled that if adequate time to achieve mastery is allowed in the early part of the course, then students will probably cover the remaining objectives more quickly. If the press to "cover the course" by the end of the semester or year forces the teacher to move on to a new objective, corrective instruction for non-mastery students should continue as new instruction progresses (see section in this module *Dealing*

with Prerequisite Skills and Corrective Instruction). This often happens when it is late in the school year and the teacher feels rushed to complete the curriculum.

As a rule of thumb, teachers should aim for at least 90 percent mastery in the classroom before going on to the next objective.

Mastery Testing and Grading

1. Following completion and review of the instructional unit(s), administer mastery or summative tests which measure final mastery of the objectives. They may be used at the ends of the marking periods, or they may be given more frequently and their grades averaged for a marking period report card grade.

2. Grade students according to the mastery performance standard established at the beginning of the course (A or B for mastery). If grades are given for participation, attendance, assignment completion, citizenship, or in other areas, they should be separate from the grades for mastery.

3. Use evaluation of achievement results to plan improvement of instruction in subsequent units or courses.

Review and Retention of Learning

Hunter (1979) did an extensive study several years ago of practices which help students to retain what they have learned. Her conclusions are still relevant. Provision is made in our description of effective instruction for these practices. They are briefly restated below:

1. Meaning

Students do not remember isolated bits of information which have no meaning for them. Structuring the curriculum and maintaining sequence of objectives lays the base for meaningful learning. Fewer and better objectives are more effective than numerous, trivial ones. Concentrate on key concepts and skip unimportant details. In the overview which precedes a lesson, or the review which follows, put what is being learned into the context of larger learning. Relate sub-objectives or lesson content to a main course objective. Occasionally discuss with students the purposes or uses of the learning which is occurring, preferably with relevance to their own lives.

2. Degrees of original learning

What is not learned well in the first place will not be remembered. The teacher should assess the degree of learning on important material before moving on, and reteach the class or correctly instruct individuals as necessary.

3. Pleasant feeling tone

The feeling of accomplishment, of "I can do it," helps students to remember and also motivates them to keep moving forward. Successes must be genuine, however small. An unpleasant feeling tone will also help students remember, but probably not what the teacher intends to be remembered. Avoidance behavior is a common student reaction to an unpleasant feeling tone.

4. Positive transfer

When something in students' past learning helps them to master and retain new learning, it is called positive transfer. This is why newer curricula aim to teach generalizations and principles rather than a string of facts: similarities and relationships between old and new learning help positive transfer, especially if called to student attention. Negative transfer, on the other hand, is interference in new learning by previous learning and results in student confusion. Teachers who try to anticipate student responses will be more aware of the possibilities of either kind of transfer. For example, an experienced math teacher will teach together from the multiplication tables 8 x 4 and 8 x 8, because they are similar, related and "support" each other: the teacher would avoid teaching 8 x 7 and 8 x 9 together because of learning interference and the possibility of "scrambling" answers.

5. Practice

At the beginning of any new learning, practice periods should be frequent and closely spaced. This is called massed practice. Such practice opportunities are described in the sections above. Once the material is learned, practice continues but the time between practicing is extended. This is distributed practice. When using sequential objectives, the teacher would review or refer back to skills learned earlier and have students practice them occasionally for retention. If the skills learned previously must be exercised to accomplish the new objective, as often happens, review and practice take place naturally with just a reminder from the teacher.

Keeping the above factors in mind will assist teachers in planning their reviews of learning. Students will "test" better at the end of the year and master later learning more efficiently.

Dealing with Prerequisite Skills and Corrective Instruction

It is possible for teachers to bring most of their students to mastery of grade level skills under the conditions described in this module. It may not be possible, however, for teachers to assume alone the total responsibility for overcoming critical skill deficiencies which prevent mastery of grade level skills, especially when these are extensive and of long standing. The resource staff of the building or district, especially any compensatory education program staff, should be mobilized to identify and deal with prerequisites in a planned fashion. The same should be true of extensive corrective instruction on grade level objectives, although these would be exceptional cases.

The teacher should selectively identify those skill deficiencies among the students that interfere with mastery of grade level objectives and then teach the missing prerequisites. If there are just a few, the teacher can handle these during regular instruction. If there are many skill deficiencies, the teacher may need the help of resource teachers, student teachers, aides, parent volunteers, a school or community learning center, or older students as tutors. The classroom teacher should still direct the process, assigning the skills to be learned, checking on progress, and evaluating outcomes.

Consistent with improving a schools' learning climate, students should not be "pulled out" of their regular grade level language or math instruction to receive this corrective instruction. Students deficient in skills must receive regular classroom instruction in an amount equal to or greater than their classmates if they are to arrive at grade level mastery.

Feasibility

The instructional methods described are not meant to make teaching easier but to make it more successful. In the early stages of implementation, extra work, and planning time are required. However, there are ways to save time, and there are certain features of these methods that help to make them feasible in the classroom.

For example, a key feature of learning for mastery is that it seems to move dependent students in the direction of independent learning. This is due in part to their growing attainment of prerequisite skills and their feelings of academic efficacy, and in their "learning to learn." While this is a gradual process, especially at the secondary level, eventually the extra teaching time required for slower students tends to decrease. Most secondary schools have an extremely wide range of student achievement with which to contend because early learning deficits in language and math were not attended to and kept expanding. While it is clear that early experience with mastery learning is the most productive of overall learning, learners at any age can overcome discouragement and acquire essential skills when this high quality instruction is provided. The sense of renewed hope that students feel on entering a new school can be used to good advantage by beginning learning for mastery at the start of junior and senior high school. Tangible and fairly immediate rewards for mastery help to re-engage the discouraged student in learning. These special external incentives become less important as the students gain in skill and confidence.

In general, most effort and planning in mastery learning should go into whole-class instruction on common objectives. This is another significant time saver when it is compared to individualized instruction or differential goal-setting and instruction for various groups within the classroom.

Key to the feasibility of building-wide adoption of this approach is coordination and cooperation by the building staff. Grade level or departmental staff, with the support of the principal and any resource staff, can avoid much duplication of effort and develop superior products by jointly undertaking the following activities:

1. Identifying instructional objectives, if not already in place.

2. Arranging objectives in a sequence from the easiest to the most difficult.

3. Scheduling the teaching of objectives so that teachers are operating from a common calendar. (The common calendar, in our experience, is the basis for ongoing joint staff effort.)

4. Lesson planning based on mastery model.

5. Development or selection of supportive materials for initial instruction, student practice, corrective instruction and enrichment or extension. Arrangements should be made for quick accessibility by any participating teacher.

6. Development or selection of any additional tests needed.

7. Identification of skills prerequisite to the selected grade level objectives and a plan to accomplish the teaching of those most needed.

Additionally, the time which is spent in meetings or in the faculty lounge in providing mutual assistance, advice and encouragement between colleagues should never be undervalued, especially as new approaches are tried. Research increasingly points toward staff cooperation and common goal-setting as a hallmark of good learning climate.

Cooperative Mastery Learning

Evidence on the importance of student cooperation to achievement is appearing with increasing frequency (Cotton, 1995). Practitioners are finding that learning for mastery promotes a greater willingness among students to help each other because of its emphasis on group learning of common objectives, as opposed to individual competition for a limited number of good grades or other rewards. Group norms and conduct tend to match mastery goals and are reinforced by cooperative learning techniques. To the extent that this is true, the teacher has many teaching allies in the classroom. It is exhausting and perhaps unnecessary for the teacher to have to initiate every motivational or learning contact each day. Some of this can be done by students themselves during regular team practice sessions if the teacher has made student team learning a basic and continuing part of classroom instruction.

We conclude by recommending that mastery teams be organized wherever possible to support and reinforce instruction by the teacher. We consider the enhanced cooperativeness known to result from student teaming to be a main facilitator of this approach to effective instruction. Four-to-six member teams should be selected carefully by the teacher to include slower and faster students and students of different races and socioeconomic backgrounds. Teams should meet on a regular basis to practice together, using materials provided by the teacher (see *Module 9, Cooperative Mastery Learning*).

Cooperative behavior among teammates should be taught and reinforced. The sensitive teacher will see that each student has chances to help and be helped as the teams study and practice for game or quiz competition. When students with different skill levels can interact comfortably with the material they are assigned, and have learned to use regular team practice time well, the teacher has some time to do corrective or enrichment instruction with individuals, small groups, or one of the teams. Most students needing corrective instruction require only an additional hour or so every two weeks, the equivalent of six minutes each school day. A few minutes spent on corrective instruction while the teams practice can be highly effective (see *Module 9* on *Cooperative Mastery Learning)*.

Summary

The major steps of effective instruction as briefly described above are:

1. Teach common grade level objectives and provide practice opportunities to the whole class.

2. Use student learning teams to reinforce instruction by the teacher.

3. Follow up with frequent ungraded progress tests.

4. Provide personalized or group corrective instruction to non-mastery students before moving on. Provide enrichment instruction to mastery students and to the whole class.

5. Using mastery test results, give grades of A or B to students meeting an established mastery performance standard.

Staff coordination and enhanced student cooperativeness lessen the burden on individual teachers. Although the full potential of this combination of effective instructional methods takes some time to be realized, the immediate gains have convinced many teachers to adopt these methods. While we have emphasized in this module the building of basic skills that enable students to become independent and lifelong learners, mastery instruction has been used with equal success in many subjects, from the elementary school through the graduate school level.

This approach provides an excellent framework for decision-making by teachers. The planned verbal and written feedback from students provide clear "stop and go" signals for both short range and long range instructional decisions. At the same time, no limitations are placed on the strengths, creativity and ingenuity of the teacher or the capabilities of the student. Teaching must have variety, and it must interest and suit the teacher as well as the learner.

Suggested Activities

1. Discuss concepts

    *   normal curve

    *   J curve

2. Assess current instructional practices and results

    *   success-failure rates of last year

    *   standards for grading

    *   common objectives

    *   special groupings, tracking

3. Establish a common expectation (or performance standard) for learning in your building for the current year, such as: _____ percent of students will master _____ percent of grade level skills. This is the goal to which planning, instruction and evaluation all relate. It should be based on a collective staff decision and commitment.

4. Review district basic skill program. Place objectives in sequence and schedule time for teaching basic skill objectives for the semester or year. Establish a common school calendar for teaching grade level objectives to facilitate joint efforts of staff.

5. Individual teachers, dyads, or small cooperating groups of teachers can begin to adopt the techniques of Direct Instruction with only a limited amount of advance preparation. These techniques are used for whole class instruction and controlled practice. Results of such use should be shared with colleagues.

6. Individual teachers, dyads, or small cooperating groups of teachers can begin to implement the corrective/enrichment instruction phase of Learning for Mastery as they choose. Wider adoption demands more lead time for preparation and staff coordination.

7. Form grade level or subject area committees to plan mastery teaching units for objectives, to be shared by all participating teachers. Units should include:

    a. lesson plan for whole class instruction;

    b. progress or formative test; mastery or summative test if needed;

    c. alternative strategies for reteaching or for corrective instruction, at least two;

    d. enrichment/extension strategies for individuals (use task analysis and taxonomy for steps c and d).

8. Use and experiment with mastery teaching units. Evaluate results, plan improvements and additional units in preparation for wider implementation in following year.

9. Discuss ways to use student team learning to support basic skills instruction. Plan and implement team selections, practice sessions on content, and team competition with some appropriate rewards.

10. Identify critical prerequisite skills for grade level instruction. Decide who is responsible for teaching skills outside the regular grade level program.

Selected Bibliography

📖 Abrami, P. C. et al. "Group Outcome: The Relationship between Group Learning Outcome, Attributional Style, Academic Achievement, and Self-Concept." *Contemporary Educational Psychology* 17/3 (July 1992): 201-210.

📖 Allport, F. "J-Curve Hypothesis of Conforming Behavior." *Journal of Social Psychology* 5 (1934): 141-81.

📖 Anderman, E. M. and C. Midgley. "Student Self-Efficacy as a Foundation of Classroom Goal Orientation" Paper presented at the Annual Meetings of the American Psychology Association, Washington, D.C. (August 1992).

Bartz, D. E. and L. K. Miller. *12 Teaching Methods to Enhance Student Learning: What Research Says to the Teacher.* Washington, DC: National Education Association, 1991.

Bentz, J. L. and L. S. Fuchs. "Teacher judgment of Student Master of Math Skills." *Diagnostique* 18/3 (Spring 1993): 219-232.

Biemiller, A and D. Meichenbaum. "How Task-Directive Dialogue Changes with Mastery and Capacity." A paper presented at the Annual Meeting of the American Educational Research Association San Francisco, CA (April 1992).

Brookover, W. B. "School Effects/Effectiveness." Paper presented at the Annual Meeting of the American Educational Research Association, San Francisco, CA (April 1995).

Block, J. H., & L. W. Anderson. *Mastery Learning in Classroom Instruction.* New York: MacMillan Publishing Co., 1975.

Bloom, B. S. *Human Characteristics and School Learning.* New York: McGraw-Hill, 1976.

Bloom, B. S. *All Our Children Learning: A Primer for Parents, Teachers, and Other Educators.* New York: McGraw-Hill, 1981.

Blumenfeld, P. C. "Classroom Learning and Motivation: Clarifying and Expanding Goal Theory." *Journal of Educational Psychology.* 84/3 (September 1992): 272-281.

Castner, K. et al. "Moving from Seat Time to Mastery: One District's System." *Educational Leadership* 51/1 (September 1993): 45-47.

Cohen, A. S. "Instruction Alignment: Searching for a Magic Bullet." *Educational Researcher* 16/4 (November 1987): 16-20.

"Cooperative Mastery Learning." *Elementary School Journal.* 91/1 (September 1990): 33-42.

Cotton, K. *Effective Schooling Practices: A Research Synthesis 1995 Update.* Portland, OR: Northwest Regional Educational Laboratory, 1995.

Dafeldecker, C. T. "Achieving Student Mastery Learning of Fifth Grade Minimal Standards for Computer Literacy through the

Development and Use of a Computer Literacy Program." *Master Practice*. Nova University, 1987.

📖 Desmond, C. T. "Mastery Learning: Teacher Belief, Language, and Practice." A paper presented at the American Educational Research Association, Chicago, (April 1991).

📖 Gray I. L., and G. M. Hymel. *Successful Schooling for All: A Primer on Outcome-Based Education and Mastery Learning*. Network for Outcome-Based Schools, 1992.

📖 Guskey, T. R. "Preservice and Inservice Professional Development Efforts Regarding Bloom's Learning for Mastery." Paper presented at the Annual Meeting of the American Educational Research Association, Atlanta, (April 1993).

📖 Guskey, T. R., and P. D. Passaro. "How Mastery Learning Can Address Our Nation's Science Education." Paper presented at the Annual Meeting of the American Educational Research Association, San Francisco (1992).

📖 Guskey, T. R., et al. "Mastery Learning in the Regular Classroom: Help for At-Risk Students with Learning Disabilities." *TEACHING Exceptional Children*. 27/2 (Winter 1994): 15-18.

📖 Hunter, *M. Reinforcement Theory for Teachers*. El Segundo, CA: TIP Publications, 1979.

📖 Hymel, G. M., and W. E. Dyck. "The Internationalization of Bloom's Learning for Mastery: A 25-Year Retrospective/Prospective View." Paper presented at the Annual Meeting of the American Educational Research Association, Atlanta, (April 1993).

📖 Jackson, D. N. *The Exploration of a Selection of Conative Construction Relevant to Learning and Performance*. Los Angeles: National Center for Research on Evaluation, Standards, and Student Testing (1994).

📖 Jenkins, A. A., and T. W. Sileo. "The Content Mastery Program: Facilitating Students' XXXX into Inclusive Settings." *Intervention in School and Clinic* 30/2 (November 1994): 84-90.

📖 Kulik, C. C., et al. "Effectiveness of Mastery Learning Programs: A Meta-Analysis." *Review of Educational Research* 60/2 (Summer 1990): 265-99.

Lai, P., and J. Biggs. "Who Benefits from Mastery Learning?" *Contemporary Educational Psychology* 19/1 (January 1994): 12-23.

Lazarowitz, R., et al. "Learning Science in a Cooperative Setting: Academic Achievement and Affective Outcomes." *Journal of Research in Science Teaching* 31/10 (December 1994): 1121-31.

Mevarech, Z. R., and Z. Susak. "Effects of Learning with Cooperative Mastery Method on Elementary Students." *Journal of Educational Research* 86/4 (March-April 1993): 197-205.

Obando, L. T., and G. M. Hymel. "The Effect of Mastery Learning Instruction on the Entry-Level Spanish Proficiency of Secondary School Students." A paper presented at the Annual Meeting of the Southeastern Psychological Association, New Orleans, (March 1991).

Oran, G. M. "Meeting the Challenge." *Preventing School Failure.* 3/1 (Fall 1993): 5-6.

Passaro, P. D., et al. "Using Mastery Learning to Facilitate the Full Inclusion of Students with the Most Intense Education Needs within Rural Schools." *Rural Special Education Quarterly* 13/3 (Summer 1994): 31-39.

Rehnberg, T., and M. Barabasz. "The Effect of a Health Belief Intervention on Safer Sex Practices." Paper presented at the Annual Meeting of the American Psychological Association, Los Angeles, (August 1994).

Riley, R. W. "World-Class Standards: The Key to Education Reform. From the Desk of the Secretary of Education." *Teaching Pre-K-8* 24/2 (October 1993): 6.

Ritchie, D., and R. Thorkildsen. "The Effects of Accountability on Students' Achievement in Master Learning." *Journal of Educational Research* 88/2 (November - December 1994): 86-90.

Schrag, J. A. *Organization, Instructional and Curricular Strategies to Support Supplementation of Unified, Coordinated and Inclusive Schools.* Reston VA: Council of Exception Children, 1994.

Sherman, J. G. "Reflections on PSI: Good News and Bad." *Journal of Applied Behavior Analysis* 25/1 (Spring 1992): 59-64.

Slavin, R. E. "Mastery Learning Re-Reconsidered." *Review of Educational Research* 60/2 (Summer 1990): 300-02.

Module 7
Academic Engaged Time

Key Concepts and Considerations

- Harnessing Classroom Power
- Time-On-Task
- Research Findings
- Engaged Time and Other Factors
- Allocation of Time

Harnessing Classroom Power

Students learn best when they are actively engaged in the learning process. It does little good to have students spending valuable school time waiting for instruction, processing administrative forms, socializing with peers, killing time with lengthy periods of non-directed seatwork, or any of the myriad of non-instructional activities common in schools. Learning is an active process that requires student participation; the more time that students spend actively engaged, the greater their academic achievement.

Time Counts

Educators and researchers have long recognized that time-on-task is vital in learning. The direct relationship between achievement and active learning time holds true for both individual students and groups of students. Numerous studies demonstrate that just a few minutes in active learning time has a direct achievement effect between otherwise comparable classrooms. Early studies (Bloom, 1976), that continue to be supported, indicate that on average, the difference between mastery and non-mastery for students needing corrective instruction is about an hour of extra instruction every two weeks. This is the equivalent of six minutes per school day (see *Module 6, Effective Instruction* for an explanation of this process).

This module focuses on increasing the amount of the time spent on direct instructional activity. While it is the classroom teacher who often has final say over how much of the scheduled time will be spent on time-on-task, increasing active learning time is a task the principal and staff should be involved in together.

Time-on-Task

Academic engaged time, as used in this module, refers to the amount of time devoted to instruction and learning. This time is largely determined by the teacher. It involves: 1) the time allocated or planned for instruction; 2) the time actually spent on instruction; and 3) the time students are actively engaged in learning (time-on-task).

Academic engaged time is not synonymous with the time scheduled for instruction in a particular subject area. The actual time spent in classrooms on teaching and learning is often much less than intended or scheduled. For example, a teacher may allocate one hour a day for reading instruction. However, if reading instruction follows recess, as much as ten minutes of reading time may be lost while students settle down to work. If students are assigned to small groups after a teacher presents a lesson, another few minutes may be lost as they move to new locations. Normal classroom problems, such as minor misbehavior, interruptions, misplaced materials, materials distribution, and so on, further intrude on the allocated time and reduce the potential for academic engaged time. While some of this time is a necessary part of any school day, much of this loss of instructional time can be minimized.

A serious detractor from academic engaged time in most schools occurs with the presence of serious discipline problems. As noted in *Module 8*, discipline largely depends on the expectations for conduct and the consistency with which these role expectations are carried out in the school social system. These expectations are alterable, and will be reflected in improved discipline, if the school as a unit decides to upgrade expectations for student behavior.

Research on Effective Schools

"Research reveals a close relationship between the amount of time students spend engaged in appropriate learning activities and their levels of academic achievement."

Chick, J.J. "Snapshop #22, Using School Time Productively," School Improvement Research Series. Portland, OR: Northwest Regional Educational Laboratory, 1992.

Research Findings

There have been many studies over the years which demonstrate that the level of student achievement in any area is related to time spent on learning (Cotton, 1995). Factors that obviously affect this relationship include absenteeism and tardiness of students. School attendance explains a significant proportion of the variance in school achievement among students (Walberg, 1994). Absent students generally receive less instruction and devote less time to learning desired skills and knowledge than students attending school.

The length of the school day also affects student achievement. There is not much difference among most full-day schools in the amount of time scheduled for instruction. Most schools allot between five and six hours of a school day to instruction. However, school variation in the allocation of instructional time is related to the level of school achievement. When some schools are on split or use half-day sessions, the allocated time for instruction varies considerably, and of course, the outcomes differ widely.

Among schools that vary little in the total number of hours scheduled in school, there is considerable variation in the amount of time allocated to instruction in language, science, social studies, and mathematics. This is a function of the school social system, including the expectations of the staff regarding what students should learn. To illustrate, if the school staff believes students are unlikely to achieve at grade level in reading and math, then the time allocated for these subjects is likely to be less than in schools where the staff expects mastery. In some schools more time is spent on activities which do not involve direct instruction (e.g., assemblies, school fairs, field trips) than other schools. In some English as a second language programs, students receive substantially less reading instruction than do students not served by these programs. When these patterns exist, overall reading achievement suffers.

Academic instructional time can differ among various groups within a school. For example, the number of hours of academic work of college-bound groups is likely to be higher than vocational or other non-college bound students receive. Obviously, the sorting of students into different groups reduces the total amount of time allocated to academic learning for at least some groups.

Although allocation of time for instruction does not guarantee that full time will be devoted to teaching and learning, high levels of learning do not occur when much of the school day is assigned to other activities. Studies recording actual engaged time and time-on-task have consistently found that the greater the time-on-task the greater the level of achievement (Cotton, 1995). Ironically, independent seatwork is one of the periods in which students are frequently not on task; yet independent seatwork is a major instructional activity in most classrooms today. While some limited seatwork can be beneficial, the absence of direct teacher-student contact during independent work time increases the opportunity for students to disengage from learning.

The evidence supporting the relationships between time and achievement is so conclusive that schools wanting to improve the achievement of their students should examine carefully the ways in which the academic engaged time can be increased.

Research on Effective Schools

Administrators and teachers:

- Schedule school events so as to avoid disruption of learning time.

- Allocate school time to various subjects based on school and district goals and monitor time use to make certain allocations are followed.

- Organize the school calendar to provide maximum learning time.

- Keep unassigned time and time spent on non-instructional activities to a minimum during the school day; then keep loudspeaker announcements and other administrative intrusions brief.

- Participate in inservice to improve their skills in making appropriate time allocations . . . and increasing student time on task.

Cotton, K. *Effective Schooling Practices: A Research Synthesis, 1995 Update,*
Northwest Regional Educational Laboratory, 1995.

Engaged Time and Other Factors

Improvement in the amount of time devoted to teaching and learning is highly dependent on the other factors discussed in these modules, including: expectations, effective instruction, discipline, and classroom management.

Attendance and Tardiness

Obviously, students absent from school are not likely to learn as many academic skills as they do when attending school. Some features of an effective plan for improving attendance are listed below. Of course, these suggestions must be combined with an effective school learning climate in which students learn well and are positively rewarded for doing so (see section on Reward Structures in *Module 4)*.

A parallel program to that outlined below also can be implemented for tardiness.

High expectations. Teachers must clearly communicate that good attendance and not being tardy is important, and that the school and the teacher expect this.

Agreement on procedure. There should be schoolwide agreement on the sequence of steps taken for absenteeism and tardiness, including reporting and followup.

Consistency. A consistent application of the plan by all staff (monitored by the principal) is required.

Written signed excuses. There should be a requirement of parental excuse for returning students, with medical excuse for extended absence.

Data on absences. A clear record of all absences should be kept for each student of why, as well as how often, absences occur.

Student conferences. There should be personal conferences with students upon returning from absences in which concern for the student, the reason for the absence, the importance of the missed work, and the need for good attendance are the focus. This surveillance of students should become progressively forceful as the number of absences increases, especially if it appears that the absences are not legitimate.

Parent contacts. Phone calls to parents or conferences, paralleling those for students, should be instituted when a record of poor attendance is forming. This should be started before a student has become a problem.

Truancy proceedings. Truancy proceedings, in line with the state or county regulations, should be instituted for problem students.

Competitions between rooms. Positive school incentive programs of competition between rooms for highest attendance should be implemented. (The procedure and strategy for this are similar to that described for *Cooperative Mastery Learning, Module 9).*

Expulsion and Suspension

For students expelled or suspended, there should be alternate education programs within the school or community, with required attendance. Time-on-task is especially important for these at-risk students. School attendance competition by rooms provides an opportunity to use positive peer pressure to change student behavior. This should be encouraged.

Suspension or expulsion from school is NOT recommended for serious truancy or tardiness problems. This defeats the goal of having students in school. Rather, for severe problems of truancy or tardiness, some form of in-school suspension or alternative school program with strict supervision and academic instruction is often preferable. In any alternative school or in-school suspension program, remedial instruction for objectives not yet mastered should be used.

Except for a few chronic problem students, the level of expectations and the extent of surveillance regarding attendance are major factors in the degree of absenteeism. When students are not held accountable for their attendance, it becomes very easy to skip school or class, and thereby miss critical time-on-task instruction.

Disruptive Students

There are better and poorer ways of responding to students who seriously disrupt the learning time of other students. Fortunately, as discussed in *Module 8,* there is an abundance of materials and ideas for helping teachers to gain greater control over otherwise unruly students. However, some students, for a variety of reasons, place too great a burden on a teacher and other students. These students should be removed temporarily to in-school or external alternative programs where they can get needed help and not unduly impair their classmates' achievements.

Free Time

When free time is given as a reinforcer, use of computer free time has been found to be an excellent incentive for reducing tardiness, even with high risk students (Inkster, 1993). And if appropriately chosen, a computer program can further reinforce desired skills and content.

Allocation of Time

It is necessary for teachers to become conscious of the amount of time allocated for teaching academic skills, and the amount of time allocated for other instruction or non-instructional purposes. Without careful advance planning, the more time devoted to other activities, the less time available for more academic time-on-task. For example, if compensatory education students are pulled-out for special instruction, they lose time going to the special room, getting started, returning to their regular classroom and getting prepared for the next instructional session. They also miss the regular instruction that took place in their absence.

Total allocated time in the school social system is related to the overall patterns of organization which characterize a school. Individual teachers cannot affect much change in this organization; this must be a process in which the entire staff participates, with leadership from the principal and the building leadership team. This must be taken into account when organizing the building for instructional time.

Planned change in the allocation of instructional time should have as its starting point the teaching of skills and knowledge necessary to move to the next higher level of learning. The creation of a common school instructional calendar, explained in *Module 6,* helps to focus staff attention on the time needed for students requiring extra instruction to attain mastery, or needing help with prerequisites. Time allotted for remediation *must supplement, not supplant,* regular grade level instruction. Only in this way will we end the massive and systemic loss of instructional time frequently imposed on those students who most need time to learn.

Time allocated for academic instruction can be increased by:

1. **adding on instructional time** by lengthening the school day, extending the days of instruction, or extending instructional activities outside the regular school day (e.g., homework, tutoring, etc.).

2. **reallocating existing time** by reducing or eliminating time spent on non-academic activities.

Increasing allocated time is difficult and, at best, limited. The most productive approach for dealing with allocated time is for the school staff to protect and manage whatever time is available. In business, time is money. In education, time is learning. Today, faced with the difficult tasks of erasing cumulative learning deficits for many students, and bringing all students to mastery levels of achievement, educators must squeeze the most learning from each school hour and day.

Managing Allocated Time

In order to make the most efficient use of allocated time, teachers and school staff should keep the following principles in mind:

- Consistent with the expectations of high academic achievement for all students, model and develop an awareness for students of the importance of using time productively.

- Within allocated time, teachers must deal with three kinds of activities: academic (reading, math); non-academic (sharing, social relations, physical activities); and non-instructional (transitions, waiting, housekeeping, disruptions). To the extent possible, reduce time devoted to non-academic and non-instructional activities so that time for academics is maximized.

- The principal and teachers should protect classroom instructional time from interruption and erosion in the following ways.

  - Schedule the maximum number of minutes each day for academic instruction and hold to the schedule.

  - Start and end classes on time.

  - Avoid interrupting classes for general announcements or special requests.

  - Discourage "drop-in" visitors, including staff members and students, during instruction time.

  - Reduce passing time between classes.

  - Reduce transition time between instruction periods, when switching from one activity or class to another.

  - Reduce loss of instructional time due to clerical activities, such as taking attendance, collecting money, issuing tickets or passes. Some suggested ways to do this are:

    - start instruction first and then do necessary clerical tasks while students are working;

    - get someone else to do clerical tasks (e.g., students, aides, volunteers) so instruction is not delayed;

    - streamline clerical techniques so tasks are performed more efficiently;

    - develop routines;

    - postpone or eliminate tasks that are not absolutely necessary during instructional time; and

    - reduce total time allocated to special activities that erode instructional time, such as breakfast program, lunch, recess and loading and unloading buses.

- Coordinate a common calendar scheduling instruction for classes that deal with the same content (e.g., all mathematics or language arts classes at the same grade level). Common scheduling encourages teachers to get the most achievement allocating time to keep up with the schedule. It also helps to ensure that teachers will cover the required materials during the time allocated to the course.

The principal should frequently monitor the level of student mastery progress for basic classes. Each review should be followed by appropriate feedback to the teacher from the principal. This process reinforces accountability for achievement with both the teacher and the principal.

Increasing Learning Time

Increasing time allocated for instruction does not mean that student time-on-task will automatically increase. However, increasing learning time will result in greater student achievement. Time-on-task is one of the most significant factors in raising student achievement. Increasing active learning time must be a priority for every teacher. While teachers cannot do the learning for students or dictate it by decree, through their attitudes, expectations and behaviors, teachers determine the amount of active learning in the classroom. Teachers must be aware of what students are doing and recognize the characteristics of students on task, some of which are:

- spends considerable time working on tasks directly related to the subject matter to be learned;

- pays attention;

- shows some enthusiasm;

- keeps busy on assigned tasks;

- spends a lot of time practicing and reviewing skills;

- enjoys learning;

- frequently experiences success in learning;

- understands the instructional task; and

- knows that he or she is expected to show results for work time to the teacher.

There are many things a teacher can do to increase time-on-task, even within a limited amount of allocated time. Proper use of student time in the classroom depends on careful advanced planning, consistent management, focused instruction and a large measure of teacher modeling on how to use academic time.

Instructional Planning

Instructional planning is the subject of reams of material. It has been shown time and again that good planning, management and effective instruction are interdependent. Good teachers seldom wing it. Rather, good teachers have a plan for the immediate and long-term needs of the class. Good teachers state succinctly the objective and communicate this to the class so students can manage their own time accordingly. Students should never be left wondering what the point is or what is expected. Classroom discussions, or questions and answers, do not depend on student or instructor interests of the day, but revolve around the content to be learned. Instructional materials selected or prepared by the instructor are ready for immediate use or distribution as needed. Good teachers anticipate contingencies with their planning so that time is not wasted.

Non-instructional Planning

Non-instructional events take students' attention, reduce teaching time and interfere with instructional plans. Nevertheless, there is an irreducible minimum of time which must be spent on recordkeeping, housekeeping details, moving from one activity to another, interruptions such as announcements, disruptions from students, and so on.

Teachers need not be helpless before this onslaught on instructional time. Advance planning means that students do not need to wait in line for teacher attention, do not need to shift frequently from one place to another or mark time while waiting for materials to be located, and do not have to ask unnecessary questions to learn what they must do. When surprises do occur in the classroom, effective teachers have a planned repertoire of responses from which to draw. Without advance planning, time spent waiting or effecting transitions can be trouble spots for restive students, with a spillover into academic time. Even during the first few minutes of the day, the class can be assigned an appropriate task while attendance is taken, papers collected, and so on. In this way, a certain businesslike tone is set which helps students to use their time well.

In anticipating and planning for these necessary non-instructional activities, it is worth remembering that minutes saved each day for instructional time count toward achievement. A few minutes of planning by the teacher may save 25 to 150 times that many minutes of student time, depending on the number of students taught by that teacher during the school day.

Instruction

Direct and focused instruction is a necessity for increasing active learning time. Throughout the modules we have stressed the need for establishing common instructional goals for all students. This creates a sense of purpose and accountability for students and thus indirectly increases learning time.

Students who are involved in seatwork activities are more likely to be involved in off-task behavior. When students are working directly with a teacher or other students, active learning time is increased. Yet, in the average classroom, two-thirds or more of the allocated time is devoted to independent seatwork, resulting in huge losses of active learning time. More ideas for increasing active learning time through instruction are contained in the activities section of this module.

Summary

The challenge to the teacher, principal and all support staff is to increase the time spent on academic tasks. This may be accomplished with a structured, orderly, teacher-directed classroom with an emphasis on academics and with frequent high level monitoring of students.

It must be remembered that the classroom does not stand alone but is part of the total school social system. Thus, the entire staff should cooperate in discussing ways to improve allocated and active learning time. Increases in the amount of time allocated to instruction resulting in higher proportions of active learning time — will be greatest if approached and solved through both the leadership of the principal and the joint efforts of the school staff.

Suggested Activities

- The Building Leadership Team of teachers and the principal should assess the existing school time schedule and organizational practices for their effect on student time, teacher time, and overall consistency of scheduling. The team should report its findings to the faculty and recommend changes where appropriate. At least two checkups a year should be made by this committee, one each semester.

- The principal should establish a time-efficient daily schedule for the building and communicate it to staff, students, and parents through the school handbook, newsletters, and bulletins. The principal is responsible for seeing that the schedule is followed.

- All school personnel are expected to model a respect for and compliance with the established school regulations for use of time.

- Substitute teachers should be informed about the daily schedules, and appropriate assistance should be given to these teachers so as to maximize their engaged time with students. Disruptions and inefficient use of time especially requires monitoring with substitute teachers.

- Because of their great potential for negative effect on student engaged time, the principal should limit the scheduling of "pull-out" classes and switching of classes as much as possible.

- Observation-feedback suggestions on individual use of time should be available to all school personnel, including substitute teachers. Ideas can be communicated by:

- Informal cooperative arrangements between staff members, where one person will occasionally observe another person for a brief period of time (at least 20 minutes) and then report back what was observed;

- Scheduled observations where an administrator, department head, or specialist teacher will use checklists or video/auditory tape. The use of recording instruments should be employed when making observations to increase objectivity and the value of the feedback. This type of observation is probably the most accurate, but can also be the most threatening if not used in a supportive manner. The purpose is not to catch people making mistakes, but rather to mirror what they are doing, not what they think they are doing.

- Occasional assessment of their actual use of time, by teachers and administrators, making notes every 10-15 minutes as to what they are doing. Over time, logs of this kind usually reveal information suggesting where improvements or changes should be made.

- Being an efficient manager of time and resources is a critical aspect of increasing engaged time. Lack of planning is the most common cause of poor management for both teachers and administrators. In particular, the failure to make written plans about what to do, how to do it, and when it is to be done results in low productivity. Daily written lesson plans for teachers should be expected and available for comment by the principal. (See comments below.)

Suggestions for Teachers

In addition to modeling a positive attitude toward learning and learners, teachers can promote active learning by increasing proficiencies in planning, managing and instructing.

1. **Planning for Instructional Time**

   a. Make weekly written plans in accord with the basic skill grade level calendar schedule.

   b. Make provisions for:

- teacher led instruction (directed lesson, lecture);

- practice activities (assignments, academic games);

- testing for mastery progress (quiz, informal test);

- correctives for non-mastery students (alternatives);

- enrichment and extension for mastery students (challenge students that have shown mastery);

- testing for mastery performance (the one that counts).

c. Share ideas for teaching skills with all teachers of your grade level. This results in better coordination, use of materials, and problem solving. In short, more effective instruction results from comprehensive, collaborative planning.

d. Anticipate off-task activities, such as socializing, daydreaming, and misbehaving, by developing lessons that provide:

- structure (definite activities, procedures);

- meaning (ties in with previous learning);

- group focus (clear purpose that students understand);

- variety (change format occasionally to combat boredom);

- lively pace (eliminate drag);

- smoothness (avoid jerkiness, stops and starts);

- minimal student movements (can lower time on task);

- student response (accountability, assists teacher's feedback).

2. **Managing Instructional Time**

a. Become a manager of learning.

b. Develop routines for efficiency.

c. Establish a minimum number of rules, but enforce them.

d.   Begin instruction promptly.

e.   Reduce interruptions.

f.   Don't become a disrupter yourself.

g.   Keep breaks to a minimum — both frequency and duration.

h.   Actively monitor students.

i.   Use positive and negative sanctions, but emphasize positive reinforcement.

j.   Increase the frequency of teacher-pupil interactions:

   • Practice teacher cruising. Circulate among entire class, checking on progress, prompting, and reinforcing. Do not sit behind a desk like an overseer.

   • Limit help to individual students to a few seconds at a time. The key is to get the student to begin working. Continue to cruise and return to the student with additional help or encouragement. Spending large amounts of time in class with one student reinforces that person's sense of helplessness and prevents the teacher from working with other students.

   • Break down learning tasks into smaller component parts to enable the "stuck" student to begin working. Reinforce all correct efforts.

k.   Make students accountable for their use of time. Specify what you expect and by what due date.

l.   Keep independent seatwork to a minimum to protect against loss of time on task.

Selected Bibliography

📖 Anderson, K. et al. "Make the Most of Every Minute," *Learning* 22/7 (March 1994): 22-23.

📖 Anderson, L. W. and H. J. Wabberg. (Editors). *Timepiece: Extending and Enhancing Learning Time.* Reston, VA: National Association of Secondary School Principals, 1993.

📖 Arlin, M. "Time, Equality and Master Learning." *Review of Educational Research* 54/1 (Spring 1984): 65-86.

📖 Bloom, B. S. *Human Characteristics and School Learning.* New York: McGraw-Hill, 1976.

📖 Bloom, B. S. "The new direction in educational research: alterable variable." *Phi Delta Kappan* 61/6 (1980): 382-385.

📖 Chick, J. J. "Snapshop #22, Using School Time Productively," *School Improvement Research Series.* Portland, OR: Northwest Regional Educational Laboratory, 1992.

📖 Cotton, K. *Effective Schooling Practices: A Research Synthesis, 1995 Update.* Portland, OR: Northwest Regional Educational Laboratory, 1995.

📖 Fielding, L. G. et al. "Reading Comprehension: What Works." *Educational Leadership* 51/5 (February 1994): 62-68.

📖 Fisher, C. W. and D. C. Berliner. (Editors). *Perspective on Instruction Time.* New York: Longman, 1985.

📖 Goldberg, M. and A. M. Renton. "Heeding the Call to Arms in a Nation at Risk." *School Administrator* 50/4 (April 1993): 16-18.

📖 Herman, J. L. "Developing a Procedure for Accountability of Student Absenteeism." M. S. Practicum, Nova University, 1991.

📖 Inkster, J. A. and T. F. McLaughlin. "Token Reinforcement: Effects for Reducing Tardiness with a Socially Disadvantaged Student," *Journal of Special Education* 17/2 (Fall 1993): 176-82.

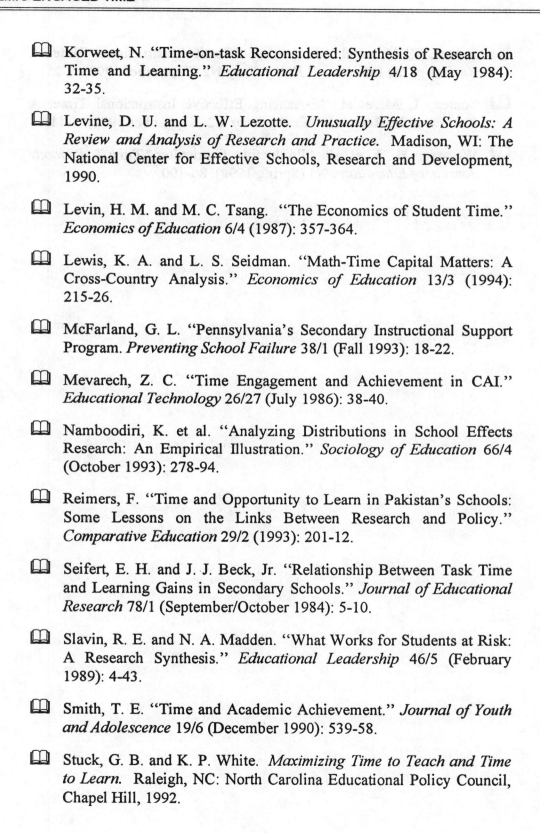

Korweet, N. "Time-on-task Reconsidered: Synthesis of Research on Time and Learning." *Educational Leadership* 4/18 (May 1984): 32-35.

Levine, D. U. and L. W. Lezotte. *Unusually Effective Schools: A Review and Analysis of Research and Practice.* Madison, WI: The National Center for Effective Schools, Research and Development, 1990.

Levin, H. M. and M. C. Tsang. "The Economics of Student Time." *Economics of Education* 6/4 (1987): 357-364.

Lewis, K. A. and L. S. Seidman. "Math-Time Capital Matters: A Cross-Country Analysis." *Economics of Education* 13/3 (1994): 215-26.

McFarland, G. L. "Pennsylvania's Secondary Instructional Support Program. *Preventing School Failure* 38/1 (Fall 1993): 18-22.

Mevarech, Z. C. "Time Engagement and Achievement in CAI." *Educational Technology* 26/27 (July 1986): 38-40.

Namboodiri, K. et al. "Analyzing Distributions in School Effects Research: An Empirical Illustration." *Sociology of Education* 66/4 (October 1993): 278-94.

Reimers, F. "Time and Opportunity to Learn in Pakistan's Schools: Some Lessons on the Links Between Research and Policy." *Comparative Education* 29/2 (1993): 201-12.

Seifert, E. H. and J. J. Beck, Jr. "Relationship Between Task Time and Learning Gains in Secondary Schools." *Journal of Educational Research* 78/1 (September/October 1984): 5-10.

Slavin, R. E. and N. A. Madden. "What Works for Students at Risk: A Research Synthesis." *Educational Leadership* 46/5 (February 1989): 4-43.

Smith, T. E. "Time and Academic Achievement." *Journal of Youth and Adolescence* 19/6 (December 1990): 539-58.

Stuck, G. B. and K. P. White. *Maximizing Time to Teach and Time to Learn.* Raleigh, NC: North Carolina Educational Policy Council, Chapel Hill, 1992.

📖 Suarez, T. M. et al. "Enhancing Effective Instructional Time: A Review of the Literature." *Policy Brief* 1/2 (September 1992): 1-25.

📖 Suarez, T. M. et al. "Enhancing Effective Instructional Time: A Review of the Research." *Policy Brief* 1/2 (September 1992): 1-11.

📖 Walberg, H. J. et al. "Productive Curriculum Time." *Peabody Journal of Education* 69/3 (Spring 1994): 86-100.

Module 8
School Discipline And Classroom Management

Key Concepts and Considerations

- Discipline and Learning Climate
- Discipline and Related Factors
- Principles of Discipline
- Creating Effective School Discipline
- Classroom Management

The Cost of Violence

As educators and as citizens, we feel growing alarm at the number of young people whose lives are circumscribed by violence. Whether as victims or as perpetrators, the most significant settings of everyday life for many children and adolescents — home and community — are environments in which violent acts are commonplace. For too many of our young these settings fail to provide the safety, nurturance, resources and opportunities for healthy development.

A sizable corpus of research clearly demonstrates that being raised in a violent climate creates fault lines in the social development of children. When this violence is allowed to persist, the fault lines widen and many young people fall into the cracks of crime, substance abuse, school failure, hopelessness, and inappropriately risky lifestyles. Simply stated, violent climates are developmentally damaging to children; they undermine the acquisition of the basic competencies required for responsible citizenship. The personal well-being of youth and the health of society are harmed.

In order for educators to address the manifold problems associated with violence, understanding of several ideas is essential. One thing that must be understood is that schools have little ability to directly alter the conditions of home and neighborhood. Poverty, unemployment, and exploitation are not in the school's sphere of direct control, even though these conditions shape the attitudes and behaviors students bring to school. Nevertheless, schools can and do influence what students feel, think and do, both in school and elsewhere. They do so by creating — or failing to create — school climates which mediate the ills which affect (or infect) students. At the very least, schools can be a positive influence by assuring a secure environment at school. This is not an impossible task. In fact, in many violent neighborhoods, schools and community centers, like those of Boys and Girls Clubs, provide safe areas.

Another way that schools attempt to mediate the negative effects of violence at home or on the streets is through school-based interventions with vulnerable populations. The past decade has seen schools throughout the nation go beyond mere identification and referral of students with special problems. More and more schools have developed peer helping programs, crisis intervention teams, conflict resolution training, support groups, and assessment and response protocols to address a range of problems related to violence and delinquency. Indeed, efforts to develop more effective school responses to child abuse, youth suicide, conflict, gangs, and acts of peer violence, ranging from bullying to sexual assault, constitute a movement within education. Yet as valuable as this movement is, it does little unless the students develop academic competence. *Research illustrates the connection between academic achievement and delinquency and crime.*

For example, Davis et al. (1991) found that students with academic deficiencies are at great risk of engaging in delinquent behavior when they get older. In fact, poor academic achievement in the early school years is one of the best predictors of subsequent delinquency in adolescence. In other words, instilling in all students a mastery of critical academic skills and content is necessary for helping them to make healthy adaptations to their social and economic environments. To use a public health analogy, schools that "inoculate" students with knowledge, values and skills, diminish their vulnerabilities and enhance their ability to resist unhealthy choices.

Such inoculation should involve both direct instruction as a regular part of the curriculum, as well as indirect instruction through appropriate role modeling by peers and teachers alike. While there may be debate as to the content of this curriculum, the common ground is that a desirable school learning climate is a vehicle for creating good citizenship — a universal goal of education.

In this sense, the academic learning climate of a school is directly linked to the goal of fostering good citizenship. A school climate which results in students achieving mastery of academic subjects is, in effect, a school climate which also promotes good citizenship. The core of good citizenship — respecting the rights and integrity of others — tends to flourish in schools where all students are provided with the opportunity and means to achieve and demonstrate their competence through participation in academic and other social arenas. Thus, academic competence and social competence are connected, and in turn, they are both linked to the school learning climate.

The critical nexus between academic and social competence among students depends to a considerable extent, however, upon the character of discipline experienced at the classroom and building level. Without effective discipline, neither academic mastery nor instilling the values of good citizenship are likely to be achieved.

Discipline

One issue which produces considerable consensus of opinion is the perceived problem of a lack of discipline in schools. Public concerns are reinforced by the troubled response of some educators. Some teachers see discipline as their number one problem. This focus on "discipline" often leads to a narrow definition of the problem and to "solutions" which treat symptoms rather than causes. Sadly, many educators feel so overwhelmed that they give up trying to discipline effectively, instead resorting to increasingly punitive "get tough" practices in order to maintain control. Such cures are often worse than the problem they are designed to remedy.

On the other hand, contrary to much public opinion, many schools provide relatively safe and effectively disciplined environments for learning. In fact, in some of the highest crime areas of our cities, students find their schools, along with community centers, to be much safer than even their homes — and certainly their streets (Randolph and Erickson, 1996). When viewed in the total context of their environments from lower income to higher income areas, many schools are relatively secure and disciplined places for students.

Security and order in a school, however, are not enough to assure an effective climate for learning. Safety is a necessary condition for a desirable school learning climate, but does not itself produce in all students a mastery of critical academic competency. There are many effectively managed schools, as far as security and order are concerned. However, many secure schools are failing schools, as far as developing student competencies are concerned. Yet there needs to be discipline. There needs to be classroom management practices that produce order while facilitating effective teaching.

"Discipline" and "classroom management" are often used interchangeably. We take a different view. Discipline in the schools is always a problem to be dealt with, and that problem is a reflection of school norms and specific techniques used in classroom management. For our purpose, "discipline" refers to dealing with student behavior with respect to manners, following instructions, disruption of routine, and consideration of the rights of others. "Classroom management" refers to the entire range of teacher-directed planning, managing, and monitoring of student learning activities and behavior. The school climate incorporates not only collective classroom management by the staff, but also school-wide rules and norms for defining and enforcing proper student behavior.

This module examines the problem of school discipline, noting the close connection to student time-on-task. The question of why some teachers feel that little can be done about discipline is addressed in terms of myths and negative, self-fulfilling prophecies. We will outline the problems and suggest solutions based on techniques and principles of effective classroom management that are used by successful schools and teachers. The relationship between the school learning climate, time-on-task, and achievement will be stressed. The module concludes with suggestions for improving behavior in school and fostering skills of classroom management among teachers. These strategies and skills focus on fostering gains in achievement for which effective discipline is required.

The Problem Defined

The popular conception of our schools is that they are increasingly out of control. Media portrayals of schools often highlight violence and disrespect for authority. While such behaviors do contribute to a disruption of schooling and may create situations that imperil the safety and welfare of those involved, violence and vandalism are only one aspect of the overall discipline problem. We are not downplaying the importance of violence and vandalism. Where serious disruption exists, it must be ended. Yet, as most educators know, a more common problem in school discipline is the continual, often trivial, undertone of inattention and interruption that occurs in most classes. The spectacular nature of more blatant offenses distorts our perception of their importance, compared to the seemingly innocuous misbehavior that is irritating but not dangerous (and consequently often ignored). It is, however, precisely these minor misbehaviors that create a serious barrier to effective education. Time spent misbehaving or goofing-off is time not spent in active learning.

Nearly two decades ago Jones (1979) tied minor interruptions directly to time-on-task. In the average class in those days, disruption resulted in 45-55 percent of time-off-task. The implication for the percentage of time-off-task in poorly managed classrooms is staggering. Considering that many schools had this "discipline problem," it is little wonder that their achievement level was low: students in these schools were seldom on task! Furthermore, teacher stress and burn-out are associated with the energy drain of trying to manage and cope with continual disruption in the learning process, producing feelings of hopelessness about the possibility of effective instruction. Thus, poor discipline may result in three other interrelated problems which undermine the educational process: a low overall student achievement level, teacher burn out, and perhaps even more serious acts of violence.

Beliefs, Myths, and Self-Fulfilling Prophecy

Despite the amount of attention given to the problem, poor discipline continues as a major force in the lives of many teachers. Many educators believe that little can be done to resolve the problem, short of increasing the use of authoritarian and repressive control tactics. Several beliefs have become prevalent and are in close parallel to the reasons often given why poor or urban children may not learn well. These myths reinforce the belief that good discipline is largely beyond the control (and responsibility) of teachers. Among these myths are:

- low achieving, low socio-economic status, minority, or emotionally disturbed students are "different," and little can be done to control them, except through heavy restriction and punishment;

- students in general are uncontrollable because of the permissiveness of society or their homes;

- parents are no longer supportive of the schools;

- parents cannot control their own children;

- schools can do little to alter the negative effects of too much television viewing by students;

- schools located in rough neighborhoods cannot be improved;

- court cases, giving due process to students, have tied the hands of the schools.

Educators who believe these myths set up a self-fulfilling prophecy whereby disruption in school is increased. Such beliefs results in lower expectations for behavior, often reflected by such remarks as, "Nothing I try makes any difference. These students just will not listen!" Teachers may interpret lack of attention, talking in class and interruptions as shortcomings of their students, or they can look for problems in their own classroom management. As a result, teachers try one gimmick after another, without using any one strategy consistently. Subsequent failure of each new plan, for want of consistent enforcement, will then confirm in the teacher's mind the hopelessness of trying to deal with "problem" students. The prophecy is then fulfilled and the students continue to act up.

Research on Effective Schools

Administrators and teachers:

- Provide a written code of conduct that all students, parents and school staff know and understand.

- Administer discipline procedures quickly following infractions.

- Deliver sanctions commensurate with offenses committed.

- Carry out discipline in a neutral, matter of fact way, focusing on the student's behavior rather than personality or history.

- Provide positive reinforcement for appropriate behavior, particularly for those with a history of problems.

- Avoid expulsions and out of school suspensions whenever possible, making use of in-school suspension with assistance and support.

Cotton, K. *Effective Schooling Practices: A Research Synthesis 1995 Update,*
Northwest Regional Educational Laboratory, 1995.

Self-fulfilling prophecies, negative expectations and failure are not inevitable. Positive, effective discipline without repressive actions is possible with all kinds of students, regardless of the community in which students reside. In the next section, evidence is examined for this claim.

Principles of Discipline

The ability to produce desirable classroom discipline cannot be understood apart from a number of principles:

- The school learning climate must be the emphasis of the school. When learning and achievement are not the priority, other behaviors detract time and effort from that fundamental purpose. In essence, school discipline can and often does become an end in itself, rather than an aspect of the school climate which facilitates learning.

- When students are unsuccessful in mastering educational skills and content, they turn to other means of satisfying needs for success and attention. Overwhelmingly, problem children are those pupils with learning problems whom we are not reaching. Discipline problems are most likely to occur among lower tracked or grouped students.

- High-achieving schools have orderly, industrious and well-behaved student bodies.

- Much of this work of fostering effective discipline involves increasing the amount of time-on-task (see *Module 7)*.

- While response to misbehavior is important, the actions taken by teachers before a problem occurs separate effective from ineffective classroom managers.

- Tolerating misbehavior by ignoring it, like tolerating academic failure by ignoring it, results in the problem growing worse over time.

In summary, effective discipline cannot be divorced from concern for achievement and learning. School and classroom learning climate go hand in hand with discipline practices.

School-wide Discipline

This section presents a framework for setting up an effective program of discipline and offers guidelines for classroom management that complement the school effort aimed at high achievement.

Many educators limit their thoughts about discipline to classroom practices. Our approach, while not neglecting the individual classroom, also emphasizes the importance of an effective school-wide discipline program. Students pass through the halls to recess, lunch hour, rest room, and assemblies; all involve activities that occur outside the classroom. Schools must have rules and standards of behavior for these common activities. Behavior in the wider milieu of the school creates a norm which is reflected in the individual classrooms. Serious problems that begin outside the classroom often appear in the classroom as spillovers.

Faculty and administration, therefore, share the responsibility for creating an orderly climate on a school-wide basis. The leadership must come from the principal; the entire staff, including grade levels and departments, must have written policies and procedures to deal with student behaviors that adversely affect the learning climate, and therefore student achievement. The following problems should be addressed with clear school policies: truancy, excessive absenteeism, tardiness, sexual harassment, fighting, bullying, insubordination, cheating, and failure to complete assignments.

Just as in academics, the key to effective school discipline is the level of expectation which the staff holds, and the consistency with which it is upheld. Staff expectations, in turn, help to shape peer group norms. Decisions on which behaviors are appropriate or inappropriate must be based on how they affect the learning climate. In too many instances, educators tolerate behavior that interferes with learning.

The School Plan

The school plan for discipline should include both in-class and out-of-class behavior. The essential features of both the in-class and out-of-class parts of the plan are: 1) identification of specific required behaviors; and 2) consequences, both negative and positive, that result from non-compliance or compliance. The challenge for the principal and teachers is to agree on a minimum number of essential rules (e.g., five rules for each area) that must be followed by all students, and then to specify what will happen as a result of breaking or following those rules. While the in-class rules for behavior should be consistent from class to class, each teacher should be allowed to modify the classroom plan to meet his or her needs as long as they do not violate school policy.

Steps for Setting Up the School Plan

1. A committee of teacher representatives, with the principal, develops a draft of a school-wide discipline plan.

2. The draft is presented to the total staff for reaction and suggestions.

3. The committee prepares a final draft.

4. The total staff is presented with the final draft for approval.

5. The adopted plan is presented to parents through special meetings, bulletins, and the Parent Handbook.

6. The principal and teachers of the committee present the plan to students in an assembly.

7. Follow-up discussions with students are conducted in classrooms.

8. Regular discussions of how to handle special discipline problems should take place, either as part of whole staff meetings or grade/department meetings.

Following Through on the School Plan

Once a discipline plan has been established and communicated to students and parents, follow through must be accomplished. A school-wide discipline plan is worthless unless it is consistently carried out by all teachers. A complete plan not only specifies what students are required to do, it also specifies what teachers and the principal are expected to do. Enforcement is essential.

When negative sanctions are employed, success depends on making prior arrangements with other adults who are expected to participate in resolving behavior problems. If, for example, a teacher expects to involve the principal in handling discipline problems, this intervention should be identified as one of the systematic steps of the classroom plan. The principal should know the steps the teacher will follow to deal with offenders. In this context, a student referral to the principal for improper behavior occurs according to agreement by the teacher and the principal. In short, intervention of the principal is one step, like others, in the classroom discipline plan. In like manner, the point of requesting parent intervention should be explained to parents ahead of time.

Teacher Responsibilities

1. Determine wants and needs regarding student conduct.

2. Establish expectations for behavior.

3. Establish minimum classroom rules.

4. Set up a classroom discipline plan: rules, negative and positive consequences.

5. Obtain the principal's approval of the plan.

6. Send a copy of the discipline plan to the parents with explanations of rules and contingencies for enforcement. (Suggest requirement of parent signature.)

7. Provide positive reinforcement to students who comply with rules.

8. Follow through by consistently and calmly carrying out a plan of negative consequences for students who choose to misbehave.

9. Revise plan and consequences if disruptions continue.

10. Persist and behave consistently according to expectations, rules, and plan.

Principal Responsibilities

1. Review, modify, and approve classroom discipline plans.

2. Check to see that teacher responsibilities are carried out.

3. Support teachers as they carry out their plans.

(For a more detailed explanation of how to reduce student misbehavior see: Moles, 1989 and Gottfredson et al., 1993).

The elements above form a planning framework for effective discipline. No matter how thorough the planning, success will require consistent implementation. Canter and Canter (1976) identified three typical modes of response to discipline problems. The effectiveness of the school plan depends on which of these modes of enforcement is employed.

1. **Avoidance.** Ignoring the behavior in the hopes that it will go away (it will not). By ignoring misbehavior, teachers communicate that the stated rules are not the actual definition of appropriate behavior. Students perceive that the staff either does not know what is going on, does not care, or is unable to stop it. In any case, the students soon control the situation, often pushing limits of tolerance to the point at which a staff member will explode, call the principal or react in some other drastic manner — but at a level far beyond what is necessary or acceptable for a positive learning climate.

2. **Punitive Action.** Because of frustrations growing out of the situation noted above, or as a means of enforcing the rules to prevent this development, schools may resort to legalistic solutions or use of outside security personnel. Teachers and principals may resort to verbal abuse, screaming, threats, or physical punishment.

3. **Firm and Consistent Assertive Response.** Effective schools and teachers respond to infractions firmly and immediately, but without harsh action. The key to this firm assertive response is communicating clearly, through both verbal and non-verbal channels, that the students are there to learn, and that interruptions of that learning will not be tolerated. The rationale is thus reasonable, the manner relaxed, calm, firm, and most important, consistent.

Most educators and communities would prefer the firm and assertive response. The preponderance of discipline problems shows that many schools fail to achieve this. Yet the existence of schools and classrooms with an orderly, positive learning climate show that this response can be achieved.

Attending to Problem Behavior

In achieving desired response to inappropriate behavior, the staff must be aware of three distinctions: 1) preventing misbehavior; 2) responding to misbehavior; and 3) obtaining help for the few students with serious problems. Each of these will be considered in turn.

1. **Preventing Misbehavior.** As noted earlier, efficient and well-organized schools and classrooms prevent many of the problems that plague most schools and teachers. Keys to preventing problems include the following:

   a. **Thorough Planning.** Poor planning for instruction is one of the biggest contributors to poor student behavior in the classroom. If the teacher appears to be disorganized, some students inevitably see such disorganization as a green light for disruptive behaviors.

   b. **Appropriate Instruction.** The planning must be accompanied by an academic program in which students' educational needs are met. Appropriate reteaching, remedial work, and enrichment must be provided as needed for all students.

   c. **Positive Reinforcement.** Proper use of time, as well as verbal and written statements of positive reinforcement, helps to motivate students to perform. The use of incentives or contingency management techniques may be in order if other approaches do not work. Creating opportunities for students to demonstrate their mastery is a powerful reinforcer and an incentive for continued mastery learning.

d. **Daily Organizational Activities.** Every school must attend to certain organizational requirements: taking attendance, lunch, recess, changing classes, rest rooms, and assemblies are a part of school. Wide variations exist in how schools manage these functions. For example, some schools and teachers waste as much as 15-20 minutes in the complex of morning activities in which students have nothing to do. Other schools use this time to have students do silent reading, or other tasks, while teachers complete required record keeping. This is prime time in which students are fresh and alert. The staff should plan independent instructional activities that take advantage of this often unused time. Other aspects of the school day are also likely to subtract from time-on-task, thus providing instances where unoccupied students create disturbance. Each school should monitor these activities, setting procedures which reduce the chance of problems.

e. **Contingency Plans.** Plans for rainy days, substitutes, assemblies, and last minute schedule changes should be prepared in advance.

f. **Effective Supervision.** Most behavioral problems occur in unsupervised situations. Research on bullying, for example, shows that most bullying episodes occur on playgrounds, in hallways, or buses, and in restrooms when students are gathered without careful adult supervision. The staff has a shared responsibility to monitor the school. Trained peer leaders can and should be part of a school's plan for effective supervision. Close supervision communicates to students that the expectations for good behavior will be enforced consistently.

g. **Consistent Rules Between Classrooms.** Individual teachers should adopt rules that are consistent with the overall school plan. This action will reinforce the norms of the school learning climate. Enforcement of rules within classes should also be carried out consistently in accord with the school plan.

2. **Responding to Misbehavior.** Despite the most careful planning, students will inevitably test the system. It is the response to this testing of limits that determines the norm for handling of discipline. The key to the school's response is consistency. The principles below (see Canter & Canter, 1976; Jones, 1979) are effective in helping the staff to achieve the needed consistency.

   a. **Setting Limits.** Enforcement must be consistent. Jones (1979) speaks of two stages: training a class and maintaining a class. While training students, the staff is setting and enforcing the limits of acceptable behavior. Until this process is complete, students will test these limits, trying to find out how firmly the line of resistance is set. During this time, the staff must meet each infraction. Generally, a simple warning is sufficient, but it may require stronger non-verbal cues (e.g., backing the student down with eye contact while moving closer, perhaps speaking the student's name with a firm request to desist at the same time). If the staff is consistent, this testing will gradually subside as the students accept the now firmly established line.

   Note: Consistency is the major difference between effective and ineffective disciplinarians. Effective disciplinarians meet each challenge until the limits are accepted. Ineffective staff allow some misbehavior to go unchallenged or give up before the limits are accepted.

   Once limits have been set, the staff will occasionally have to remind the students of those limits. This can be done with a simple verbal or non-verbal cue (e.g., snapping the fingers, softly speaking the pupil's name, walking toward the offender), which does not disrupt the on-going class. However, teachers must continue to meet infractions quickly and firmly with the message that, even though a simple cue is usually necessary for enforcement, they are prepared to go further if needed.

   b. **Choice.** Inevitably, there will be some students who either do not stop their disruptive behavior when confronted, or who repeatedly exceed the acceptable limits. The student must realize that his or her choice to continue misbehaving results in a consequence that is self-inflicted. This is an important aspect of the student's learning responsibility. Cause and effect must be clearly established in the student's mind.

c. **Consequences** (negative reinforcement). Consequences must be planned in advance. The consequences should be reasonable and capable of being carried out. It should also be something the student does not like, yet is not psychologically or physically harmful (sarcasm, corporal punishment, or personal condemnation are not appropriate). Finally, the consequences should be given in terms of the student's actions, "Since you chose to continue your actions, you have chosen to receive . . . " (Canter & Canter, 1976).

Some effective consequences can be: loss of privileges, restitution of damages, isolation, calling parents, and making up wasted time. The consequences should follow logically from the action (e.g., paying for a broken window, cleaning up a mess, sanding a name off a desk).

d. **Incentive Systems** (positive reinforcement). In situations where negative consequences do not produce the desired change in student behavior, use of positive reinforcements may work. Setting up special incentive programs involving rewards for acceptable performance may be motivating for the student, whereas continuous negative consequences may cause more and greater non-compliance. Usually, alternating a negative consequence with a positive incentive approach is more productive than a steady diet of totally negative consequences. It is important for the teacher to emphasize and reward appropriate behavior with positive consequences, while providing negative consequences each time a student chooses to misbehave. It is also important to provide all students with opportunities to attain rewards for their behaviors.

e. **Additional Follow-through.** The process of enforcing limits, providing choice, and giving consequences will work for most students. For some students, further action may be needed. Parents and the principal should be involved in setting up such procedures and consequences. In addition, students who need this extra attention may also need supportive counseling, remedial academic work, and a caring teacher. Students who continue to act out can learn to control their behavior, but they often require help in learning appropriate responses and in meeting their needs for success and attention.

f. **In-school Suspension.** Sometimes students may have to be removed from class because they endanger other students, show flagrant disrespect, or engage in other serious misbehaviors. These same students are often in need of remedial educational help. Suspension may be just what the student wants. More and more schools are recognizing the need for alternatives to suspension. An in-school suspension room, staffed with counselors or teachers to provide intensive remedial academic work and firm behavioral limits, can be one possibility.

3. **Obtaining Help for Non-conforming Students.** Students are not evil by nature. Individuals who have trouble conforming to established limits use acting out behaviors to satisfy their social, academic, and emotional needs for success, recognition, and attention. These problem students must learn to meet their needs in acceptable ways. Additional help in socialization or academics may be necessary. For the vast majority of students, firmly set and enforced limits in a positive learning climate enable them to function successfully. For the generally small number of students that are serious, chronic discipline problems, the teacher or principal should refer the student to specialized agencies or trained personnel for professional help.

The staff which consistently follows these guidelines should be able to maintain successful discipline as a part of a positive school learning climate. The important point is that raising the academic performance of students results in fewer disciplinary problems. The above strategies for maintaining discipline are an adjunct to creating a climate for mastery learning. Simply enforcing disciplinary codes in the absence of improving the learning climate will inevitably fail.

Classroom Management

Classroom management and classroom discipline need to be consistent with school-wide programs. Because the principles of setting and enforcing consistent limits for behavior were discussed above, under the school plan this section will address specific time-saving and instructional techniques that improve discipline and raise achievement. Much of this section on classroom management focuses on management of time. It complements *Module 7, Academic Engaged Time.*

Research on Effective Schools

Without adequate ongoing inservice for participants, school management will be reduced to a "muddling through" decision-making activity, with adverse learning consequences.

Holt, A. and P. J. Murphy. "School Effectiveness in the Future: The Environment Factor." *School Organization* 11/3 (1993): 175-86.

Time-saving Techniques

The following techniques have been shown to improve the management process, increase time-on-task, and prevent behavior problems. They are consistent with research on effective instruction that results in better achievement.

1. **Planning and Preparation.** Well-planned lessons improve the quality of instruction and reduce boredom and restlessness. Advance preparation of materials avoids delays for duplicating and assembling. Teach by design — not by improvisation.

2.   **Fluency of Transitions.** Much time is wasted switching from one subject or class to another. Teachers who can move a class easily from one topic to another, or students from one class to another increase time-on-task and reduce behavior problems.

3.   **Monitors.** Student helpers can ease the burden of trivial paper work, distribution of materials and errand running. Student monitors save the teacher time during transitions and learn personal responsibility. Being a monitor is a reward to many students.

4.   **Routines.** Early in the year students should learn acceptable ways of dealing with daily routines, such as orderly entering and leaving class, getting ready for instruction, moving into groups or teams, and sharpening pencils.

5.   **Traffic Patterns.** Classrooms should be arranged to permit easy movement in and out of class and to areas for activities. Arrangement of furniture and desks so the teacher has quick access to every student is essential.

6.   **Enrichment Activities.** Audio-visual materials, instructional games, and learning centers should be available for students who finish their work ahead of the rest of the class. Instructions on how to use such materials independently and quietly must be provided.

7.   **Attendance Taking.** Much time can be wasted during necessary administrative details. Classes should have standing instructions to be working on some form of independent material or project as soon as they enter the class, so instruction can proceed as attendance is taken. For secondary teachers, this time saver can occur from 4-6 times a day.

8.   **"Tired" Time.** The period of time just prior to lunch or dismissal is often wasted because students and teachers are hungry and tired. These are excellent times for academic games, stories, silent reading, or group-response activities.

Instructional Techniques

Studies have shown that certain techniques used during instruction may improve time-on-task and prevent disciplinary problems. Perhaps the biggest difference between effective and ineffective classroom managers is their skill in using the following preventive techniques:

1. **"With-itness."** The "with-it" teacher is aware of all class activities even during individual and small group instruction, and intervenes to prevent misbehavior from escalating to disruption. With-itness includes clear vision of the entire classroom and frequent scanning of the class.

2. **"Overlapping."** The skilled teacher has the ability to do more than one thing at a time, such as conducting a study group and helping a single student.

3. **Group Focus.** Establishing a single purpose for student activity, then not allowing other activities to compete for student attention, is an important teacher task.

4. **Maintaining Smoothness and Momentum.** The teacher's careful attention to transitions, maintaining continuity of thought, and avoiding jerkiness of sudden stops and starts, helps instruction proceed in a deliberate, orderly fashion.

Jones (1979) described two common classroom activities that waste time:

1. **Seatwork.** The rate of time-off-task is two or three times as great during seatwork as during whole-group instruction. Seatwork must be challenging, varied, and easy enough to permit independent work. It must be perceived as important by students rather than as a filler of idle time.

2. **Helping Contacts.** Helping contacts average 4 minutes per student. At this rate, in a 30-minute session only 7 students are helped. Students who work independently are ignored, while students who depend on assistance from the teacher are rewarded with attention. Jones suggest improving helping contacts by reducing them to 20-30 seconds. During that time the student is

rewarded for completed work and is given cues for the next step. Thus the number of contacts can be increased and students are rewarded for independent work. This technique has shown success with slow and learning-disabled students.

Cooperative learning techniques can be especially helpful in promoting more effective seatwork and in fostering helpful contacts. Cooperative learning results in a higher rate of time on task for a larger percentage of students.

These are sample classroom management techniques. Many others exist in the literature and in the repertoires of skilled teachers. Classroom management is a learned skill. Self-evaluation, peer and principal observation, staff discussion, and time-use analysis are all means of discovering and correcting weaknesses in efficient use of time. All effective teachers are good managers of instruction. No teacher, even the most popular and talented, is immune from the need for management skills.

Suggested Activities

1. Establish a school-wide plan for discipline that is consistent with and supportive of individual classroom plans. This is an operational plan that provides a systematic, orderly, and effective method of reacting to acts of student misconduct.

    Suggestion:

    a. Review guidelines in *Module 1*.

    b. Read *Assertive Discipline* and *Competency-based Resource Materials and Guidelines* by Lee Canter.

    c. Use other media identified in the Resource section of this module for additional ideas that can be built into the school or classroom discipline plan.

2. Make the school-wide plan for discipline available to teachers, students and parents. This plan should be included in the school handbook for teachers and also in handbooks for students and parents.

3. Copies of the school discipline plan should be sent home, with provisions for parents to sign and return to the principal a slip indicating they have received and read the plan. Expect all students to return a signed parent slip. Follow-up meetings with parents should be scheduled to discuss the plan and promote support.

4. The principal should explain the school discipline plan to students: what it is, how it will operate, and how the staff will follow through on the plan. Conducting grade level assemblies for this purpose is suggested.

5. Check up on yourself periodically by evaluating your disciplinary techniques.

6. Discussion of discipline problems should be a regular feature of whole staff meetings or grade/department meetings. Individual students should not be identified; rather, emphasis should be placed on a specific behavior and how to remedy it. Sharing and making suggestions are encouraged.

Classroom Management

1. Review the factors for improving the use of teacher and student time identified in this module.

2. Thoughtful advance planning for operating your classroom and delivering instruction will eliminate many problems for maintaining an orderly, productive classroom. At least, two kinds of plans should be made:

   a. **General Operational Plan,** establishing the routine daily operation of your classroom, including starting and ending times, procedures and time for taking role, grouping schemes, sequences or flow of activities and subjects. Describe any special procedures you expect to be followed. This plan should be placed in the front of your lesson plan book (for substitutes) and posted in the classroom for students to read.

b. **Specific Instructional Plan.** Indicate how you will spend time and deliver instruction. Merely recording times and page numbers from text books is not sufficient. This does not give adequate information about what you intend to do during a time period, what you expect students to do, and how you expect instruction to proceed (e.g., grouping, activities, units, content development). The instructional plan should serve as a record of how you intend instruction to proceed, which can be reviewed for future planning and shared with other teachers. Daily instructional plans should evolve from a longer range plan for instruction (e.g., semester, month, week) that attends to concerns of subject scope and sequence, as well as time/task requirements.

3. Use audio and visual recordings to extend your understanding of classroom management concerns. These can be effective discussion starters for grade level or departmental meetings. The use of audio/videotape by a teacher to record classroom events is recommended as a means of getting a true picture of what is happening.

4. Cooperative observation of classroom instruction by other staff members is also encouraged. This should be followed up with adequate discussion between the teacher and observer to identify strengths and weaknesses. Peer evaluation should be a part of instructional assessment for *all* teachers, regardless of how long they have been teaching.

5. As with discipline problems, discuss and seek solutions to problems of classroom or building management in staff meetings or in the smaller grade/department meetings.

Selected Bibliography

📖 Boyd, V. "Creating a Context for Change." *Issues* 2/2 (Spring 1992): 1-92.

📖 Canter, L., with M. Canter. Assertive discipline: A take charge approach for today's educator. Los Angeles: Canter and Associates, Inc., 1976.

📖 Cantrell, R. P. and M. L. Cantrell. "Countering Gang Violence in American Schools." *Principal* 72/3 (November 1993): 6-9.

📖 Cotton, K. *Effective Schooling Practices: A Research Synthesis 1995 Update.* Portland, OR: Northwest Regional Educational Laboratory, 1995.

📖 Davis, A. D. et al. "Language Skills of Delinquent and Nondelinquent Adolescent Males." *Journal of Communication Disorders* 24/4 (August 1991): 251-66.

📖 *Family Strengthening in Preventing Delinquency — A Literature Review.* Rockville, MD: Juvenile Justice Clearing House, 1994.

📖 Fergison, E. and S. Houghton. "The Effects of Contingent Teacher Praise, as Specified by Canter's Assertive Discipline Programme, on Children's On-task Behavior." *Educational Studies* 18/1 (1992): 83-93.

📖 Good, T. L. and J. E. Brophy. "School Effects." In *Handbook of Research on Teaching,* 3rd edition, edited by M. C. Wittrock. New York, NY: Macmillan, 1986.

📖 Good, T. and J. Brophy. *Looking in Classrooms,* 6th ed. New York: Harper Collins, 1994.

📖 Gottfredson, D. C., Gottfredson, G. P. and L. G. Hybl. "Managing Adolescent Behavior." *American Educational Research Journal* 30/1 (Spring 1993): 179-215.

📖 Gottfredson, G. D. and D. C. Gottfredson. *School Climate, Academic Performance Attendance and Dropout.* College Park, MD: Johns Hopkins University, Center for Social Organization of Schools, 1989.

Holt, A. and P. J. Murphy. "School Effectiveness in the Future: The Environment Factor." *School Organization* 11/3 (1993): 175-86.

Jones, F. H. "The Gentle Art of Classroom Discipline." *The National Elementary Principal* 58/1 (Winter 1979): 26-32.

Kamelnui, E. and C. B. Darch. *Instructional Classroom Management: A Proactive Approach to Behavior Management.* White Plains, NY: Longman, 1995.

Levine, D. U. and L. W. Lezotte. *Unusually Effective Schools: A Review and Analysis of Research and Practice.* Madison, WI: National Center for Effective Schools, 1990.

Moles, O. C. (ed.). *Strategies to Reduce Student Misbehavior.* Washington, DC: U.S. Department of Education, Office of Educational Research and Development, 1989.

Randolph, N. and E. Erickson. *Gangs, My Town and the Nation.* Holmes Beach, FL: Learning Publications, Inc., 1996.

Sammons, P. et al. *Key Characteristics of Effective Schools: A Review of School Effectiveness Research.* London (UK): University of London, International School Effectiveness Centre, 1994.

Wilson-Brewer, R. et al. *Violence Prevention for Young Adolescents: A Survey of the State of the Art.* Cambridge, MA: Education Development Center, 1991.

Module 9
Cooperative Mastery Learning

- Harnessing Classroom Power
- Key Concepts and Considerations
- Cooperative Learning Models
- Research on Cooperative Learning
- The Process of Cooperative Learning
- Team Learning Games

Harnessing Classroom Power

Educators committed to the belief that all children can learn make a deliberate choice to untrack their schools. This decision is based on compelling reasons. Above all, effective educators can and will improve all of their students' academic performance. These educators actively enhance student attitudes about themselves. They work to make a positive influence regardless of race, past achievement, minority status, gender or socioeconomic background. Effective educators work to untrack their schools including out of classroom behavior. Clearly, untracking has potential in all areas of schooling (George, 1992; Oakes, 1985; Wheelock, 1992).

On both a classroom and a school wide-basis, an institutional commitment to untracking is fundamental. It is also fundamental for effective educators to employ techniques that harness the power of students in a classroom. The research evidence is clear — cooperative mastery learning is successful at involving students in the instructional process in heterogeneous groups by mobilizing powers inherent in the peer group. Fortunately, in the last several years, numerous cooperative learning materials have been developed for the classroom teacher of every subject area and every grade level — all of which stress the importance of harnessing peer power (Harbison, P. et al., 1995).

Educating for Excellence

Educators often talk about peer power but all too often fail to harness this power effectively. This module presents a rationale for tapping a strong resource in any classroom — the students. The power of students lies in their ability to reinforce the attitudes, actions, and behaviors of other students. The student culture in general, and cooperative mastery learning groups in particular, are powerful forces in shaping the social and academic behavior of individual students. This in turn enhances the academic achievement climate of the entire school.

For most of us it is important to be an accepted member of a group. All of us are sensitive to rejection or disapproval by our peers or fellow group members. Correspondingly, all of us are receptive to praise, being liked, and other signs of approval by our peers. This is, in fact, how groups "keep their members in line." If group members act or even talk in a way contrary to the group's values or norms, they are likely to receive negative sanctions. By the same token, if group members subscribe to and act upon shared values and norms, they are likely to be popular, well-liked, praised, and rewarded. Using these techniques of social control, groups tend to persist, show consistent patterns of behavior and attitudes, and very powerfully "shape" members' actions.

Research on Effective Schools

Increases in the number of classroom friendships is positively associated with increasing achievement.

Vandell, D. L. et al. "Peer Social Status and Friendship."
Merrill-Palmer Quarterly 40/4 (October 1994): 461-77.

In any classroom, students form friendship groups, common-interest groups, boy groups, girl groups, and sometimes racial or ethnic groups. These groups pursue various goals and hold shared values. One group may be interested in trading bubble gum cards, another may be interested in sports, another in theater, and still others may exist as gangs. In very few such cases are students organized around academic values or the reinforcement of learning. The task, then, is to find ways that student groups traditionally formed for non-academic purposes may be used to reinforce academic learning and appropriate social skills.

Cooperative Learning Models

There are several models of cooperative learning, but they all share certain goals and methods. For example, they have small groups of students (usually heterogeneously grouped) that function as teams to help one another to learn some academic skill and knowledge. Robert Stahl (1994) summarized the other shared attributes of the various types of cooperative learning including:

- a clear set of specific student learning outcome objectives,
- the students accept the targeted outcome;
- an equal opportunity for success;
- positive interdependence;
- face to face interaction;
- positive social interaction;
- access to the information to be learned, opportunity to complete required task;
- sufficient time spent learning;
- individual accountability;
- public reinforcement for academic success; and
- post-group reflection.

Cooperative mastery learning functions to reduce individual failure while reinforcing group norms of academic success. These group norms, in turn, tend to be internalized by individuals. Usually, cooperative learning is designed to supplement a teacher's instruction, but also may require that students find or discover information on their own (Slavin, 1991).

According to Slavin (1991), among the four most commonly studied cooperative learning models are:

- Student Team Learning (STL),
- Jigsaw,
- Learning Together, and
- Group Investigation.

The *STL* models stress team awards, individual accountability, and equal opportunities for success. "The teams are not in competition to earn scarce awards; all (or none) of the teams may achieve the criterion in a given week, individual accountability means that the team's success depends on the individual learning of all team members. This focuses the activity of team members on explaining concepts to one another and making sure that everyone on the team is ready for a quiz or other assessment without teammate help. Equal opportunities for success means that students contribute to their teams by improving over past performances. This ensures that high, average and low achievers are equally challenged and that the contributions of all team members will be valued" (Slavin, 1991).

In the *Jigsaw* model (Aronson, 1978), several teams of students are brought together to study and share what they learn from each other. The teacher begins with a general topic such as, "The Building of the Panama Canal." The teacher breaks up the topic into several sections. One team might investigate the political conflict over building the canal; another, economic and health costs; and another, the significance of the canal for people in the region and in the United States. Each team would then teach the members of the other teams. Since each student can only learn from what the students on the other teams teach, there is incentive to pay attention and learn from the others. This Jigsaw method has been elaborated by Robert Slavin and colleagues and will be discussed later in this module.

The *Group Investigation* model seems to have been incorporated into the teaching repertoires of many teachers who employ other cooperative learning methods (Sharan, 1980) . The emphasis is on the team engaging in investigations which emphasize cooperative discussion and planning, cooperative data gathering and interpretation, and cooperative reporting of findings and implications. Like the *Jigsaw* method, students are involved in selecting the topic to be studied, and then are divided into teams to address subtopics. In turn, the teams arrange for individual responsibilities and finally, each team presents their findings to the class.

The *Learning Together* model offered by David Johnson and Roger Johnson (1991) has a long and relatively popular track record in the cooperative learning movement. Recently, these authors have expanded their model to include not only how a classroom might be cooperatively structured, but how the school should be structured to facilitate the impact of cooperative learning classrooms (Johnson and Johnson, 1993). They favor the structuring of small schools within current large schools, whereby a class becomes a base learning community. They assert that 5 steps must be taken in restructuring the schools to maximize the effectiveness of cooperative learning:

- cooperative learning must dominate each student's day, being used 60 to 80 percent of class time;

- long-term cooperative base groups, composed of students and faculty, must be formed the first year that students enter a school and continue until they leave;

- positive interdependence must characterize the structure of the student's activities in small groups, classrooms and base groups;

- the students must be taught how to resolve conflicts constructively; and

- the students must function in base learning communities.

The 5th Step — the creating "base" learning communities of 90 to 120 students, with 3 to 6 teachers each, who stay with the students throughout the students' attendance in that school — is extremely important if the impact of cooperative mastery learning is to be maximized over its already successful impact. The purpose is to foster enduring relationships among students and between students and staff, and thereby reduce the sense of isolation felt by many students in large schools.

Research on Effective Schools

Students with the same teacher for 3 years have a stronger bonding to school.

Kester, V. M. "Factors that Affect African-American Students' Bonding to Middle Schools." *Elementary School Journal* 95/1 (September 1994): 63-73.

Reducing the size of the students' school (within the larger school) makes it easier to reduce alienation and estrangement from education when employing cooperative learning. It increases the number of personal relationships and also allows for greater student accountability to be a good citizen. When a community is created where everyone knows everyone else, the school experience becomes personalized and there is fostered a sense of belonging. Such a personalized learning community not only helps students, but it also reduces alienation, burn out, and turnover among teachers.

A permanent teaching team is also said to have a number of other advantages as well. Students need permanent relationships with teachers, just as they do with each other. Teachers in enduring relationships can be effective in 1) diagnosing learning needs; 2) finding ways to motivate; 3) establishing routines to prevent discipline problems and manage classrooms; and 4) resolving unique problems. The quality of help that teachers can provide increases every year they work with a student.

David Johnson and Roger Johnson are to be commended for their efforts to enhance the relevance of cooperative learning methods. While we believe that more research needs to be done on the creation of small schools within large schools, initial reports are promising. Hence, their model deserves consideration.

Whether a school chooses to restructure itself into small base learning communities or not, at the current time there is ample reason for every school in the country to untrack students, to group students heterogeneously, and to employ cooperative mastery learning models. The research is very strong on this point.

In summary, research on cooperative mastery learning provides us with evidence that this type of model is valuable for a number of reasons, all of which relate to improving the academic learning climate and overall student achievement in a school. Cooperative learning techniques, for example, have been found to be effective in increasing academic performance, mutual concern, pro-academic norms, positive attitudes towards school, self-concepts of ability and time on task. These results indicate the importance of their use for developing an effective learning climate. Although additional research needs to be done on the total effects of cooperative learning, it seems to be a valuable tool. Like all tools, it must be used correctly to produce desired results. Please see the *Added Resources* section at the end of this chapter for illustrative materials that are available.

Research on Effective Schools

A great deal of research has been conducted comparing the relative effects of cooperative, competitive, and individualistic efforts on instructional outcomes. The research began in the late 1800s. During the past 95 years over 550 experimental and 100 correlational studies have been conducted by a wide variety of researchers in different decades with different age subjects, in different subject areas, and in different settings. The evidence indicates that, compared with competitive and individualistic efforts, working together to achieve common goals produces: (a) greater effort, motivation, achievement, retention, and higher-level reasoning; (b) interpersonal attraction and social support (students care more about each other, form more friendships, provide both academic and personal support, and are more committed to each other's success and well-being); and (c) psychological health, social competencies, and self-esteem.

Publishers' footnote to Johnson, D. W. and R. T. Johnson. "Cooperative Learning: Using Gang Dynamics to Enhance Learning," *School Intervention Report* 6/3 (Spring 1993).

Cooperative Learning: The Process

Student team techniques change both the task and the reward structure of a classroom. Rewards given to students are based on the performance of the team as a whole. Slavin (1977) noted several years ago that team learning can be called a cooperative task structure, and the reward structure can be called a cooperative reward structure. Students performing well in a team help improve the functioning of their teammates by modeling and encouraging positive attitudes and correct responses. Team learning research has shown that students prefer and learn better in settings in which they teach and learn from each other (see Devin-Sheehan, Feldman & Allen, 1976).

The traditional classroom, on the other hand, uses an individual task structure (students work independently or listen to the teacher) and a competitive reward structure (grading on a curve) where students seldom help each other. Rather, the students compete for a limited supply of good grades (Slavin, 1977). In fact, with curve grading, to help or encourage another student to get better grades is to reduce one's own chance of a good grade (see also *Module 6* on *Effective Instruction*). This tends to be a "zero sum" environment where the success of some students is advanced at the failure of others. The personal attention each student receives is necessarily limited. Students compete against one another because everyone cannot get an "A."

Built into activities for learning skills should be time for practice, peer tutoring and modeling. Practice is imperative for effective instruction. If the activity, for example, is some sort of spelling bee or math fact drill, members of the team should have a considerable amount of time to spend practicing together and tutoring one another. Tutoring may consist of peer-to-peer drill, a form of modeling, or having one of the students function as a quasi-teacher for the rest of the group.

The exact nature of peer-to-peer teaching can usually be left to the group so that it develops spontaneously its own instructional dynamics. This will not hinder the internal dynamics of the group, but will give the team members more effective options from which to choose. If the learning activities are perceived by students as important, a peer reinforcement system usually will emerge. The "academic heroes" of the day will come to receive more and more praise and adulation by their peers as they lead their groups to victory in group games and tournaments. Motivation, interest, and time-on-task are enhanced, while individual failure is reduced.

The peer group will reward academic performance as well as other successes (i.e., sport performance). On the other hand, it is likely that some negative reinforcement will be aimed toward team members who bring down team scores and fail to do well on the team competition learning tasks. This should not be construed in a negative manner by the teacher. Such peer-to-peer reinforcers are likely to "motivate" the team members to work harder and to increase their performances. The team mediated positive and negative reinforcements should be allowed to flourish, as long as they are within the bounds of good sportsmanship.

Team learning sessions should become part of the regular classroom routine. These are not activities which are done once in a while "to give the kids something fun to do." Team learning is an instructional technique which maximizes peer encouragement, positive social relations among students, time actively spent in learning, self-concept, and academic performance. Growth will occur when team activities become part of the classroom operation, and are tied closely to the main course objectives.

Team Rewards

Most of the cooperative learning games described below rely on team competition. In order for group learning games to work, teachers must create symbolic or tangible team rewards that will be attractive to the student peer culture.

The Importance of Team Rewards. Most students are in touch with the symbolism, language system, and reward structure of competitive team sports. When organizing a class for team games, begin with a gender neutral sports analogy and then modify it as necessary to ensure that the goal of achievement by all students is advanced. Team names, standings, and percentages form a part of the analogy. Reward systems similar to those used in team sports have been used. Teachers may obtain inexpensive trophies that can be passed from one winning team to another at various stages in competition. Pennants or flags are indicators of group success. A newsletter highlighting team standings is attractive to the students and their parents.

Teachers and principals may also use tangible rewards. The parent-teacher organization may raise money for group prizes such as movie tickets, sporting events tickets, or coupons for hamburgers and milk shakes at a local fast-food restaurant. Second and third place groups, or teams showing improvement, ought to receive lesser rewards occasionally to recognize their efforts. The composition of your learning teams should occasionally rotate so that no team continually dominates.

Symbolic and tangible rewards for distribution in classrooms should be kept readily available. Pennants, trophies, coupons, jacket patches, team photographs, posters and recognition assemblies are rewards that the school staff can employ at little cost. Students also may be asked to indicate their preference for various rewards. Frequent favorites are "free time" or a weekend without homework.

Time and Team Learning

In many classrooms, a teacher instructing the whole class may be interacting with only one or a few students at a time, while the other students are expected to listen or follow along. To the extent that other class members attend to the lesson or pay attention to the teacher-student interaction, learning is active and productive. However, unless students are motivated to pay attention when not being called on by the teacher, engaged time drops and learning decreases. The reality is that many students simply "tune out" when the teacher is not interacting with them directly.

Well-structured team learning offers two distinct advantages to the problem of time-on-task. The first is that teams practicing for competition are likely to spend all their available time working hard to learn the material. The level of engaged time is high. The second is that during practice sessions, the teacher has the opportunity to work closely with individuals, small groups or particular teams without the rest of the class engaging in off-task or disruptive behavior. In effect, the team structure absorbs some of the instructional, reinforcement, management and discipline functions of the teacher, giving him or her time to work at a higher level of teaching skill in providing corrective or enrichment instruction.

Team Games. Effective team games include several essential features. There are many commercial pre-programmed learning games for both reading and math, but certain of their characteristics differ from the ones suggested below. For example, some commercial games suggest homogeneous teams to ensure "fair" competition, or allow only the most skilled members to compete. This is contrary to research on effective grouping (see *Module 5* for explanation). Consistent with the goal of high achievement for all students, the point of team learning is not to "select out" the best, but to make each student a participant and a winner.

The important features to remember in selecting and developing team games are:

- Teams are not necessarily used for initial instruction but for supplementing instruction presented by the teacher. The teams practice on common grade level objectives. Students are not expected to learn on their own in teams but to practice, drill, study, and apply; also to encourage, correct, tutor and help each other on learning objectives and materials provided by the teacher.

- Teams should be heterogeneous in terms of skills and knowledge. Selection of team members should not function to reinforce existing friendship cliques. The teacher may divide the class into teams in any number of ways, balancing academic strengths and weaknesses, race and sex, and breaking up undesirable behavior combinations. The teacher makes the team selections rather than permitting students to choose their teammates. (The latter method might be quite appealing in terms of the team sports analogy that it represents, but it can damage the self-esteem of those chosen last, or restrict participation to a select group of "buddies.") In competition of team against team or room against room at the same grade level, the competing groups ought to be heterogeneous and matched against roughly equivalent competing teams. In other words, teams should have a fairly equal chance to win so that it is their own effort that makes the difference.

- Teams should be together for a period or time, at least six weeks, which allows members to come to know and trust each other and work well together. If the teacher has made careful selections, he or she should simply ignore initial protests on team assignments and move ahead. If teams are formed and reformed too frequently or have frequent "substitutes," team spirit does not build. Experience in districts with poor attendance suggests the wisdom of increasing slightly the size of the teams (6 instead of 5, 5 instead of 4) so that teams can function without missing members. At the same time, because tardiness or absence would put the team at some competitive disadvantage, the errant member will receive group pressure to attend. Bonus points may be awarded to teams with perfect attendance.

- Prior to every competition, time should to be devoted to practice. The full strength of the peer culture will be mobilized only if students have an opportunity to teach one another and exert group pressure upon team members in ways that cannot be used in the context of the game itself. The teams should have regular structured practice time to drill, using the same kinds of information, spelling lists, number facts, or learning objectives that will be used in the contest.

- It is in team practice sessions that peer instruction and encouragement influence learning. The actual contest or competition provides the incentive for students to improve skill performance, but it is the practice in teams that makes the greatest contribution to improved achievement. Practice and drill on academic subjects are necessary but can be less than exciting. Just as in sports, the academic contests with their intrinsic and extrinsic rewards provide the motivation for students to practice and improve.

- Rules should be developed to ensure orderly and fair competition. Cooperative behavior is not learned immediately in sports or in academics; it is acquired gradually. As in teaching classroom behavior, this instruction takes place every day until the appropriate behavior becomes routine. Observe how the teams operate as you circulate around the room, and sit in occasionally as they practice. The teacher should reinforce all examples of cooperative or helping behavior and bring them to the attention of the class. For example, during the first few contests, points can be awarded or taken away from teams on the basis of sportsmanship and conduct; or a special trophy may be awarded for exemplary team behavior.

- In any of the learning games, extensive use should be made of both symbolic and tangible rewards to the teams. The teams ought to feel that performance is important and instrumental to learning (i.e., mastery of grade level basic skills). The use of external rewards such as pennants or trophies, however, is a supplement to the intrinsic reward of peer encouragement.

- Contests can be oral or written. They may contain questions for individual team members or for the entire team, either as a deliberative body or in sequence for multiple operations or parts of a problem. Teachers should balance several factors in determining the type of contest or question format. For example, younger students have shorter attention spans while older students can be "contested" over more objectives. Short, right answers, as in spelling or number facts, call for a different setting than complex problem-solving. An oral contest may generate more excitement and motivation while a written contest may increase time-on-task by requiring all students to participate in providing answers. Alternatively, the "challenge" process may be used in oral contests to induce all students to work each problem, or answer each question, in order to win game points.

- All students should have frequent successes in practice and in competition, both as individuals and as teams, if maximum learning is to result. Some points to keep in mind:

  - Encourage all team members to contribute to the learning of the team. If the teacher acts on the assumption that only the most advanced students can help others, much of the potential of team learning is lost. For example, a common error is to appoint permanent "captains" who are the most advanced students on their teams and to give them great leeway for making decisions, assigning tasks and so on. This tends to lessen the sense of responsibility of the other team members and may even arouse their resentment if the captain usually insists on being "teacher." Jobs such as captain, scorekeeper, answer checker, drillmaster or resource gatherer, while necessary, should be rotated among team members. Slower students often surprise the class with their ability and willingness to help others if the structure and operation of the teams gives them, as well as the faster students, the opportunity.

  - If there are students who consistently fail to answer questions correctly, vary the difficulty of the questions. In some contests, students could choose the kind of question to answer. For example, the difficulty of questions might vary according to getting a single (easiest question) to scoring a home run (hardest question) where the risk of "striking out" is greater. Students may select a level of risk and still add points to the team total.

  - If you have a team that remains in last place for two weeks, with no sign of improvement, it is probably time to reshuffle the teams to give them an even chance at winning. Alternatively, the team might be given advice and help on how to proceed in mastering the material on which they will compete. It is usually possible to spot the problems of a losing team by closely observing their practice sessions.

Team Learning Games

The "Bee" Game

The "bee" is a classic game that has been used for generations at all skill levels and with all ages. The past focus has been on individual competition, such as "spelling bee," where each student competes on his or her own. We suggest that this be modified to a team format. Academic contests are easily arranged for short-answer learning drills such as spelling, number facts in addition and subtraction, multiplication and division. The stimulus materials may take the form of spelling lists or flash cards to be used during practice sessions.

During the competition, the teacher presents questions to team members, who have a limited time to respond. A right answer will give the team a point and a wrong answer will give them a zero. Each team should present a "batting order" to the teacher at the beginning of the game. A variation is to give the next team an opportunity to answer a question missed by the previous team. Such a "corrective" response may be given two points in scoring. To facilitate the game, a student should keep point scores and make sure that the questions are being directed to individuals in the pre-determined order.

The bee may be used with spelling and number facts. It is a fast verbal drill and is likely to be accompanied by a great deal of spontaneous interaction, cheering and group excitement. For older students, however, written tests can be employed and the same kind of scoring used. One school had students spell the word or solve the problem on a transparency and then display the answer on an overhead projector. This allowed contestants to write their answers, which many found more comfortable than verbalizing them. The transparency allows the audience, and the scorekeepers, to see the answers more clearly than a chalkboard does, and is easily erased after each contestant is finished.

Team Games Tournament (TGT)
(Source: The Johns Hopkins Team Learning Project)

Note: We recommend that schools considering *Team-Games-Tournaments (TET)* contact The Johns Hopkins Project for its manual and directions, as well as grade-appropriate learning objectives in reading and math. These are complete with practice and game questions, answer sheets, scoring sheets and so on. The following brief description introduces the reader to this technique.

In *TGT* one member from each of several standing teams goes into a new group for the tournament and competes there for points to take back to his or her team. Each of the standing teams should have practice time in which to study the same stimulus materials and prepare all team members for the competition.

The game uses a set of question cards that are in the middle of the table. A student picks a question card from the shuffled pile, reads the question aloud, then arrives at and announces an answer. The rest of the people at the table, in turn, may challenge the answer and refer to a common set of answer sheets (or the teacher) to check for correctness. The correct answer or correct challenge earns one game point. The student with the right answer keeps the question cards as a tally. The game proceeds for a specified length of time or until all the question cards have been used up. At the end of the game individual standings at a given table are computed on the basis of total game points. These places, in turn, earn team points for an individual's team. For example, with four players, the winner at a table will get eight points for first place, the second place person will get six points, the third place person will get four points, and the lowest scoring member gets two points. These team points will be summed from all tables in the class and then applied to team standings. Note that every player takes adjusted points back to his or her team. Quizzes occasionally may be substituted for the game with team points determined as indicated.

Rutabaga
(Source: The Johns Hopkins Team Learning Project)

Rutabaga is a form of *TGT* that is used for building oral reading skills at any grade level. In practice sessions, team members read aloud to each other. On game day, students are assigned to 3-6 member tournament tables as in *TGT* and compete for points to take back to their own teams. Students take turns reading aloud to the other players who have the same reading material in front of them. The reader substitutes the word "rutabaga" for words of his or her choice. The first player to fill in the missing word gains a point. A wrong guess loses a point.

Jigsaw II
(Source: The Johns Hopkins Team Learning Project)

Jigsaw II can accommodate complex learning tasks. Each team member is designated "expert" for his or her team on one part of the material to be learned, although all team members read the material. The "expert" studies the assigned section and meets with the experts from all the other teams who have responsibility for the same material. The experts discuss the material in detail and make sure they have mastered it well, because their job is to go back and teach it to their own teams to prepare them for competition.

Twenty Questions

This is a team game version of the well-known game. It is particularly appropriate for complex reasoning tasks.

The teacher identifies a person, place, or thing which teams are to identify through a series of questions that receive yes-no answers from the teacher. Each team will identify an interrogator to ask the questions of the teacher. The teams rotate their questions and may ask only one question at a time. For every question that is answered "yes" the team receives points; for every answer that is answered "no" the team loses points.

Between-Classroom Formats

Most team learning games will occur within a single classroom. Occasionally teachers may wish to challenge another classroom or even have a grade level contest. Although other formats can be devised, two that we have used successfully are described briefly below.

a. *Winning Teams Compete:* A week before the grade level contest, each room has its own contest. The team that wins the room contest then competes for the grade championship. If the contest is held in the gym or auditorium, all other students in the rooms can be spectators, cheering their own teams on to victory. The cheering by spectators often reaches great intensity. Under these conditions, practice and learning are facilitated by a team's strong incentive to be the room representative, then the grade champion. Cheering of classmates can also be a strong factor in promoting a sense of room spirit and pride. *Caution:* the pressure to win is great enough that some rooms may be tempted to send as their "representative team" the 5 or 6 fastest students in the class. This defeats the entire dynamics of team learning as described in this module. Teachers must police themselves against such an eventuality.

b. *All Teams Compete:* In this format, all of the teams from each room compete. This intramural style has the advantage that all students compete in the grade level contest as well as in the room contests. A seventh grade at one school illustrates this format.

Each of 5 classrooms had 5 heterogeneous teams of 5-6 members. The week before the grade contest, each classroom had its own contest to determine within-class ranking. On the day of the grade contest, the #1 ranked team from each classroom went to one room. Likewise, each of the #2 ranked teams gathered in another room, and so also for #3, 4 and 5 ranked teams. Prior to the contest, the teachers prepared questions covering the agreed-upon learning objectives. The 5 teams in each room, representing 5 different classrooms, competed for points under the direction of one of the teachers. The teams were awarded points based on order of finish (e.g., 10, 8, 6, 4 or 2 points). Team points were added up for each of the classes, and the top scoring room became the grade grand champion.

The all-team competition system eliminates spectators and makes every student a participant. We feel that both of these methods facilitate common planning of grade level objectives by teachers at any one grade level. Teachers work together to establish standards of behavior, contest rules, award assemblies, and so on. One teacher commented that the sharing of ideas and instructional techniques that resulted from such a contest was the most positive experience of his teaching career.

Research on Effective Schools

"The use of cooperative learning as a means to improving intercultural relationships is supported by more well-designed research than any other single schooling practice. Organizing learners into culturally heterogeneous teams, giving them tasks requiring group cooperation and interdependence, and structuring the activity so that the teams can experience success, comprise an extremely powerful means of enhancing intergroup relations."

"Fostering Intercultural Harmony in Schools: Research Findings," *Topical Synthesis #7, School Improvement Research Series*. Northwest Regional Educational Laboratory, 1994.

Summary

In this module we have presented methods of student cooperative learning which increase basic skill achievement and improve the school learning climate. These strategies, like those suggested in other modules, need structure, collaboration, and joint decision-making consistent with emphasis on student achievement. Cooperative learning furnishes practice opportunity in the mastery learning strategy and should not be seen as separate from other instruction. It is a motivating technique which keeps students on task. It is an efficient means for practice and reinstruction on skills which have been introduced by the teacher to the whole class. In team learning students get immediate attention from their group members and are kept interacting with the learning material.

The cooperative learning approach can improve the effectiveness of a class or school program significantly and reduce the amount of time it takes for some students to master grade level skills. This approach has the added advantage of reducing the negative consequences to self-esteem and motivation associated with individual failure. Cooperative learning should become part of the school social system, used by all teachers. If only a few teachers employ this method, the effect on the total school will be reduced.

The motivational power of the peer group and a cooperative learning model tends to "turn on" students who might not ordinarily be excited about academics. This makes cooperative learning an important method by which teachers can structure learning so that changes in student attitudes and academic motivation are likely to occur. It is also a potent tool for reducing behavioral problems within the classroom.

Suggested Activities

1. Read *Using Student Team Learning*, 3rd ed., by Robert E. Slavin (1986) for information and ideas on using team learning successfully. Teams-Games-Tournaments (TGT), Jigsaw I and II, and Rutabaga are explained.

2. Grade level teachers should develop an approach to team learning games with which they feel comfortable and can support. Come to agreement on:

   a. areas or subjects for competition;

   b. composition;

   c. schedule of interclass competition;

   d. rules for competing;

   e. sportsmanship requirements;

   f. format of competitions;

   g. rewards.

3. Discuss with students the concept of team learning, team competition, and sportsmanship. Developing an appreciation for being a team player and a good sport are critical to the success of using team learning. Being a good winner and good loser are attitudes that must be taught and modeled by the teacher. Slighting this important topic can easily destroy your team learning program. (See Suggested Sportsmanship Rules.)

4. Regarding the formation of teams:

    a. each team should reflect the range of performance, and the ethnic and sex mix of the class;

    b. equalize teams for performance;

    c. teachers place students on teams rather than having students pick teammates;

    d. team decides on name.

5. Schedule team practice at least once a week — more often if possible. Practice is where the greatest potential for team learning payoffs is found. Do not neglect this vital element.

6. Team competition should be held regularly within a classroom. Treat this like regular competition, with standings and appropriate rewards.

7. In setting up an interclass contests:

    a. teachers decide the content to be used and supply all teams with the same information to study;

    b. establish the date of the contest in advance so teams can have sufficient practice beforehand;

    c. specific rules should be decided and discussed with students;

    d. the object of the competition is to identify the winning class in the grade level that is involved.

8. Team learning games can follow a variety of formats: verbal, paper and pencil, and simulation. Alter the game format occasionally to maintain student interest.

Suggested Sportsmanship Rules for Team Learning Games

Note: These rules were compiled by one school's 6th grade students. Rules were then enforced during the contests by the teachers.

1. Come into room in an orderly way.

2. Stay in seats.

3. Avoid distracting players while they are thinking and taking tests.

4. Avoid laughing at wrong answers.

5. Avoid arguing over answers, points, and accusing people of cheating.

6. Have a good attitude toward others such as: tell others they have played well, avoid bragging, and try to have fun even if you lose.

7. Do not tease others when they lose.

8. Follow directions.

9. Congratulate the winning team.

10. Be respectful when others are talking.

11. Do not make fun of your own teammates when they fail to get any points for the team.

12. If any of these rules are broken, 5 points will be taken off the teams' score for each rule broken.

Suggestions to Teachers for Interclass Contests

1. Agree on all rules prior to practice sessions and the contest.

2. When reading results to students, be positive in announcing positions and giving standings of teams.

3. Have answer sheets available ahead of time to facilitate scoring.

4. Have extra ditto copies of materials on hand to prevent problems due to faintness of copy.

5. Penalize points for inappropriate talking. Decide on consistent enforcement among teachers before the contest.

Resources

Dishon, D. and P. Wilson O'Leary. *Cooperative Learning: A Technique for Creating More Effective Schools,* 2nd ed. Holmes Beach, FL: Learning Publications, Inc., 1994.

Fogarty, R. and Bellanca, J. *Patterns for Thinking, Patterns for Transfer: A Cooperative Team Approach for Critical and Creative Thinking in the Classroom.* Palatine, IL: IRI/Skylight Publishing, 1993.

Johnson, D. W.; Johnson, R. T.; Slavin, R.; and B. T. Vasquez, program consultants. *Cooperative Learning Series.* Videotapes, Alexandria, VA: Association for Supervision and Curriculum Development, 1990.

The Johns Hopkins Student Team Learning Project. Baltimore: Center for Social Organization of Schools, The Johns Hopkins University.

The International Association for the Study of Cooperation in Education (IASCE)
P.O. Box 1582
Santa Cruz, CA 95061-1582 USA
Phone: 408-426-7926; Fax: 408-426-3360

The Cooperative Learning Network
Sponsored by the Association for

Supervision and Curriculum Development (ASCD)
Administrative Center
2000 N.E. E. 46th Street
Kansas City, MO 664116
Phone: 816-453-5050

Animal Town Game Company
P.O. Box 485
Healdsburg, CA 95448

Family Pastimes
RR #4
Perth, Ontario, CANADA K7H 3C6

Selected Bibliography

(Materials marked with an * would be particularly valuable for inservice workshops.)

📖 Albert, L. *A Teacher's Guide to Cooperative Discipline.* Circle Pines, MN: American Guidance Service, 1989.

📖 Aronson, E. et al. *The Jigsaw Classroom.* Beverly Hills, CA: Sage, 1978.

📖 Artzt, A. F. and C. M. Newman. *How to Use Cooperative Learning in the Mathematics Class.* Reston, VA: National Council of Teachers of Mathematics, 1990.

📖 Bellenca, J. and E. Swartz (eds.). *The Challenge of Detracking: A Collection.* Palantine, IL: IRI Skylight Publishing Inc., 1993.

📖 Bellenca, J. and R. Fogarty. *Designing Professional Development for Change: A Systematic Approach.* Palantine, IL: IRI Skylight Publishing Inc., 1995.

📖 Bernard, B. *The Case for Peers.* Washington, DC: Department of Education, 1990.

📖 Bigelow, B. "Getting Off the Track." *Rethinking Schools* 7/4 (1993): 1, 18-20.

Cartledge, G. and J. F. Milburn (eds.). *Teaching Social Skills to Children and Youth: Innovative Approaches,* 3rd Ed. Needham, MA: Allynwood and Bacon, 1994.

Cohen, G. *Designing Groupwork: Strategies for the Heterogen Classroom.* New York: Teachers College Press, 1994.

Clarke, J. *Together We Learn.* Scarborough, Ontario: Prentice-Hall Canada Inc., 1990.

Costa, A. *The School as a Home for the Mind.* Palatine, IL: Skylight Publishing, 1991.

Davidson, N. (ed.). *Cooperative Learning in Mathematics: A Handbook for Teachers.* Menlo Park, CA: Addision-Wesley, 1990.

Davidson, N. *Cooperative Learning in Mathematics: A Handbook for Teachers.* New York: Teachers College Press, 1992.

Davidson, N. and T. Worsham. Enhancing *Thinking Through Cooperative Learning.* New York, NY: Teachers College Press, Columbia University, 1992.

Deutsch, M. "A Theory of Cooperation and Competition." *Human Relations* 2/2 (1949): 129-52.

Devin-Sheehan, L., R. Feldman and V. Allen. "Research and Children Tutoring Children: A Critical Review." *Review of Educational Research* 46/3 (Summer 1976): 333-385.

Dishon, D. & P. Wilson O'Leary. *Cooperation Unlimited INK,* newsletter for teachers and administrators. P.O. Box 68, Portage, MI 49002, (616) 327-2199, 1986 to present.*

Duren, P. E. and A. Cherrington. "The Effects of Cooperative Group Work Versus Independent Practice on the Learning of Some Problem-Solving Strategies." *School Science and Mathematics* 92/2 (1992): 80-83.

Faber, A. and E. Mazlish. *How to Talk So Kids Will Listen & Listen So Kids Will Talk.* New York, NY: Rawson, Wade Publishers, 1980.

Feldman, D. "Toward a Non-elitist Conception of Giftedness." *Phi Delta Kappan,* 60/9 (1979): 660-63.

📖 Fogarty, R. *Designs for Cooperative Learning Together.* Santa Rosa, CA: Center-Source Publications, 1994.

📖 "Fostering Intercultural Harmony in Schools: Research Findings." *Topical Synthesis #7, School Improvement Series.* Portland, OR: Northwest Regional Educational Laboratory, 1994.

📖 Gamoran, A. and M. Berends. "The Effects of Stratification in Secondary Schools: Synthesis of Survey and Ethnographic Research." *Review of Educational Research* 57/4 (1987): 415-35.

📖 George, P. S. and K. Rubin. *Tracking and Ability Grouping in Florida: A Status Study.* Sanibel: Florida Education Research Council, 1992.

📖 Good, T. and J. Brophy. *Looking in Classrooms,* 6th ed. New York: HarperCollins, 1994.

📖 Goodenow, C. and K. E. Grady. "The Relationship of School Belonging and Friends' Values to Academic Motivation Among Urban Adolescent Students." *Journal of Experimental Education* 62/1 (Fall 1993): 60-71.

📖 Graves, L. and T. Graves, editors. *Cooperative Learning: The Magazine for Cooperation in Education.* P.O. Box 1582, Santa Cruz, CA 95061-1582.*

📖 Harbison, P. et al. "Incorporating Cooperation: Its Effects on Instruction" in *Beyond Tracking* edited by P. Harbison and J. A. Pool. Bloomington, IN: Phi Delta Kappa Educational Foundation, 1995.

📖 Hart, T. E. and L. Lumsden. "Confronting Racism in Schools." *OSSC Bulletin* 32/9 (May 1989).

📖 Hilke, E. V. *Cooperative Learning.* Fastback 299. Bloomington, IN: Phi Delta Kappa Educational Foundation, 1990.

📖 Hoffer, T. B. "The Effects of Ability Grouping in Middle School Science and Mathematics on Students' Achievement." Paper presented at the annual meeting of the American Educational Research Association, Chicago, April 1991.

Johnson, D. W. and R. T. Johnson. *Learning Together and Alone: Cooperation, Competition and Individualization.* Needham Heights, MA: Allyn and Bacon, 1991.*

Johnson, D. W. and R. T. Johnson. "Cooperative Learning: Using Gang Dynamics to Enhance Learning." *School Intervention Report* 6/3 (Spring 1993): 14-19.

Johnson, D. W.; Johnson, R. T. and E. J. Holubec. *New Circles of Learning: Cooperation in the Classroom and School.* Alexandria, VA: Association for Supervision and Instruction, 1994.

Joyce, B. "Common Misconceptions About Cooperative Learning and Gifted Students." *Educational Leadership* 48/6 (1991): 72-74.

Kagan, S. *Cooperative Learning.* Kagan's Cooperative Learning Company, 27128 Paseo Espada, Suite 602, San Juan Capistrano, CA 92675, 1992.

Kester, V. M. "Factors that Affect African-American Students' Bonding to Middle School." *Elementary School Journal* 95/1 (September 1994): 63-73.

Kohn, A. *No Contest: The Case Against Competition.* Boston, MA: Houghton Mifflin Co., 1992.

MacIver, D. *Motivating Disadvantaged Early Adolescents to Reach New Heights: Effective Evaluation, Reward, and Recognition Structure.* Baltimore: Johns Hopkins University, Center for Research on Effective Schooling for Disadvantaged Students, 1992.*

Madden, N.A. et al. *A Comprehensive Cooperative Learning Approach to Elementary Reading and Writing: Effects on Student Achievement.* Center for Research on Elementary and Middle Schools Report No. 2. Baltimore: Johns Hopkins University, Center for Research on Elementary and Middle Schools, 1986.

Marcus, S. A. and P. McDonald. *Tools for the Cooperative Classroom.* Palantine, IL: IRI Skylight Publishing Inc., 1990.

Mattingly, R. M. and R. L. VanSickle. *Jigsaw II in Secondary Social Studies: An Experiment.* Athens: University of Georgia, 1990.

📖 McPartland, J. M. and R. E. Slavin. *Policy Perspectives: Increasing Achievement of At-risk Students at Each Grade Level.* Washington, D.C.: U.S. Department of Education, 1990.

📖 Oakes, J. *Keeping Track: How Schools Structure Inequality.* New Haven, Conn.: Yale University Press, 1985.

📖 Oakes, J. "Can Tracking Research Inform Practice? Technical, Normative, and Political Considerations." *Educational Researcher* 21/4 (1992): 12-21.

📖 Oakes, J. et al. "Curriculum Differentiation: Opportunities, Outcomes, and Meanings." In *Handbook of Research on Curriculum: A Project of the American Educational Research Association,* edited by P. W. Jackson. New York: Macmillan, 1992.

📖 Oakes, J. et al. *Multiplying Inequalities: The Effects of Race, Social Class, and Tracking on Opportunities to Learn Math and Science.* Santa Monica, CA: Rand Corporation, 1990.

📖 Oakes, J. et al. *Educational Matchmaking: Academic and Vocational Tracking in Comprehensive High Schools.* Santa Monica, CA: Rand Corporation, 1992.*

📖 Okebukola, P. A. "The Relative Effectiveness of Cooperative and Competitive Interaction Techniques in Strengthening Students' Performance in Science Classes." *Science Education* 69/4 (1985): 501-509.

📖 O'Neil, J. "Can Separate Be Equal? Educators Debate Merits, Pitfalls of Tracking." *ASCD Curriculum Update* (June 1993): 1-3, 7-8.*

📖 Page, R. and L. Valli, eds. *Curriculum Differentiation: Interpretive Studies in U.S. Secondary Schools.* Albany: State University of New York Press, 1990.

📖 Rogers, J. *The Inclusion Revolution.* CEDR Research Bulletin No. 11. Bloomington, IN: Phi Delta Kappa, May 1993.*

📖 Sanders, C. S., Jr. "The Effects of High School Staffing Patterns on Low-Achieving Students." Doctoral dissertation, University of Florida, Gainesville, FL, 1992. *Dissertation Abstracts International* 54, 52A.

Sharan, S. "Cooperative Learning in Small Groups: Recent Methods and Effects on Achievement, Attitudes and Ethnic Relations." *Review of Educational Research* 50/2 (Summer 1980): 241-271.

Sharan, Y. and S. Sharan. *Expanding Cooperative Learning Through Group Investigation.* New York: Teachers College Press, 1992.

Slavin, R. E. "Classroom Reward Structure: Analytical and Practical Review." *Review of Educational Research* 47/4 (Fall 1977): 633-650.

Slavin, R. E. *Using Student Team Learning,* 3rd ed. Baltimore, MD: Johns Hopkins University, 1986.

Slavin, R. E. "Ability Grouping and Student Achievement in Elementary Schools: A Best-Evidence Synthesis." *Review of Educational Research* 57/3 (1987): 293-336.

Slavin, R. E. "Synthesis of Research on Grouping in Elementary and Secondary Schools." *Educational Leadership* 45/1 (1988): 67-77. 79-82.

Slavin, R. E. "Achievement Effects of Ability Grouping in Secondary Schools: A Best-Evidence Synthesis." *Review of Educational Research* 60/3 (1990): 471-99.

Slavin, R. E. "Are Cooperative Learning and Untracking Harmful to the Gifted?" *Educational Leadership* 48/6 (1991): 68-71.

Slavin, R. E. "Synthesis of Research on Cooperative Learning." *Educational Leadership* 48/5 (1991): 71-77, 79-82.*

Stahl, R. J. *Cooperative Learning in Social Studies.* Reading, MA: Addison-Wesley Publishing Company, 1992.

Stahl, R. J. "The Essential Elements of Cooperative Learning in the Classroom." *ERIC Digest.* Washington, DC: Office of Educational Research and Development, 1994.

Topping, K. *The Peer Tutoring Handbook: Promoting Cooperative Learning.* Cambridge, MA: Brookling Books, 1988.

Vandell, D. L. and S. E. Hembree. "Peer Social Status and Friendship: Independent Contributors to Children's Social and Academic Adjustment." *Merrill-Palmer Quarterly* 40/4 (October 1994): 461-77.

Wheelock, A. *Crossing the Tracks: How "Untracking" Can Save America's Schools.* New York: New Press, 1992.*

Module 10
Reinforcing Achievement

Key Concepts and Considerations

- Basic Reinforcement Principles
- Types of Reinforcement
- Classroom Examples
- Suggested Activities
- Additional Resources

In developing an effective school learning climate, with high expectations for all students, we should understand the power of reinforcement techniques which motivate and sustain behavior consistent with these expectations. The following techniques provide a general framework of reinforcement principles which are applicable to student learning and student conduct.

This module focuses on the proper use of reinforcement so that desired student behavior, both social and academic, can be maximized. It covers the principles and values of reinforcement, types of rewards, proper use of rewards, praise and encouragement in the classroom, and the qualities of reinforcements which make them most effective. In addition, we will present specific examples of proper reinforcement during oral and written drill.

Basic Reinforcement Principles

The Stimulus: In order to create a desirable learning situation, we must reinforce the responses that lead to the achievement of high levels of academic skill and knowledge. These responses by students can only occur in relationship to something that is presented to them. This "something" is the "stimulus." An example of an academic stimulus would be questions asked of a student. It also may be an exercise in a book, a word presented on a spelling test, or a subtraction problem. A smile, a frown, or other facial expression can also be a part of the stimulus. We present stimuli to students, and either by example, lecture or a variety of creative teaching techniques, we provide our students with the information we hope will elicit a correct response.

One point to bear in mind is that students must be clear about what is being asked of them. For example, a subtraction problem that is being presented to them must stand out from the general classroom hubbub. The word that they are being asked to spell must be understandable. The question that has been verbally directed to them must be unambiguous, and should generally have no more than one correct answer. The problems, questions, and exercises that we present to students must be ones that enable the student to distinguish relevant information from background information.

The Response: The response is the answer or behavior that the student produces in relation to the stimulus that is presented. It can be the verbal, written, or overt behavior that the student produces when asked a question, given a problem, or asked to spell a word. One of the things we often forget as teachers is that a response should be either right or wrong, or at least, acceptable or unacceptable. Teachers must make a discrimination between answers that are right and answers that are wrong.

Reinforcement: After a stimulus has been presented to a student and the student has produced a response, what happens next? This is where the teacher, if he or she chooses, can reinforce the answer or behavior exhibited by the student. Thus teachers should determine the correctness of the response given by students and then act to reinforce or extinguish that response. Reinforcements can be positive or negative in nature. A positive reinforcement (sometimes thought of as a "reward") is likely to cause the response to be strengthened in a student. Reinforcement is like psychological glue; every little dab that we use is likely to attach the answers more firmly in students' minds. When we positively reinforce something — no matter whether it is right or wrong — we are likely to increase the probability of its being repeated. Sometimes teachers reinforce wrong answers. Sometimes teachers reward incorrect behavior. Usually, this is done inadvertently, or because a teacher feels it puts other goals than student achievement level first. One example of this is when teachers act as if it is most important to be always warm and accepting of students' answers, even when those answers are factually incorrect or exhibit poor thinking. Unfortunately, the frequent result is that students unintentionally "learn" to be poor students.

Negative reinforcement is the reverse of positive reinforcement. Sometimes we motivate student behavior by withdrawing something that students value. For example, if students value the teacher's praise when answering questions, withholding that praise for incorrect responses can be a powerful motivator. This is analogous to parents withdrawing an allowance from children who refuse to do their dishwashing chores. Negative reinforcement can be as effective as positive reinforcement.

Most of us prefer to be "positive people" and so may avoid using negative reinforcement. We must be aware that sometimes telling a student, "No, that's not correct," while providing support and encouragement, "Now try again, I know you can do it," will help the student learn the correct response. By telling students they are wrong and providing encouragement for the correct response, students will feel that learning is possible and thus be more motivated to respond correctly. Any reinforcement used in a non-discriminating manner is likely to impede student learning.

If a reinforcer is to be effective in modifying behavior, it must be delivered contingently; that is, the reinforcer is not given until the desired behavior occurs. The individual or group receiving the reward must clearly understand that the reward is given only on the performance of correct behavior. In a school or classroom these behavioral expectations should be clearly understood by the students. They should know what is expected of them academically and socially, and what students view as rewards or punishments should then be consistent with the expectations for all students.

Tangible and Social Reinforcers

In the classroom or school there are two basic types of reinforcers which can be delivered: tangible and social rewards. Tangible reinforcers are items such as snack treats or free time. These are given for appropriate responses. More complex or sophisticated systems, in which the rewards may be points or check-marks that are given at the time of response and then accumulated for exchange or purchase of tangible rewards later, are known as token economies. Also, tangible reinforcers can be symbolic; the use of trophies, banners, honor roll and certificates of merit are a few such rewards. The stars we place on student assignments are another example of a symbolic reward. By using such reinforcers, teachers are communicating to students their satisfaction with student performance; by withholding them they communicate dissatisfaction.

Some difficulties in providing tangible reinforcers should be recognized. They can be expensive and time consuming for the teacher. Also, if a reward is to be effective, students should be responsive to it. A reward for some students may not be valued by others. The teacher will have to try various types of tangible reinforcers to identify those most desirable for affecting behavior in the classroom. Some reinforcers lose their effectiveness if used too often or too long. Vary material reinforcers, or use them sparingly, in order to stimulate desired behavior.

A second type of reinforcer is social in nature. Praise given by the teacher or student peers has been advocated as a useful method. Praise is relatively easy to apply and is a direct statement of the contingency between the behavior and the reinforcer. Yet praise does not always operate as a reinforcer. For example, some students may see it as embarrassing and thus undesirable. Teachers should be sensitive to situations in which praise will be valued by students.

When intrinsic motivation does not exist, extrinsic reinforcers, both social and tangible are appropriate (Good and Brophy, 1994). Yet intrinsic motivation (enjoyment and achievement) is a more lasting and powerful motivator. Thus, the teacher should be concerned with helping the student make the transition from working at academic tasks for extrinsic to intrinsic reasons, gradually reducing or "fading" the number of extrinsic reinforcers. Calling students' attention to "how good it feels" and to their sense of personal accomplishment, and relating classroom learning to the outside world of jobs and later education, are means that can be used to make this transition.

As mentioned above, for a reinforcement schedule to be effective, it must be contingent upon behavior. Teacher praise, however, is often given inappropriately, as in the case when an incorrect student response is praised. This inappropriate praise is often found among teachers who have low expectations for student learning (Brookover et al., 1978). Teachers sometimes use it as an attempt to encourage students or to reward them for simply participating in the class. It is seen by many as a way of getting low-achieving students to feel good about themselves. Yet to the extent that students recognize what the teacher is doing, the result will be embarrassment, discouragement, or other undesirable outcomes. Furthermore, reinforcing an improper response sends an inconsistent and confusing message to all the students in class.

Another problem with typical classroom praise is its lack of specificity. Anderson, Evertson, and Brophy (1979) found several years ago that only five percent of teacher praise followed good work or good answers by students. Hopefully, this has changed. If the situation has not changed, it is unacceptably low, since praise is intended to motivate academic or other behavior from students.

Another factor which reduces the effects of teacher praise is the teacher being perceived as lacking in credibility. In other words, the verbal content is not supported by, or is even contradicted by, non-verbal expressive behavior. Students are very aware of the sincerity or credibility of teacher talk; praise which is seen as insincere is often dysfunctional. Unfortunately, troublesome students receive as much praise as do better behaved and more successful students. Perhaps, in such cases, the teachers wish to minimize their interactions with these students. Reinforcement provided in this manner tends to lead to undesirable learning outcomes.

Studies of teachers indicate that praise, when used properly, is most effective in raising achievement levels of students of low socio-economic level or low-achieving classrooms. It appears that teachers' praise for academic progress is more meaningful to low achievers than to high achievers who are accustomed to consistent success. This does not mean, however, that we should praise low-achieving students for every single response.

Frequency of Reinforcement

Teachers have only so much time to attend to a classroom of students. A teacher cannot be expected to reinforce all the responses students make. Several years ago Meacham and Wilson (1971) provided two general and still valid rules to follow:

1. Teachers should reinforce most heavily when the student is learning a new task and less when he or she is maintaining a behavior that has been well-learned.

2. When the desired behavior is social and to be maintained over a long period of time, it is recommended the teacher use an intermittent schedule of reinforcement. In this method, several correct responses may be required for a reinforcement (ratio schedule) or a given time may elapse before it is given (interval schedule).

Some Classroom Examples

The following examples are based on our initial framework of stimulus, response, and reinforcement. They should provide further clarity of the principles of praise and encouragement discussed above. These are practical examples which are encountered in most classrooms. Note that in these examples, the teacher is seen as the reinforcer, but the peer group can also be motivated to follow these principles. They may be an even stronger force in maintaining or sustaining appropriate behavior. Just as in team learning, the group can be mobilized to reward or sanction the behavior of students in the classroom.

Stimulus — Asking Questions. Questions, whether verbal or in a written form, should be asked in such a way as to enable the student to understand

and discriminate what is being asked. Generally, there are two types of questions, or learning stimuli, that we present to students. One type of question calls for a short factual answer. These convergent questions often deal with matters of fact which a student either knows or does not know. For students this questioning process is, in essence, an exercise in memory. Examples of convergent questions include those involving famous dates, state capitals, number facts, president of the United States, etc. Convergent questions often begin with "when," "where," and so on.

One thing to remember in asking this type of question is not to ask two questions at the same time. For example, we should not ask, "Who was the first governor of Michigan and how many terms did he serve?" Double questions tend to confuse both students and teachers.

Generally, questions of this type can be asked or presented in a very rapid manner (see *Module 6, Effective Instruction*). Thus, if we are involved in an oral drill on number facts, we should pace ourselves fairly rapidly. Correspondingly, we should not allocate a great deal of time for similar written exercises.

A second type of question involves a reasoning process on the part of students. These questions, divergent in nature, not only include who, what, where and when, as before, but they also include how and why. In responding to such a question, the student must become involved in more complex thought processes and more complex answers. However, the same guidelines about clarity of the question and the associated clarity of the answer suggested for convergent questions, also apply to divergent questions. Just as in rote or mechanical learning, the student must understand what is being asked. These types of questions, of course, should be paced more slowly than rote learning questions, as students will need more time to think over their responses.

Responses — Correct and Incorrect. Unless the student does not respond at all, he or she is likely to give a response that can be evaluated in terms of its "rightness" or acceptability. As implied in the above discussion, most questions should have clear, unambiguous, right or wrong answers. Factual-memory questions are definitely of this sort.

When questions are more complex the teacher's evaluation may be that an answer is "mostly right" or "mostly wrong." This demands more elaborate feedback on the part of the teacher, and a more astute application of reinforcement principles. This process resembles that of reinstruction, with teachers providing encouragement and support, but at the same time ensuring that students know whether their answers are basically right or wrong.

Reinforcement and Feedback Behavior on the Part of the Teacher. Whatever a student does, whether he or she answers correctly or incorrectly, or doesn't answer at all, some reciprocal response is demanded on the part of the teacher. Let us consider a situation in which a student does not respond. If the question is a simple factual one, such as a math or work drill, the teacher should encourage the student, wait a few seconds, and then give the answer. However, if the question is more complex, involving reasoning, the teacher should give the pupil time to think over the answer and should try to ascertain whether the student does or does not know the answer. If a student does not respond to a complex question, the teacher should always attempt to get a correct or nearly correct response from the student. This may involve simplifying or restating the question, or breaking it down into its component parts.

What happens if the student gives a wrong answer? If we are talking about a factual question, presented in a rapid-paced learning session, the teacher should indicate that the answer is incorrect, give the correct answer, and either move on or immediately reinstruct and requestion. The student should clearly understand that the answer given was wrong. However, it is important that this information be given to the student in a positive, instructive manner. The teacher should politely point out the error, give the correct answer and move on. Whenever an incorrect answer is given, the teacher must be very careful to avoid either discouraging the student or reinforcing incorrect answers.

What about situations where an incorrect or mostly incorrect answer is given to a reasoning question? In these circumstances, a more complex process is called for on the part of the teacher. On the one hand, the feedback should be elaborated with attempts to nudge the student into giving a fully correct answer. This may involve restatement in a different vocabulary, or a shortening of the question itself. Another strategy is to provide the student with hints or prompts, or to break the question into smaller, shorter questions. If attempts to simplify the question do not yield a correct response from the student, the teacher should point out the incorrectness, possibly advise more study, and move on to the next question or student.

The strategy of "staying with" a student in order to help him or her come up with the correct answer is a part of the process of "probing" that follows questions. This practice is especially necessary for students who are behind in their work, or who lack confidence. Probing must be done in an encouraging and supportive manner while communicating clearly the expectation that the student can and will learn. As noted earlier, this is necessary in order to ensure that the students will receive reinforcement. Unless you probe or stay with students who have not mastered the material, they are unlikely to receive the kind of success and reinforcement that helps to motivate and sustain appropriate behavior.

Let us now consider the happy situation in which the student produces a correct response. It is here that a clear, positive reinforcement should be given. At the very least, the student should understand that a correct answer has been given. In other words, the correctness of the answer must be acknowledged. It should be clear to both the student who produced the answer and to the rest of the class that this was the correct answer to the question. This type of reinforcement may be supplemented by more elaborate use of praise, or even tangible rewards. Thus, the teacher may comment "Very good" or "Exactly right" as a quick acknowledgment for factual questions but give a longer, more complete response for reasoning questions, significant accomplishments, and extra efforts. This allows the teacher to differentiate the level and quality of praise in response to the difficulty of the questions, and thus prevent praise from becoming so common that it is no longer effective. The teacher should attempt to give praise that is varied and individually oriented. Thus, rather than saying, "That's good" to everybody's correct answer, the teacher can individualize it by adding the student's name to the comment or praising the specific skill the student exhibited (e.g., "That's excellent work, Janice! You have shown you now understand how to write topic sentences.").

Using Reinforcement with Written Exercises. Often teachers use correct reinforcement in verbal learning situations but not when students are involved in written exercises. Reinforcement principles are equally valid here. Thus, if students are being asked to perform a set of math problems at their desks, the teacher should be circulating around the room, pointing out wrong answers, possibly restating questions, acknowledging correct answers, correcting errors, occasionally giving praise, and so on. If students merely work by themselves on workbook drill, with no involvement on the part of the teacher, their active learning time is reduced. Furthermore, they may not be aware of the rightness or wrongness of their responses.

Summary

Teachers and principals often praise incorrectly or fail to praise at all.

1.   The school staff needs to be reminded to praise when praise is earned.

2.   If staff members are unsure of the effects of praise, they should be shown why, when and how to use it for best results.

    A. Positive reinforcement of correct student responses with encouragement and support will result in:

- mastery of intended behaviors;

- feeling that learning is possible and valuable;

- ability to appropriately assess one's functioning in school social situations; and

- positive perceptions of self and sense of well-being.

    B. Positive reinforcement of incorrect response, without reinstruction, results in:

- incorrect knowledge, skills, and behavior;

- confused self-assessment and feelings of futility regarding school;

- inability to apply basic skill principles.

C. Negative reinforcement of incorrect student responses, with reinstruction, results in:

- feeling that learning is possible;
- learning correct behavior;
- acquiring reasonable perceptions of self; and
- ability to perceive accurately and respond appropriately to others.

Reinforcement which is misused can have disastrous effects on learning and conduct. Teachers and staff can improve learning through the proper use of reinforcement techniques in the classroom and in the school generally.

Suggested Activities

1. Examine your current level of use of reinforcement practices (see *Teacher Check List*).

2. Periodically, take a look at what you're actually doing in the classroom with students to reinforce achievement. This can be done by use of audiotape or videotape recordings or by getting another teacher to observe your reinforcement practices. The use of audiotape can be done by yourself, placing the recorder next to a desk where students come to you for assistance. If desired, video recording can also be done without having someone to operate the equipment, providing the camera is positioned to cover teacher-student interaction. If this approach is too restrictive or does not produce the recording quality you desire, consider using a student to operate the camera. Otherwise, ask a staff member or volunteer to videotape for you.

3. Involve other staff members in looking at reinforcement practices by using role-playing to illustrate correct-incorrect techniques. This can be fun and very informative at the same time. If time allows, prerecord the role-playing on videotape so only the best "takes" are

presented at meetings of the whole staff or smaller grade/departmental meetings.

4. Survey your students to find out about their likes and dislikes. You may be surprised to find that something you are using as a positive reinforcer is actually viewed negatively by some students. Also, there may be some actions or activities preferred or valued by students which could be more effective. (See *Suggested Survey* below.)

5. Determine how you can best use tangible rewards to reinforce achievement in your class. Remember, tangible rewards can be very motivating for students to improve behavior or performance but you must use them appropriately:

    a. contingently — awarded only for desired performance;

    b. selectively — used when social reinforcers cannot produce the desired results;

    c. temporarily — used only as long as students need it. Don't condition students to expect tangible rewards for every effort.

Teacher Check List

Reinforcing Achievement

Positive Reinforcement

❑   Do you positively reinforce every student in your class at least once each day?

❑   Do you give positive reinforcement immediately, or as soon as possible, after a desired response has occurred?

❑   Do you give students positive reinforcement for correctly doing things you expect them to do?

❑   Do you use positive reinforcement in a planned way?

Negative Reinforcement

❑ Do you use negative reinforcement with students to initiate a change in behavior?

❑ Do you use punishment to suppress undesirable behavior?

❑ After using negative reinforcement do you identify an alternative desirable behavior for the student?

❑ If so, do you then encourage the student to achieve the desired change by using a regular schedule of positive reinforcement?

Extinction

❑ Do you ignore undesirable responses that are new or occur infrequently?

❑ If ignoring doesn't eliminate the undesirable response, do you switch to using negative reinforcement?

❑ Do you understand why ignoring academic errors of students is inappropriate?

Schedule

❑ Do you use a regular schedule of reinforcement during the initial steps of learning?

❑ Do you continue to use a regular schedule of reinforcement up to the point at which learning occurs?

❑ Do you reinforce learned behavior periodically to sustain it?

Social Rewards

❑ Do you know your students well enough so you can take advantage of their likes and dislikes?

❑ Do you know your students well enough to determine the sources of approval they value most and least?

❑ Do you use verbal praise often with students?

❑ Do you make your praise contingent, specific, and sincere?

❑ Do you deliberately position/locate yourself or students in the room as social reinforcement (proximity).

❑ Do you purposely use body language as a positive or negative reinforcer?

❑ Do you allow your students to participate in activities of their choosing as positive reinforcement?

Tangible Rewards

❑ Do you provide special rewards to students to encourage desired behavior?

❑ Do you make sure all students clearly understand that acceptable or specified behavior will be rewarded and other behavior will not be rewarded?

❑ Do you reward students only when they perform in the manner specified?

❑ Do you avoid making students dependent on artificial reinforcers by giving tangible rewards only when necessary or appropriate?

❑ Do you attempt to switch your students from tangible rewards to social rewards?

Performance Feedback to Students

❑ Do you check and return student work promptly?

❑ Do you give every student a clear picture of his or her performance status?

❑ Do you offer performance feedback to every student every day?

❑ Do you use feedback language that is easily understood, not complex?

❑ Do you give feedback information that is specific or related to particular errors, correct responses, or accomplishments?

❑ Do you provide opportunities for performance feedback from peers (e.g., student team learning practice, group checking, peer tutoring, etc.)?

SUGGESTED STUDENT SURVEY

Name:_____

Concerning this class, I am a person who . . .

likes _____

hates _____

can _____

cannot _____

would never _____

would rather _____

wants to learn how to _____

would be better if _____

is really good at _____

gets really angry when _____

"bugs" other people when _____

has the good habit of _____

has the bad habit of _____

wishes I could change the way I _____

wishes I could change the way other people _____

Outside of school, I am a person who . . .

never misses watching the TV show entitled _____

will someday _____

enjoys doing _____

Selected Bibliography

Anderson, L., Evertson, C. and J. Brophy. "An Experimental Study of Effective Teaching in First Grade Reading Groups." *Elementary School Journal* 7/3 (Summer 1979): 193-223.

Bandera, A. "Perceived Self-efficacy in Cognitive Development and Functioning." Paper presented at annual meeting of the American Educational Research Association, San Francisco, CA, April 1992.

Black, S. "In Praise of Judicious Praise." *Executive Editor*. 14/10 (October 1992): 24-27.

Brookover, W. B. et al. "Elementary School Climate and School Achievement." *American Educational Research Journal* 15/2 (Fall 1978): 301-318.

Brophy, J. "Teacher Praise: A Functional Analysis." *Review of Educational Research* 51/1 (1981): 5-32.

Faber, A. and E. Mazlish. *How to Talk to Kids Will Listen and Listen So Kids Will Talk.* New York, NY: Rawson Wade Publishers, 1980.

Good, T. and J. Brophy. *Looking in Classrooms,* 6th ed. New York: Harper Collins, 1994.

Harris, A. M. and M. V. Covington. "The Role of Cooperative Reward Interdependency in Success and Failure." *Journal of Experimental Education* 61/2 (Winter 1993): 151-68.

Inkster, J. A. and T. F. McLaughlin. "Token Reinforcement: Effects for Reducing Tardiness with a Socially Disadvantaged Student." *Journal of Special Education* 17/3 (1993): 284-88.

Kemeenui, E. J. and C. B. Darch. *Instructional Classroom Management: A Proactive Approach to Behavior Management.* White Plains, NY: Longman Publishers, 1995.

Meacham, M. L. and A. E. Wilson. *Changing Classroom Behavior: A Manual for Precision Teaching.* Scranton, PA: International Textbook Co., 1971.

Mory, E. H. "The Use of Informational Feedback in Instruction." *Educational Technology, Research and Development* 40/3 (1992): 5-20.

Nelsen, J. *Positive Discipline.* New York, NY: Balantine Books, 1987.

Spencer, R. and O. Martin. "The Effect of Teacher, Paraprofessional and Peer Monitoring on Student Learning." Paper presented at the Annual Meeting of the Mid-South Educational Research Association. Knoxville, TN, November 1992.

Stipek, D. J. *Motivation to Learn: From Theory to Practice,* 2nd ed. Needham Neights: MA: Allyn and Bacon, 1993.

Tobias, R. "Math and Science Education for African-American Youth: A Curriculum Challenge." *NASSP Bulletin* 76/546 (October 1992): 1-92.

Module 11

Assessing Student and School Performance

Key Concepts and Considerations

- Testing for Mastery Learning
- Formative and Summative Testing
- Record Keeping
- Suggested Reports
- Improving the Quality of Assessment
- Evaluating School Programs

Types of Evaluation

All kinds of data on students are gathered for the purpose of making important decisions — decisions relevant to what students have learned, decisions about how to help them, and decisions about how to improve education in the classroom, the school, and the district. Data also are obtained on students to meet requirements for communicating the performance status of classrooms, schools, districts, and special categories of students. In all of these purposes, the usefulness of the data depends on the validity of how and what is gathered to make the evaluations and decisions. The questions are: "Did we collect data that was pertinent to the decisions we made?" and "Did we analyze the data correctly?"

It is easy to make errors in judgment about the relevancy of data collected. This has been made apparent by researchers. They have noted that it is relatively common for teachers to have material on their tests for students that is not taught in their classes, and to leave out important information that is taught. Teacher tests and other forms of evaluation, in other words, are often out of alignment with their instruction. And sometimes their instruction is out of alignment with the learning objectives set forth by the school. The point is that if test data or other observations gathered on students are not in alignment with what is covered in instruction, there is little or no substantial basis to make an assessment as to what or how much was learned in the course. Such data for evaluating what students have learned in a course or program has no place in mastery learning.

There are occasions where it may be proper to gather data on students that were not taught the course objectives, if there are purposes other than the evaluation of instructional effectiveness. Educators and persons outside of education often have a need to know about the presence of skills, knowledge, attitudes, and other student characteristics in planning programs, selecting objectives to focus upon, and other reasons. Such data, however, provides little clue for evaluating the effectiveness of a school's curriculum or a teacher's classroom instruction in achieving objectives.

This module is most concerned with collecting and evaluating data that is directly related to student mastery of the competencies intended by the school and the classroom. As such, it is concerned with avoiding a condition that is present in many schools. This is where, at best, testing is irrelevant to enhancing the effectiveness of instruction, and at worst, interferes with teachers' abilities to teach course objectives.

Paper and pencil tests are not the only form of assessment that are appropriate for mastery learning. While such tests and quizzes can provide a valuable tool for determining some types of learning, in many cases, they do little to reveal whether critical knowledge of skills have been learned. For example, if the objective is for students to be able to use a word processor to write a term paper, a test asking students to identify word processing commands would reveal little about a student's ability to use a word processor. Rather, a performance-based assessment where students are asked to produce a computer-generated document would provide much greater insight into how well a student has mastered the skills necessary to use a word processor.

Teachers need to consider alternative forms of assessment to match specific learning objectives. Among these alternatives are rubrics, performance-based assessment, portfolios, and even some limited forms of self-assessment. This is not to say that teachers should not test. On the contrary, tests and quizzes can, depending upon the material to be covered, be vital forms of assessment. The determination of how to assess student mastery should be linked to specific learning objective. In fact, an appropriate objective defines or provides direction to assessing completion of that objective.

Testing and Course Objectives

Educational objectives should serve three functions: they should specify what students are expected to learn, they should guide the instructional activities of teachers, and they should provide direction to assessing student mastery of the objective. There are two ways of gathering information on students relative to assessing instructional objectives — one, generally wrong and the other, generally right. A teacher may look to the test and organize classroom instruction to teach what will be on the test, or the test may be based on what the instruction was intended to teach. Testing that is aligned with classroom instructional objectives, which in turn is aligned with curriculum objectives, is what is supposed to occur. When it does, it is correct to "teach to the test." It is wrong to teach to a test unless there is a clear and significant overlap of test content with both curriculum and classroom objectives. The appropriate use of testing as a means of assessment is an integral part of instruction.

When to Test

When a patient visits a medical physician because he or she is not feeling well, the first thing the doctor does is to make a number of observations. These observations may derive from how the patient looks, what the patient says and does; and perhaps, the physician runs some tests on the patient. All of this data is for *diagnostic* purposes. A diagnosis is made, and on the basis of this diagnosis the physician makes a recommendation as to whether there should be treatment, and if so, the character of that treatment. Given that treatment is provided, the physician usually asks for a second set of diagnostic data to confirm whether the treatment was working as intended. If not, another treatment may be prescribed with further testing. Obviously, the purpose of doing the diagnostic testing before and after treatment is to increase the odds of doing the right thing by the patient — to help the patient.

There is another type of testing or data gathering that physicians sometimes engage in that is not for the prime purpose of treating a person. This is called a *screening examination*. Screening exams are usually done when a person needs to meet certain criteria in order to receive insurance, a license, a job, or a grade. The examination is not done to affect medical treatment. Rather, screening examinations are done mostly for the purpose of determining and certifying a condition of the persons tested.

Except in schools using mastery learning methods of instruction, testing in education typically functions as a screening device. Seldom do teachers, except in physical and health education classes, test before instruction to first see what a student knows and doesn't know. Seldom do they appropriately use diagnostic testing to provide instruction so as to remedy deficits, and then follow up with another examination to see if different or additional instruction is needed. Teaching for mastery requires diagnostic examination. In educational parlance, diagnostic evaluation is commonly referred to as *progress* or *formative* evaluation, while screening examinations in schools are commonly referred to as *output* or *summative* evaluation. The purpose of a formative test is to guide and improve instruction while it is in progress. The purpose of a summative evaluation in education is to assess the presence or absence of particular skills, knowledge, or attitudes in students. Summative tests are often used as indicators of what students learned in a program, that is, program *output*. Both *formative* evaluation and *summative* evaluation are valuable to ensure mastery learning.

Formative Evaluation

Formative's first meaning in most dictionaries is *having the power to shape, form or mold: a formative influence.* To be formative, the evaluation cannot occur only after the instruction is complete, as is the case with most testing in schools. Formative evaluation should be viewed as a phase or series of observations over time. Initial observations must occur before instruction is first presented, to be followed by instruction that is based upon demonstrated or failed competencies in the first test, and then retested to determine the success or failure of the instruction. Instruction and evaluation should be continued until the desired competency is learned. Formative evaluation in mastery learning programs should occur at a minimum of every two weeks. Formative observations constitute a truly personalized diagnosis followed by instruction, even though the same objectives are held for every student. In classes where all students have mastered the critical level of objectives taught for the next higher level of class, there will be little need for much variation in instruction to learn the new objectives.

Formative evaluation data should not be used for grading unless it is the last data collected at the end of a unit of instruction. This would defeat its motivational purposes. As the case with diagnostic testing by physicians, there is cooperation between student and teacher when formative evaluation is done correctly. Students should not have to worry that the teacher will learn about deficiencies in their competency, and as a result, be given lower grades. If done correctly, students will expect the teacher to use negative information to help them learn what is required so as to earn a high grade. This means, of course, that formative evaluations should be in alignment with any summative evaluation instruments used for grading students.

Unfortunately, summative evaluation, without telling students what they are expected to know, often creates adversarial relationships where students only want teachers to learn what they know. It would be a sad situation if physically ill persons approached their physicians and did not want them to discover their illness or its causes. Similarly, educators should not use any type of evaluation procedure in a way which causes students to hide their knowledge and skill deficits from their teachers.

Summative Evaluation

The root of summative is sum. Like the term "summation," *it is the act or operation of obtaining a sum.* Like "summary," it is giving a concise or sum description of performance. Summative is the expression of an aggregate sum. The aggregate of summative evaluations, when using objective criteria over specific skills and content, is often expressed as a percentile, as a percent of competencies demonstrated, as a profile of competencies learned, or as a grade.

Summative procedures, aside from motivational purposes, may have some relevance for assessing program effectiveness and grading, if the content of the evaluation process appropriately overlaps the course content, and there is relevant pre- and post-instruction data available. Summative evaluations procedures that do not cover course content may be useful, but only for describing the status of a student or program on some dimension other than course content. For example, the assessment results for a group of students who receive the services of a special program may be compared to the assessment results of similar students not receiving the same services. The differences in the aggregated performance for the two groups may be one inferential indicator of the effects of the special program if there is appropriate information on the students prior to instruction.

Another important use of summative results is that of monitoring progress for groups in the classroom or school on dimensions not necessarily taught as course objectives. This use of such results can be informative and may be undertaken by teachers and administrators. An example of such an application of this evaluation process might be used to answer the following question: "Is math development the same for boys and girls?" To answer this question, teachers might aggregate math assessment scores for the boys and girls separately, and then compare the results while controlling for factors which would otherwise distort conclusions. As educators make their assessments of students it is critical that they pay close attention to determine to what extent all students, regardless of family background, have mastered critical skills and knowledge. As illustrated in *Figure 11-1*, the scheduling of testing and other procedures of data gathering on students differs considerably for mastery learning and non-mastery learning models of instruction.

Figure 11-1
TYPICAL SCHEDULING

Formative Evaluation Scheduling: Mastery Learning Model

Time 1	Time 2	Time 3	Time 4	Time 5
Formative 1st Test	Instruction	Formative Retest	Alternative Instruction	Summative Test or Formative Retest

Summative Evaluation Scheduling: Non-mastery Learning Model

Time 1	Time 2	Time 3
Instruction	Test	Move on to next Unit of Instruction

or

Time 1	
Test	No pre- or post-test instruction intentionally related to test

Norm-Referenced Tests

Although nationally based norm-referenced or standardized tests, such as the Metropolitan Achievement Test (MAT) and Scholastic Aptitude Test (SAT), can identify persons with different levels of achievement as compared with national norm groups, they are of questionable utility in evaluating the effectiveness of instruction. Often such tests do not measure what a local educational program was designed to teach, or what was taught. Since the test items are designed to differentiate between the "best" and the "worst" students, writers of norm-referenced tests are generally to exclude test questions that measure the common skills that most students have learned. Equally important, because norm-referenced testing means that a student's grade depends upon his or her performance relative to that of classmates, the potential for effective cooperative learning is reduced. Also, such tests are not designed to reveal particular problems that are keeping pupils from achieving at a mastery level. Thus, they provide little information for a teacher or a school staff to use to improve the instruction. They are helpful, however, if used as a general assessment of the status of a school, as it compares to national or other norms on the content the test measures.

Criterion Referenced Evaluation

These types of evaluation are meant to determine whether or not a student has mastered "particular" knowledge or skills, rather than how he or she compares to some norm group. The evaluation reveals what students have accomplished in specified situations. The Criterion referenced tests are objective reference tests with built-in mastery indicators that should pertain to instructional objectives. Items used in these tests should match the set of student skills called for in the objective itself, and should not be eliminated (as they are in the norm-referenced tests) merely because most students answer them correctly. Criterion referenced tests can be sensitive measures of what has actually been taught to the students. They are critical for implementing mastery learning because they indicate the kind of instruction that is needed by students. They also indicate when students are ready to proceed to subsequently higher level tasks.

Teacher-Made Tests

Summative test results administered once or a few times a semester or year, are seldom sufficient for measuring student mastery of specific objectives. In addition, there are few criterion referenced tests that are commercially available that are likely to be in alignment with course objectives. As a result, teacher-made evaluation and other forms of evaluation must be developed for formative assessment. Formative teacher-made evaluation is to enable more frequent modification of instruction by furnishing ongoing measurements of classroom achievement of specific objectives over shorter periods of time. Teacher-made evaluations can be both written and oral, or the student can behaviorally demonstrate the target behavior to the teacher's satisfaction. Teacher-made formative evaluations, however, should also meet the objectives for the school.

Thus teachers at the same grade level should, whenever possible, develop common instructional materials and common formative tests to facilitate teaching and assessment of mastery in basic skills for every academic course, at each grade level. This helps to assure congruence in objectives, materials and tests among teachers, and alignment with school objectives. This also reduces the workload on any one staff member.

The use of frequent teacher-made formative tests is beneficial in a number of other ways. They familiarize students with testing through practice. They quickly provide feedback information to students. They provide students with an opportunity to demonstrate or "show off" what they have learned. Such demonstrations often reinforce what has been learned, while serving as a powerful motivator for new learning. And, frequent progress checks reduce anxiety regarding how well students will perform on summative mastery tests.

Rubrics, Performance Based Assessment, Portfolios, and Other Forms of Evaluation

Rubrics are excellent formative and summative assessment tools because they provide a well-defined set of criteria for both teachers and students. A rubric is simply a series of competencies that relate to a specific objective. Often in the form of a series of statements, rubrics assess student performance to determine if each component of an objective has been met. For example, a rubric for determining students oral presentation skills may include a series of statements such as maintained eye contact, spoke in a voice loud enough for the audience to hear, checked for audience feedback, adjusted presentation based on audience feedback, and sought to actively engage audience. Of course, these are only a few examples of components for successful oral presentation skills. However, it students have a rubric listing each of these criteria they will be able to better prepare for the evaluation since they know the criteria used by the teacher for the evaluation. In addition, the rubric helps teachers identify what to consider during an evaluation, and actually makes the evaluation much easier. A teacher can simply check off, or use plus and minus, to indicate if each component of an objective has been mastered. Rubrics also provide an excellent framework for working with students because it identifies specific strengths and weaknesses of each student related to the learning objective.

Performance-based assessment is gaining popularity because it can more easily match objectives that are at higher levels of learning. While written tests are excellent tools for determining if students have factual knowledge, it is much more difficult to use a traditional test to assess a student's ability to analyze or synthesize information. For example, if the objective is to have students dissect a frog then it makes sense to have students actually perform the dissection as the evaluation. Often performance-based assessment uses rubrics so students are fully aware of each component skill and so teachers can easily diagnose which, if any, deficiencies exist for each student. The type of performance based assessment depends on the specific learning objective. Here too the objective determines or provides direction as to the type of performance-based assessment to use.

Portfolios are en excellent assessment tool because they reflect a large body of learning. Often portfolios are used to establish the sum of a student's body of work. For example, in a creative writing course, having students keep copies of their work from the beginning of a course to the end can demonstrate to teacher, parents, administrators, and students how they have progressed throughout the course, and the presence or absence of certain competencies. Far too often students do not realize what they have in fact learned. Portfolios provide concrete evidence.

Reflection is an important part of learning and asking students to provide an assessment of how they are progressing can provide a great deal of insight into how students are learning and how students perceive their learning process. There are a variety of tools for reflection and self-assessment including journals, portfolios, rubrics, self-assessment essays, and oral conferences. The danger with any form of self-assessment occurs primarily with summative evaluations. If you simply ask students at the end of a course to give themselves a grade then the temptation to give themselves a high grade will be high. However, if the self-assessment is used periodically throughout a course and does not "count" for a grade will likely yield a more accurate self-assessment.

Informal Instructional Assessment

Ongoing, formative assessment of student progress is most often done informally by teachers. While paper and pencil tests may be used, the pervasive interactional give and take within the classroom is most salient in shaping the teacher's instructional decision making. Effective teachers take into account the verbal responses of students, their facial expressions, their attention level, and other reactions to determine whether they are achieving educational objectives. Such cues are important indicators of how well the lesson is progressing. In other words, teachers engage in a type of informal formative assessment when they consider student responses to instruction, and then modify the instruction accordingly. This is somewhat analogous to a professional actor who modifies a performance based on interpretation of audience feedback. In school, such informal assessments of instruction are an important adjunct to formal feedback from quizzes, homework, and other materials.

The most common forms of informal teacher evaluation of students involves the teacher's oral questioning of students. According to Morgan and Sexton (1991), teacher questioning of students enhances learning in the following important ways:

- promotes pupils' attention by actively engaging them in the lesson;

- fosters deeper thinking by encouraging students to clarify and verbalize their ideas;

- facilitates peer teaching by giving pupils an opportunity to articulate their thought in front of their classmates;

- reinforces important points by emphasizing them through question cues;

- provides immediate feedback which allows teachers to diagnose problems and to pace instruction.

To maximize the power of this process, teachers should involve the entire class in questioning, rather than relying on only a few (usually the same) students to volunteer answers. The questions should follow logically from the instructional objectives, with adequate time given to students so they may consider a response. Equally important, the questions should include a range of difficulty, from simple factual questions to those which stimulate analysis, synthesis, and problem-solving applications. When appropriate, teachers should probe student responses with follow-up questions.

Because such a questioning process itself tends to generate new questions, teachers should be prepared to deviate occasionally from the prepared lesson plan. Such deviations often serve to enhance the instructional process, causing students and teachers alike to seek new insights and to chart a knowledge path which goes beyond the confines of the classroom. The bottom line, however, is that the process of informal questioning is an important tool in the formative assessments which characterize an effective learning climate.

SIZING-UP STUDENTS

Teachers form initial judgments of students based upon several sources of information, including formal assessments, informal observations, school records, and comments from teachers, parents, and other students. All of these information sources are part of a teacher's assessment of students. Such assessment has important consequences for how each pupil is treated. In a recent book, Peter Airaisan points out that teachers have an ethical responsibility to make their "sizing-up" of students as valid and reliable as possible. He recommends that teachers keep in mind the following:

- "[Teacher] prejudgment can stem from prior knowledge, first impressions, or personal prejudices and often interferes with fair and valid assessments.

- Teachers should be careful not to interpret cultural differences as cultural deficits.

- Teachers should be careful not to injure students by mislabeling them based on observations that don't justify the label.

- Teachers should be careful not to form a permanent perception of pupils based on one or two observations that may not be typical behavior.

- Teachers should treat initial impressions as hypotheses to be confirmed or corrected by later information.

- Teachers should supplement their informal observations with more structured activities. Reliable assessments usually require multiple observations in order to identify typical student behavior.

- Whenever possible, teachers should base their decisions on different kinds of information that support each other."

Airasian, P. *Assessment in the Classroom.* New York: McGraw-Hill, Inc., 1996.

Record Keeping

If instructional improvement is to result, record keeping is an indispensable part of testing for progress and mastery. It provides teachers with ongoing objective information, in writing, on the progress or lack of progress each student is experiencing, and serves to jog both memory and teacher judgment. It is an important vehicle for providing accurate and comprehensive academic feedback to students and their parents, and to other teachers if necessary.

In some districts, computerized scoring partially replaces the teacher's hand recording and summarizing of test results, particularly for school-wide tests. We refer in this section to the more frequent evaluation done within the classroom. In particular, we refer to the upgraded progress tests given approximately every week or two, which are considered part of student practice, and to the summative mastery tests which cover the same material but are used for grading or reporting. The results should be used for daily and weekly lesson planning and student work assignments. We suggest two basic record keeping forms: a student form and a teacher form (see *Figures 11-2* and *11-3)*.

With teachers gaining literacy in computer use, the increased availability of computers for teachers, and the commercial availability of "friendly" software for teacher record keeping, the chore of record keeping has become much easier. Students can also participate by recording information. This helps students become more agile in a technology that is increasingly important. And one further note, since the first edition of this manual, many computer programs have been developed that have been shown to be effective in formative evaluation and interaction.

Whatever the case, each student should have a folder, notebook or other location where samples of work, print-outs, completed assignments, notes, homework and so on are kept. This folder should contain a simple form for listing essential course objectives and recording the results of progress and mastery tests, that also can be used to inform parents. Samples are shown in *Figures 11-2* through *11-4)*.

Figure 11-2
RECORD KEEPING REGARDING ACHIEVEMENT IN MATH

Your Name _____

Hour _____

(Not used for grading) 85% = Mastery

Whole Numbers Units	Progress Tests	Date	Mastery Tests	Date
(Use of objectives)				
Multiplication 1 digit 2 digit 3 digit				
Division 1 digit 2 digit				
Rounding Off				
Inequalities Greater Than Less Than Equal to				
Averages				
Story Problems				
Factors Prime Factors Factor Trees Prime Factorization Greatest Common Factor				
Multiples Least Common Multiple				
Expanded Notation				
Roman Numerals				
Principles Commutative Associative Distributive				
Functions				
Bases				

Figure 11-3
SAMPLE TEACHER CHART

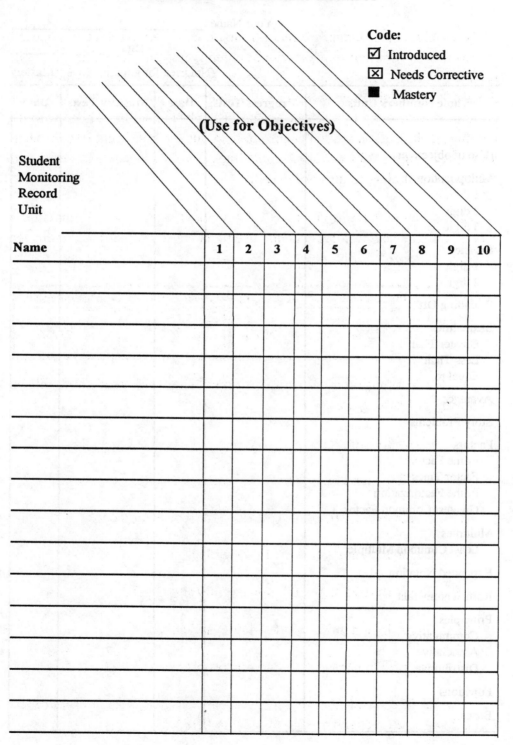

Figure 11-4
SAMPLE PARENT REPORT

Your child is in a mastery learning math class. What does this mean? It means that for each unit of work, students are told the skills they will review or learn. Each skill is taught to the class and then an ungraded practice test is given to everyone. Those who master skills (get 85% correct) can do extra things that extend or apply the skills. Those who do not master skills get a second chance to learn, using a different lesson. Then a final test is given for a grade. Sometimes a student needs extra time and help outside of class to master the skills.

Listed below are the units we have worked on so far. Your child's scores on the last test are given. Remember, a score of 85 indicates mastery.

UNIT:	Place Value	Rounding	Add/Subtract	Multiplication
Final test:	75%	85%	95%	87%

We are working on a division unit now. The skills your child will be reviewing or learning are:

1. know division facts;

2. divide by a number from 1-9 and check answer;

3. divide by 10, 20, 30, 40, 50, 60, 70, 80 or 90 and check;

4. divide by a number from 11-99 and check;

5. divide by 100, 200, 300, 400 . . . 900 and check;

6. divide by a number from 101-999 and check;

7. estimate the answers to division problems.

In order to do well in division, a student must know the multiplication facts, how to subtract and how to round numbers.

Additionally, wall charts and other observable record keeping devices are excellent examples of symbolic rewards for achievement. Some kind of check mark or symbol is used each time a student masters one of the objectives or units. Student names may or may not be used on such charts. If they are used, chalking up successes publicly can be a real stimulus to students. If a teacher feels this would upset rather than encourage students, names can be eliminated altogether. The chart would then measure movement of the total class toward mastery, and individuals could still assess privately how they compare to the class.

Parents, as well as students and teachers, should be kept informed of students' progress in mastering the basic skills. Teachers should provide parents with information about their child's performance in a format parents will understand, and which will facilitate discussion at parent-teacher conferences.

Improving the Quality of Assessment

By improving the quality of tests and other forms of evaluation, we can be sure that assessment results are representative of what students have learned and are not due to extraneous factors. It is important that any form of evaluation be a valid measure of a student's actual state of knowledge or skill. For example, we know that some students do poorly because they are not comfortable in a testing situation. Nervousness and anxiety can lessen a student's motivation and thought processes. Furthermore, we cannot assume that students are equal in their understanding of how to take a test, their motivation to do their best, and their understanding of the importance of the test. Thus not only is it important for tests to be technically sound, but the testing situation itself must not be neglected. The following suggestions can help to ensure that all students are prepared to perform to the best of their ability.

First, teachers must believe that tests are important and must communicate this to students. Students should be told that formative tests will be used to help them learn and to improve their instructional program. Frequent ungraded formative tests results should be considered part of practice and used to give the student feedback regarding his or her learning, without using results for final evaluation of learning. When test results are explained and used positively instead of negatively (to help rather than punish), and students get lots of practice in taking tests, they become more comfortable and perform better. Second, it is important that teachers cover the material in class in the same form to be used for testing. This means they must be fully acquainted with the test items. For example, if a test uses a horizontal format $(25 + 5 = N)$ for addition, students must be taught this format. There should be no surprises in item format. This has been found to cause poor results on the part of students.

Another problem is caused by computer-scored answer sheets which are typical of norm-referenced instruments. Some children put answers in the wrong places and their poor results are due to this mistake rather than not knowing the material. Also the failure of students to erase completely when changing answers, or neglecting to erase all stray pencil marks, may lower test results. Students should be taught the format and method of using test answer sheets so these problems will not occur. Some schools have purchased stand-alone scanners for teaching the use of answer sheets as well as scoring tests. These are passed from classroom to classroom so that all students can learn the correct techniques. Students are given directions, take a test and then run it through the scanner themselves. Bells or buzzers sound, sheets are scored incorrectly or not at all when directions have not been followed. Students enjoy and are not likely to forget this lesson.

It is unfair to penalize students for not knowing proper test procedures and for not being comfortable and familiar with a test format. Since testing is school-related practice, it is the job of the school staff to see to it that test-taking skills are developed.

Finally, be sure to let students know the test is coming and when it will be given. Arrange for any review necessary on objectives or material covered by the test. Such reviews should use questions similar to but not identical with the test. If students are unfamiliar with the kinds of items which appear on the test, then the test is unlikely to result in a valid assessment.

In mastery learning, both summative and formative assessments that are used for grading and the resulting grades are based on a predefined set of criteria. It is very important that both teacher and student be fully aware of the grading criteria prior to instruction. After all, if students are expected to master an instructional objective they must know the level of performance required to demonstrate mastery. For example, if the objective is for students to perform two-digit addition then students must know how they will be tested and how many two-digit addition problems they must complete correctly to demonstrate mastery.

With mastery learning, the grades an individual student earns is not based on comparisons to other students or based on other non-mastery considerations such as participation, attendance, citizenship, or any other criteria not directly related to specific student performance. Norm reference tests (those that compare students performance) do not necessarily indicate mastery. These types of tests only indicate how well students are performing relative to others on selected materials. If a student receives an A solely because she or he has the highest test score tells us little as to how much the student actually knows. A whole class could be failing to meet course objectives yet some would still receive "A's".

Assigning grades based on a bell-curve basis (e.g., 10% A's, 20% B's, 40% C's, 20% D's, and 10% F's) is also not reflective of mastery learning because it too is based on comparisons rather than meeting performance criteria in mastery learning. It is possible, in fact desirable for all students to earn an A or B as long as all students demonstrate mastery of course objectives at a high level. It is also possible for all students to fail if mastery is not attained. With mastery learning the goal is a j-curve where most students are at the high-end of a performance continuum and where most students are demonstrating mastery of instructional objectives.

One of the potential pitfalls of grading in a mastery learning model is setting criteria too low. It is easy to give all students an A or B by setting a criteria that is so low that nearly all students will achieve mastery with little or no learning. Just because all students earn an A or B is not an indication of successful teaching if the criteria for mastery was set too low. In mastery learning the expectations for achievement must be high. So too must be the criteria for demonstrating mastery.

Evaluating School Programs

Responsibility for assessing the effectiveness of the school instructional program should be shared by the principal and teachers. The school principal must be the facilitator of school program evaluation. This means it is the responsibility of the principal to be aware of the reported data, to communicate it to teachers, and to see to it that the data is used to improve the basic skills program. Furthermore, the principal should initiate school modifications to overcome major skill deficiencies made evident by test data. Since more than one staff member may be responsible for students of a particular age group within a school, evaluation of school effectiveness should be based on the school as a unit. The quality of a school's performance can be determined by the extent to which students are achieving the specified objectives of the school program.

Specifically, the yardsticks for measuring the school's effectiveness in teaching the basic skills should be based on established building goals for student performance. This is usually expressed in terms of a specified percentage of grade level skills. For example, if the school goal in a particular year is for all students to master at least X percent of the grade level skills, then the match of post-test results to this goal is the basis for evaluating the school's success. It is important to remember, however, that the school goal for mastery performance should be clearly established at the beginning of the school year so students and teachers can work to achieve it. This kind of criterion should not be used to measure the effectiveness of the program unless it was clearly communicated to teachers and students with sufficient time to achieve it.

All students, including those in alternative education programs, must be expected to master the critical knowledge and skills. It is not sufficient that only the "average" of "normal" students achieve grade level performance. All students should be expected to reach high levels of achievement on the expressed teaching objectives. These students may be included in district-wide evaluation, as well as school or classroom assessment. Each school must be responsible for all students achieving the objectives specified for all students. The practice of some districts or schools to exclude certain children from testing suggests that these children are neither expected, believed able, nor (presumably) taught to achieve mastery of grade level objectives. The lack of assessment data for these students provides an incomplete picture of the school's effectiveness, and obstructs efforts to improve the instructional program.

Finally, judgments about students and about a school's effectiveness should be based upon multifactor assessments. In other words, a variety of assessment techniques is essential for maximizing valid and reliable results. Policies derived from test results are helpful only if the assessment items and procedures match the instruction given.

Suggested Activities

- The principal should establish and publish the school schedule of formal summative student testing for the year or semester. The teacher should also inform students about any summative tests that may be used for grading. This should be done early, indicating dates for any pretesting. This information should be communicated in writing to students and parents.

- The principal should familiarize the staff with the types of formal summative tests that will be used, with the kind of data that will be generated, and how the data can be used to improve student performance if minimal levels of competency does not occur. (In too many cases, this last step is overlooked or neglected, resulting in little teacher understanding or use of test data. This is a glaring example of educational waste — in dollars, time, and information.) Teachers should be instructed in how to communicate the meaning of test results to parents and to students.

- Discuss record keeping at a department or grade level meeting. Ask teachers to share information on what forms or ways they record student progress. If the district provides a record keeping procedure, make sure everyone has copies and understands how to use it. (See example in this module.)

- The principal should meet with the special education staff members concerning how the grade level basic skills program will be delivered to their students. Also, since these students are expected to learn the same objectives as regular students, communication and coordination between regular education teachers and special education teachers for mainstreamed students is a necessity.

- Preparing students for testing will help eliminate anxiety and reduce errors.

- Establish a realistic achievement goal for the school year, while ultimately striving for 100 percent of the students' mastery of basic skills. Examine your school's most current achievement results. How far away are these results from the performance standard you are considering for the school achievement goal? Remember, set your goal above your present level to make teachers and students stretch to achieve it. If you are going to err, err on the high side. The more you expect from students, the more they will give you.

- Announce your goal to students and parents with resolve and enthusiasm at the beginning of the school year so that everybody understands what is expected. This is an important event and should be treated as such.

  - Conduct a special assembly for students to announce the achievement goal and to explain what students are expected to learn.

  - Conduct a special meeting for parents for the same purposes as above. Issue a school plan for parent support and involvement, and explain how it fits in with achievement goals. Solicit the backing of parents.

Selected Bibliography

📖 Airasian, P. *Assessment in the Classroom.* New York: McGraw-Hill, Inc., 1996.

📖 Block, J. H. and L. W. Anderson. *Mastery Learning in Classroom Instruction.* New York: MacMillan Publishing Co., 1975.

📖 Brown, F. G. *Measuring Classroom Achievement.* New York: Holt, Rinehart & Winston, 1981.

📖 Calfee, R. C. and P. Perfumo. "Student Portfolios: Opportunities for a Revelation in Assessment." *Journal of Reading* 36/7 (April 1993): 523-37.

Cohen, S. A. "New Alignment Experiments: Using Outcome-based Instruction to Teach Transfer of Learning." *Outcomes: The Quarterly Journal of the Network of Outcomes Based Schools* 10/3 (Fall 1991): 11-16.

Costa, A. L. and B. Kallick. "Reassessing Assessment." In *If Minds Matter,* Vol. II (ed.) by A. Costa, J. Bellanca and R. Fogarty. Palatine, IL: Skylight Publishing, 1992.

Crossland, H. "Screening Early Literacy: Ideology, Illusions, and Intervention." *Educational Review* 46/1 (1994): 47-62.

Crow, L. W. and R. J. Bonnstetter. "Formative and Summative Assessment of a Reform Project: Models of Change. A Glimpse of the Texas, Scope, Sequence and Coordination Project." Paper presented at the Annual Meeting of the National Association for Research in Science Teaching. Atlanta, GA, April 1993.

Dassa, C. et al. "Formative Assessment in a Classroom Setting: From Practice to Computer Innovations." *Alberta Journal of Educational Research* 39/1 (March 1993): 111-25.

Good, T. and J. Brophy. *Looking in the Classroom,* 6th ed. New York: Harper Collins, 1996.

Helgeson, S. L. and D. D. Kumar. "Technological Applications in Science Education." Paper presented at the Annual Meeting of the National Science Teachers Association, Atlanta, GA (April 1993).

Hord, S. M. *Facilitative Leadership: The Imperative for Change.* Austin, TX: Southwest Educational Development Laboratory, 1992.

McMullen, B. G. "Quantitative Analysis of Effects in the Classrooms." Paper presented at the Annual Meeting of the American Educational Research Association, Atlanta, GA, 1993.

Morgan, N. and J. Sexton. *Teaching, Questioning, and Learning.* New York: Routledge, 1991.

Nitko, A. J. "Curriculum-based Criterion — Referenced Continuous Assessment: A Framework for the Concepts and Procedures of Using Continuous Assessment for Formative and Summative Evaluation of Students." Paper presented at the International Meeting of the

Association for the Study of Educational Evaluation, Pretoria, South Africa, July 1994.

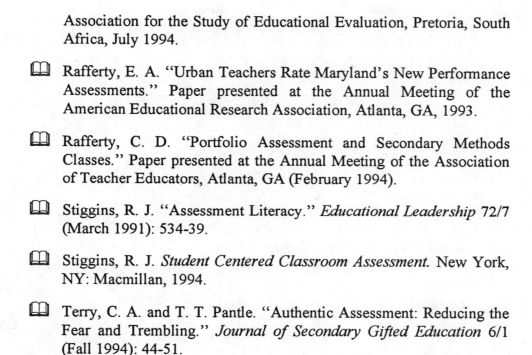 Rafferty, E. A. "Urban Teachers Rate Maryland's New Performance Assessments." Paper presented at the Annual Meeting of the American Educational Research Association, Atlanta, GA, 1993.

Rafferty, C. D. "Portfolio Assessment and Secondary Methods Classes." Paper presented at the Annual Meeting of the Association of Teacher Educators, Atlanta, GA (February 1994).

Stiggins, R. J. "Assessment Literacy." *Educational Leadership* 72/7 (March 1991): 534-39.

Stiggins, R. J. *Student Centered Classroom Assessment.* New York, NY: Macmillan, 1994.

Terry, C. A. and T. T. Pantle. "Authentic Assessment: Reducing the Fear and Trembling." *Journal of Secondary Gifted Education* 6/1 (Fall 1994): 44-51.

EPILOGUE: UNDERSTANDING WHAT WORKS

We conclude this book with what we believe is a fundamental truth: academically literate citizens are a prerequisite for a productive economy and for creating bonds essential to a healthy society. At each level of schooling, students must be taught to master the competencies necessary for meaningful participation in a technologically complex and diverse democracy. Unless our schools hold high academic standards for all students, and unless our schools provide the means by which students can achieve those standards, the value of education is trivialized. Failure to properly teach our young harms them, and it undermines the foundations of our society.

What must we do to enhance the academic competencies of all students? We must achieve three concomitant goals that are preconditions for an effective academic learning climate for all students. One precondition is to guarantee that all schools are safe and orderly. Students will not learn as we wish where violence or disruption is tolerated.

The second precondition is to structurally organize schools so that they become true academic learning communities. This means that we can no longer allow schools to produce failure in large numbers of students through the practice of tracking them on the basis of presumed fixed abilities to learn. We know that ability grouping has at least three profoundly negative consequences: it creates the conditions of academic and social failure rather than mastery; it heightens tensions between groups, usually along racial and social class lines; and it undermines good citizenship by fostering feelings of injustice and resentment among those denied equal educational opportunity.

To improve our schools, we must build a consensus that tracking is inimical to creating an effective school learning climate. We must admit that years of investing in tracking is a mistake, and that tracking is inherently unfair because it is a "zero sum game" in which there are always too many needless losers. Achievement expectations, allocation of resources, and even the distribution of self-conceptions of academic ability among students will reflect this unfairness. Therefore, we must detrack schools.

Related to detracking is our third precondition: we must be clear on what we want all students to learn in math, science, social studies and language at each level, plus certain knowledge acquisition skills (such as computer literacy). This means that each school's curriculum objectives must be specified in a scope and sequence model. This also means that there must be effective instruction to assure mastery of these learning objectives by all students at each level. This mastery must be documented with valid assessment of both teaching and learning.

We recognize that the transition from tracking to a system of mastery learning will pose difficulties in some situations. In the initial phase of detracking, students formerly in the lower tracks will require more instructional effort in order for them to master common learning objectives. Along with relatively low academic skill levels, poor self-conceptions of ability, pervasive feelings of futility, low motivation and behavioral problems may need to be addressed. These difficulties will be particularly evident among older students (those in middle school and high school) who have been in the lowest ability groups from the early grades.

The difficulty of this transition from tracking to mastery learning is likely to be compounded by those who claim that the transition in itself undermines equality of educational opportunity. An investment in time and resources during the period of detracking in those with the poorest skills, some might argue, is unfair to those who have already attained mastery. This argument reflects the following logic: if tracking is unfair because it treats students differentially, then detracking should mean treating all students the same. The problem with this line of argument is that in the transition, an entire generation of those who have experienced the disadvantages of tracking will be lost. Treating students who have not been taught critical competencies in a manner identical to those who have been winners under a tracking system constitutes an invitation for them to continue their failure.

Within the context of transition from tracking to creating an effective academic learning climate model of instruction, fairness does not mean the identical treatment of all students, with little or no variation based upon individual need or circumstance. Rather, fairness is based upon *setting a common minimal, but high standard* of achievement for all, then *providing the means* necessary for each student to attain that standard. Individual variation in skill level among students at the onset of instruction should not serve as a justification for large numbers of students failing to achieve the desired level of mastery. Despite such variations, the standard set for all students should be attainable by each student because of appropriate resource allocation and because of the mastery learning approach to instruction.

Finally, as a national policy objective, we should invest in reducing class size, especially in schools plagued by high rates of academic and social failure among students. Smaller class size, particularly in the early school years, has a number of positive benefits for creating an effective school learning climate. In smaller classes, with more monitoring and formative evaluations of students' behavior, two significant outcomes occur: fewer behavioral problems and higher rates of mastery of learning objectives. Smaller classes also foster a more personalized, mentoring learning community which reduces feelings of alienation and futility.

An effective academic learning climate is one where students feel empowered by their positive connection to others and by their own academic success. Acquiring academic and social competencies in school becomes a self-fulfilling prophecy for lifelong, self-directed learning. In this sense, to create effective schools is to create a healthy society.

ISBN 1-55691-058-4

© 1997, 1982 by Wilbur Brookover, Fritz Erickson, and Alan McEvoy

Learning Publications, Inc.
5351 Gulf Drive
P.O. Box 1338
Holmes Beach, FL 34218-1338

Printing: 5 4 3 2 1   Year: 10 9 8 7

Printed in the United States of America.

Creating Effective Schools:

An Inservice Program for Enhancing School Learning Climate and Achievement

Second Edition

by Wilbur B. Brookover
Fritz J. Erickson
Alan W. McEvoy

with

Laurence Beamer, Helen Efthim, Douglas Hathaway, Lawrence Lezotte,
Stephen Miller, Joseph Passalacqua, Louis Tornatzky

LP LEARNING PUBLICATIONS, INC.
Holmes Beach, Florida